Psychotherapy Grounded in the Feminine Principle

Psychotherapy Grounded in the Feminine Principle

Barbara Stevens Sullivan, M. S. W.

Chiron Publications
Asheville, North Carolina

Library of Congress Catalog Card Number: 89-9713

Printed in the United States of America.
Edited by Siobhan Drummond Granner.
Book design by Nancy R. Snyder.

Library of Congress Cataloging-in-Publication Data:

Sullivan, Barbara Stevens, 1943-
Psychotherapy grounded in the feminine principle / Barbara Stevens Sullivan.
p. cm.
Bibliography: p.
Includes index.
ISBN 978-1-63051-522-5 (pbk.)
1. Psychoanalysis. 2. Femininity (Psychology) 3. Psychotherapy. 4. Feminist therapy. I. Title.
[DNLM: 1. Psychoanalytic Therapy—methods. 2. Unconscious (Psychology) 3. Women—psychology. WM 460.5.U6 S951p]
RC506.S84 1989
616.89'14—dc20
DNLM/DLC
for Library of Congress

89-9713
CIP

gratefully dedicated to
Don, Lynda and Dave

Contents

Acknowledgments

My greatest appreciation and thanks go to my patients, who, to paraphrase Winnicott, have paid to teach me. For the most part, they stuck with me through all my trips, including the dead ends, patiently providing me with the space to work out the attitudes and ideas contained in this book. Even those who quit in midstream taught me a great deal and I am grateful to them—though I may, of course, have felt many other things about them as well. Some of their lives and therapeutic experiences fill the pages of this book, in disguised, even fictionalized forms. To each of them and to all the people who are not mentioned but who shared the depths of their souls with me, I offer thanks and the hope that they have gained as much from the experience as I did.

I want to thank also my husband, Mark Sullivan, and my children, Abby Sullivan and Michael Israel, who provided a warm nest for my existence, an emotionally nourishing cave to which I could retreat during the draining months and years of this writing. Mark and Abby, who lived with me through this period, suffered long hours during which I abandoned the family for my computer; they tolerated my moods, my periods of exhaustion, elation, despair, and rage. Mark, who is himself a therapist, offered invaluable clinical, intellectual, and editorial assistance, reading many drafts of many chapters many times and discussing my ideas endlessly as I worked them out. Thank you all, very much.

Many friends and colleagues read all or part of this manuscript, in some cases more than once. Each of them contributed something to its finished form, untangling some knot in my thinking, smoothing out my language, moderating my hyperbolic style. Beth Barmack, Hilde Burton, Sue Elkind, Mariam King, Pilar Montero, Marjorie Nathanson, Rachel Peltz, and Tom Richardson are all outstanding therapists whose clinical and intellectual acumen contributed to the finished version of this book. Dorothy Witt gave generously of her literary talents and editorial expertise, smoothing out my rougher sentences and paragraphs, correcting my grammar and spelling, and challenging me with insightful questions about the book's structure, tone, and meaning. Finally, Murray Stein and Siobhan Granner, my editors, contributed substantially of their time and energy, providing important guidance and advice on the content of the book and reviewing each and every word with great care. To each of you, may I somehow, someday repay the favors.

Preface

This book is about depth psychotherapy. By that term I mean therapy that seeks to heal by orienting toward the unconscious—the patient's unconscious, of course, but the therapist's as well, for it is through reverberations in one's own depths that the therapist receives the patient's messages. Such therapy is inevitably lengthy and difficult, proceeding as it does in the medium of an intense, intimate relationship between patient and analyst. If it goes any distance at all, it affects the analyst as well as the patient in deep and unexpected ways.

The work proceeds largely out of each participant's unconscious. We like to imagine the therapist knows what he is doing—that his conscious intent and his behavior are unified, that counterproductive currents originate only in the patient. But we know this is not true. The therapist as well as the patient must struggle with destructive tendencies; the patient like the therapist offers constructive energy to the work.

One difficulty shared by both participants may be conceptualized as resting on the ways our culture devalues the feminine principle. The thesis I shall explore is that this devaluation has had a severely negative impact on therapeutic work. In the following chapters I will discuss the nature of the feminine principle and how and why we need to reclaim it in order to be clinically effective.

I have referred to my subject as "depth therapy" in an attempt to avoid the kinds of hair-splitting discussions that develop when analysts try to describe the difference between "analysis" and "psychotherapy." A simplistic approach is often favored: if an individual is trained as an analyst and says he is doing analysis, it is analysis. Or, if the patient lies on a couch and is seen four or five times a week, it is analysis. If he is seen three times a week, it is not; if he is sitting up, it is not.

These definitions beg the essence of the question: what qualities make analysis analysis? Having studied for many years before becoming certified, analysts naturally want to believe they do something different from what ordinary therapists do, therapists not formally trained as analysts. It has unfortunately proved impossible to explain exactly what that difference is. This is not to say there are not profound differences in depth between the work of different practitioners, even between the work of the average analyst and the average therapist, but these differences are difficult to describe and impossible to measure. They do not rest on objectively ascertainable criteria such as the frequency of sessions, the posture of the patient, or the training of the therapist. It is possible to see a patient every day, using the couch, without ever managing to facilitate an experience of depth between the patient and his own unconscious or between him and his therapist. It is also possible to constellate a transformative therapeutic experience with someone who comes only twice a week and who never uses the couch.

The procedure I want to address in this book is one that enables the patient to reach into his inner depths—his unconscious—in increasingly powerful, continuous ways. This becomes possible for the patient because the therapist or analyst is working out of a partnership with his own unconscious. The partnership between the two individuals, patient and therapist, mirrors each person's inner partnership with his self. I will use the words "analysis" and "therapy" interchangeably to refer to work that attempts to affect the patient's basic character structure through the medium of an emotionally charged interpersonal relationship.

The work I am describing has traditionally been the preserve of psychoanalysis, but I do not want to call it simply analysis, partly because traditional analysis frequently does not seem to be terribly effective and partly because of the increasing number of therapists untrained in analysis whose work is nonetheless imbued with significant depth. But most of all it is because I do not like the word "analysis." "Analysis" means cutting something up into its component parts, examining each part and describing or understanding it. "Analysis" does not even imply putting the pieces back together again when one is finished! "Therapy," on the other hand, is a healing process that brings together pieces that have been torn asunder. My patients may or may not want to understand themselves but insofar as they do want "understanding" ("analysis"), it is as a stepping stone to healing. People seek psychological help because they are suffering, and when they claim otherwise (as, for example, for training purposes) it is because they are afraid at first to face the extent of their suffering. No one would submit to the demands of depth work unless compelled to do so by reason of inner pressures, and no one goes any farther on an inner journey than he must to achieve an adequately satisfying resting place. The work is rich; it is exciting and rewarding. But it is not fun, and it is painful. It is work taken up and continued only under inner duress.

The patient brings to this work his most private, vulnerable essence, the deepest reaches of his heart. The therapist, in the normal course of events, finds himself involved in profoundly personal ways, loving (or occasionally hating) his patient to a degree that may frighten him because it seems so clearly beyond the bounds of a "professional" relationship. Not infrequently, the patient is more intimate with his therapist than he has ever been with anyone else, certainly including his spouse. In one way or another, the therapist normally responds to this emotional intimacy with some comparable feeling. A considerable chunk of therapeutic energy may go into the therapist's own struggles with his involvement. Much of the literature can be seen as offering a variety of distancing mechanisms and defenses to clinicians who might otherwise fear losing themselves in the constellated sea of emotion.

It is true that the therapist must retain some objectivity and separateness from his patient; if he becomes personally enmeshed in the same way he does with friends or lovers, the relationship will quickly become a friendship or a love affair. But it is also true that the therapist must allow his heart to respond as fully as his head does, and there must be room in the work for some kind of expression of the deep concern for his patient generated within him. One of my hopes for this book is that it will provide a substantial cognitive foundation for the therapist's humane instincts. Too often therapists are afraid to like their patients and to act concerned or responsive with them. Warmth and caring are often offered in secret ways that are not reported to supervisors or colleagues. Somehow the ideal analyst has come to be seen as cold, impervious, objective, and scientific. That is not *my* ideal and I want to share a rationale that can help clinicians find constructive ways to utilize their nurturing instincts.

The case examples and vignettes presented in the following pages come from my practice, from the work of therapists I have supervised, from the clinical experiences of my friends, and from my own experiences as a patient. I have done my best, of course, to disguise the patients involved, and this has unfortunately meant in many cases that the therapist cannot be given recognition either.

Credit to my intellectual predecessors is also short. I have not attempted formal reviews of the literature concerning any of the subtopics I discuss, and I often know that a given thinker contributed an idea without knowing *where* he or she discussed it. When I know a source, I cite it; when I know that someone had an idea but do not know where it was put forward, I give the person credit without a citation. I undoubtably fail at times to give credit to those who came before me. Attempting to write about the feminine principle from a deeply personal point of view has precluded, in terms of energy and focus, the masculine activity of scientifically surveying the field. I cannot emphasize too strongly the fact that this in no way reflects a lack of respect on my part either for that activity or for the many psychologists upon whose work I am building.

Chapter 1

The Feminine Principle

It is the thesis of this book that therapeutic work of all theoretical persuasions has been significantly impaired by the dominant cultural imbalance between the masculine and feminine principles. Good therapists—Freudian, Jungian, Interpersonalist or whatever—must do much of their best work in opposition to a severe cultural bias that denigrates nurturing, receptive, accommodating behavior and idealizes active, assertive, controlling behavior.

This book is intended for depth psychotherapists of all persuasions. Every faction of the field of psychology has begun to recognize that the factors involved in analytic work are so diverse and complex, so extensive, that no theory has yet begun to encompass clinical work. Our understanding of the human psyche is considerably more solid than is our understanding of psychotherapeutic work. The elements comprising a good clinician have not yet been defined, and they are certainly not captured by any one theoretical orientation. I myself am a Jungian psychoanalyst, but it has long been clear to me that no particular school of therapy holds The Truth in its hands. There are excellent Jungian analysts and, unfortunately, there are also incompetent and even destructive ones. The same is true for every other group of therapists or analysts with whom I have had any contact, either personally or through my study of the literature. In the course of this book, I will argue that our society's bias against the feminine has skewed our understanding of our work so that profoundly healing aspects of the clinical encounter—aspects that cut across theoretical lines—have been overlooked and have functioned outside therapists' awareness to make therapy work in spite of their theories about how it *should* work.

But what is "the feminine"—or, "the masculine"? If we have learned anything in the last few decades from the women's movement, we have surely learned that neither women's nor men's personalities can be categorized. We are people first, each of us carrying unpredictable possibilities for development. Traits that have been assigned to one or the other sex reflect a given culture's stereotypes rather than anything inherently true for women or men. Sometimes the particular assignment stems from the nature of each sex's genital organs, as in the idea that women are receptive and men are aggressive. It is true the vagina is receptive and the penis behaves aggressively in sexual intercourse. But any given woman may be more aggressive than any given man, and many men have taken advantage of the women's movement to actualize their inherent receptive tendencies. It seems probable that none of the traditionally sex-linked characteristics are biologically linked to men and women at all.

And yet the concepts, masculine and feminine, persist. One can disagree with every traditional element, knowing that no man or woman could ever be simply masculine or feminine, and at the same time, one encounters individuals about whom one's gut feeling is that they are very "masculine," be they men or women. Where it seems conceivable that racial stereotypes may some day fall into oblivion, I find myself unable to imagine a human culture that does not continue to weave fantasies about the nature of maleness and femaleness. There seems to be an elemental inclination, beginning in very early childhood, to sort people and experiences into male and female categories. The particular qualities associated with each category vary from culture to culture, but every culture devises some sense of the masculine and the feminine, and the tendency to sort life into these two categories is universal, an inherent psychological activity of the human species.

We often imagine that if something is culturally rather than biologically determined, it can be changed. But our culture is our collective character structure, and changing even one person's character structure is an extraordinarily slow process. These culturally developed images of maleness and femaleness, inherently inaccurate regardless of their content, when applied to men and women, have an *intrapsychic* life that we can modify only by working with them. We cannot change these stereotypes by fiat; we cannot say, for example, thinking and feeling will no longer be considered masculine or feminine. The unconscious psyche has no interest in our injunctions and will simply go on its way, experiencing thinking as masculine and feeling as feminine. But the unconscious is open to a relationship with us. If we will begin by trying to understand how the unconscious imagines male and female energy, it may shift its images in response to our interest. If we will be open to the unconscious, it will be open to us.

In thinking about character structure, most analytic traditions begin with concepts: defenses, superegos, drives, and so on. Let us begin instead at a phenomenological level, looking at individual people and trying to tease out what they imagine the feminine or the masculine to be. Freud considered dreams wish-fulfillments, and Jung suggested they were complementary to consciousness. Beyond either of these formulations (and contradicting neither) dreams can be seen simply as the psyche painting pictures of itself. These pictures include landscapes and structures, story lines, plants and animals and—men and women, images of an unconscious sense of masculinity and feminity. I want to begin this search for the nature of the masculine and feminine principles (as they are understood in our culture) by looking at the struggles of two individuals, Sydney (a woman) and Stanley (a man). For each of them, healing an injured inner woman became a lifelong task of central importance. Perhaps we can develop an intuitive feel for the concept of intrapsychic feminine or masculine energy patterns by exploring their manifestations in these two cases. From this phenomenological beginning we will turn to an attempt to conceptualize masculine and feminine intrapsychic energies on a more general level.

Sydney

Toward the beginning of her analysis, Sydney, a 30-year-old woman, had a dream which she came to identify as central to her developmental issues.

> *I'm sitting with my feet in a bathtub, about two-thirds full of water, in a bathroom very like the one in the apartment where I grew up. My father is standing behind me. I've bled menstrual blood into the water. The clot of blood begins swirling around and separates into two clots. One clot, on my left, moves down toward the drain. It turns into a crab which scurries down the drain. The other clot, on my right, moves towards the surface of the water and turns into a woman, all white, a bloodless spirit, who rises up out of the water in a long flowing white gown and begins to float out of the window right above the tub. I'm terrified of losing the woman and want my father to do something to stop her from disappearing out the window. I want him to grab her and choke her. I'm not worried about the crab, that seems okay, safely tucked away someplace in the plumbing. My father is absolutely immovable, standing there as though turned to stone, with no expression on his face.*

Sydney is partially immersed in a bath of water, the element from which all life emerged. She is connected to and facing her own unconscious, contained in a tub. This is a hopeful image of a solid beginning for her analytic work. The container is firm, the psychological material is available, she is facing into it and attempting to deal with it. Sydney is in her childhood home: she is still living in the psychological world of her parental complexes, and the man in the picture for her is her father. But he is not prepared to immerse himself in the bath with her—or to respond in any way to her distress. He is almost nonliving, a statue. So

Sydney, the woman (with a man's name, we notice) has no real man to accompany her on her journey. She must find a way to do the man's job as well as her own.

Her challenge is a profoundly feminine one. Sydney is facing a situation that emerges from menstrual blood, the life-giving blood of one of the major feminine mysteries. The blood in the dream is itself alive, swirling around and dividing into two living things in the water. Blood is a central symbol in the dream: the menstrual blood from which all else emerges, the bloodless woman, and the crab, streaked bloody-red in the dream. (Sydney believed live crabs look like the cooked crabs she had seen.) Blood carries an individual's passion. It is the home of the soul, bringing one's ancestral heritage forward to one and carrying one's immortality toward the future in one's bloodlines. Indeed, blood is the carrier of life, and excessive loss of blood will rapidly cause death. The blood in this dream, menstrual blood, carries the creativity of Mother Nature herself, promising an ordinary, mortal woman the opportunity to partake in the miracle of human birth. This blood therefore doubly represents the center of a woman's feminine side.

Out of this magical blood the feminine is born and splits into two separate elements, a crab and a bloodless wraith. The crab is a very primitive animal consisting almost entirely of a stomach. It is a body with claws, essentially without a head, encased in an exoskeleton. Sydney's crab has disappeared into the deeper layers of the plumbing—slang for the human sexual organs or the body. It begins on Sydney's left-hand side and moves still farther to her left, the side of the maladapted unconscious. Perhaps her lack of concern about this crab reflects its unconscious nature as it moves more and more deeply into the water of the unconscious and out of sight; consciously Sydney felt her attachment to the crab was not threatened while her connection to the spirit woman was.

In fact, Sydney's relationship with her body and with her crabby, pinching, preverbal emotional self—the elemental psyche where emotions originate deeply embedded in the physical reality—was troubled in many ways. She somatized in moderately difficult (though not incapacitating) ways such as headaches and backaches. She treated her body badly in the sense that she ignored pain, believing that since it was psychogenic ("all in her head") it was not real. She would force herself to continue activities that were intensely painful for her when there was no reason to do so. While her sex life was quite good at times, at other times she dissociated from her body and was unable to experience the physical reactions taking place. Her disturbed relationship to the feminine was reflected in this disturbed relationship to matter.

Sydney suffered a similar dissociation from the nonintellectual raw emotions of her instinctual psyche—rage, despair, overwhelming need. These emotions would possess her in autonomous storms of affect which she could neither control nor integrate. Although she was aware of what she said and did in these storms, on a deeper level she could not appreciate the emotional meaning of her utterances and actions. The crab's exoskeleton, protecting Sydney's vulnerable, primitive emotionality, kept Sydney's developed adult mind away from her tender center, just as it shut out others. Her lack of concern for the crab and her terror over the potential loss of the spirit woman reflected her inadequate concern for her body and her body's natural emotions. It paralleled an overestimation of the traditionally masculine world of the spirit, a disturbance that had undoubtably been active in drawing her to *Jungian* analysis with its emphasis on the spirit rather than to a more body-based therapeutic experience.

But the spirit woman, who captured the intense feeling of the dream, was also an important part of Sydney. The dream supports Sydney's belief that the spirit woman's total and permanent loss was imminently threatening in a way the crab's was not; that loss would indeed have been tragic. Provided her Jungian analysis does not stop with the reclamation of this spiritual side, it was apparently imperative that she begin the work here rather than with the crab.

This disembodied woman is alabaster white reflecting her total lack of blood, and she floats, lighter than air, up from the water, out of the window. The threatened loss of this spiritual feminine side reflected the fact that her family of origin, being staunch atheists and materialists, had been unable to accord validation to her psychic reality, focusing only on the objective, "realistic" side of life. From a Self-Psychological perspective we could say Sydney had received grossly inadequate levels of empathy for her emotional experiences; subjective experiences were simply not recognized by her parents. Perhaps because she is in a Jungian analysis, or perhaps because of some innate personal disposition that led her into Jungian work, she experiences this lack of empathy in spiritual terms, as a threat to her soul. Sydney has internalized the absence of parental mirroring as part of a broader pattern, a pattern that indoctrinated her so insistently with the notion she had no soul that she was in real danger of losing it.

Sydney's strange wish—that her father throttle the woman—reflects her inchoate sense that the woman's lack of substance is a problem. She wants her father to tackle the woman physically, with an approach that would not be effective, in fact, on this bloodless ghost, an approach designed to *force* the woman into an embodied state. This wish reflects Sydney's awkward relationship with both the feminine and masculine principles. She is expressing her sense that a violent, forcing expression of power is the only response she can muster for a difficult situation. The response that comes to mind indicates a hypertrophying of the masculine, not a healthy expression of it.

This strange wish also speaks to the most fundamental problem imaged by the dream: the splitting of Sydney's feminine side into two incomplete halves. The spiritual side needs to be embodied; the body needs to be revered. Sydney is caught in a modern dilemma whose roots reach back to the Christian rejection of the body. Her proposed solution to the dreadful dissociation in her feminine side would bring the two sides together by force. This can never work, for it disregards the nature of the psyche's reality: the psyche is not material and must be approached psychologically, with respect for its true nature.

One week later Sydney had the following dream:

> *I'm in the kitchen of my childhood home with my sister. We're chatting, having a nice visit. My son, we know, is ill. While we visit we receive word that he has died. We are not in any way disturbed by this information, we just go on visiting. Then my father comes in, very upset. Now we're in the bathroom. Father has heard that Daniel is ill. "How is Daniel," he asks, frightened. "Oh, Daddy," I reply, "Daniel is dead, he's all dead." My father falls to his knees, tears streaming down his face.*

Sydney woke from this dream shocked and very frightened for Daniel's health. He was sleeping at a friend's house, and Sydney was unable to go back to sleep that night, waiting, tearful and anxious, until late enough in the early morning to call and reassure herself that the outer Daniel was fine.

This dream seemed to Sydney to be a coda to the first dream. Her father has come decidedly to life. The activity he brings is quite different from the throttling Sydney hoped for from him: he brings feeling to the situation. Where the two sisters' cozy, companionable visit had not included any emotional depth, the father's entry brings an awareness of meaning. He carries Sydney's capacity for concern. This is what was needed in the earlier dream. A feminine response was called for in the face of the feminine mystery Sydney was watching, not a masculine, take-charge-and-act approach.

It is interesting that Sydney's father found his feeling when faced with the death of the boy-child but not when faced with Sydney's wounded feminine nature, torn asunder and dispersing outward, fragmenting under centrifugal forces. His reaction to that situation recalls the Greek myth of Medusa, the sight of whom turned any man to stone. From the perspective of Sydney's childhood family the feminine is inherently horrendous; any expression of the feminine principle is experienced as Medusa. The capacity to feel for the masculine is available to her through her father, but feeling for her feminine side seems utterly lacking. It is also interesting that, in the face of the feminine mystery of her first dream, Sydney is accompanied by her father rather than her mother, but this reflects her personal family's dynamics rather than anything of broader cultural or archetypal relevance.

A disturbed relationship to the feminine principle always implies a disturbed relationship to the masculine as well. For many years Sydney struggled with Nazis in her dreams, pursued by them, trapped in concentration camps and trying to escape, finding herself suddenly transformed into a Jew, hiding from the Nazis in the heart of Berlin. The Nazis embody a severely distorted relationship to both the feminine and the masculine—grotesquely exaggerated manliness, sickening sentimentality in the place of true feeling, a denigration of the feminine principle, though not of (Aryan) women, beyond any other culture.

Nearly two years after Sydney's dream of the woman and the crab, her psyche announced with a dream that some transformative healing had begun.

> *I'm at the beach with Daniel. I know the Nazis are coming in amphibious tanks from the ocean. I make various attempts to get away but it becomes clear that this is impossible—they are going to get me this time. I do manage to get Daniel to safety, but I am trapped, with a high sand dune at my back. There is a slight rise between me and the ocean so I can't see the shore line, though I can see some of the ocean. I see the tanks coming up out of the water. I am naked under my long brown woolen cape, and I kneel down in the path of the coming tanks with my arms out to the sides. [Here Sydney demonstrates, holding her arms straight out so that her body has the shape of a cross.] The first tank comes over the rise and sitting on its turret is a blond American G.I., looking like a picture of the Americans liberating Italy.*

Sydney is at the ocean, here, at a place of ultimate vulnerability, the edge of our habitat, the end of land. She is nearly naked, stripped down to her female body almost unprotected. After years of running she must turn and face her pursuers. There is no way left to fight, she must submit to her internal fate. The fact that she gets Daniel to safety shows both her concern for him and the fact that this ultimate ordeal must be confronted alone, from a completely feminine center. She sinks down into a posture of total humility, accepting Christ's fate as her own, preparing to bear the suffering of her situation rather than struggling to evade, transcend, overpower or otherwise refuse it. She has turned herself over to a completely receptive feminine mode.

From this union with her female soul—this embodiment of the feminine principle—comes an amazing transformation in her masculine side: instead of Nazis, the ultimate oppressors, her deep unconscious brings her a liberating army headed by an American soldier who looks a lot like her (she had blond hair). Sydney almost never dreamed of Nazis again, and on the rare occasions when they did appear it was at a great distance, carrying no immediate threat. The terrible disjunctions in the connections between her feminine and masculine sides had begun to shift in fundamental, constructive ways.

Stanley

Stanley was a man in his early 30's who entered analysis with a strong but gentle therapist in his early 40's whom I will call Michael, a man secure in his masculine identity but with a good relationship to the feminine. Stanley sought treatment partly in response to an upsetting and shocking dream:

> *I'm in a room: there's a large fish tank with murky water. I'm fishing in the tank with a round stick. I pluck out a small octopus or squid. It looks like a baby clam. Mucouslike.*
>
> *Then I'm in a hospital setting: before me are two women lying on examination tables. They are alive but all the skin is off their bodies, you can see their muscles and veins. I'm horrified, repulsed, in terror. They are attached by flesh to the tables. I think I should stick my feelings down—this is a medical procedure going on.*
>
> *The little squid I had jumped off the stick and jumped up one of the women's vaginas. Then a man comes in and reaches inside the woman's vagina and pulls out a HUGE clear bag of some membranelike material, filled with old clothes and bloody body parts. The man berates her for trying to hoard these things. He is like a pimp—these things are worth money and she was trying to keep them to herself.*
>
> *Then I'm underneath a third woman who is suspended above me in the air, hanging from bars by pieces of skin. Her blood is dripping down on me.*

Here is the wounded feminine in horrifying dimensions.

Stanley was sophisticated in his thinking about women's rights and even about the feminine principle. He had read considerably in the Jungian literature and knew about the value of Being as opposed to Doing, about the importance of experience as opposed to knowledge, about the need for feelings, meaning, relatedness, and tenderness. But all that knowledge had been built over his wounded soul which he had feared—with good reason, one would have to say—to experience. He was an arresting example of the fact that conscious ideas and knowledge are of minimal value when one needs inner transformation. In seeking therapy he was looking for an intellectual experience within which his dreams could be "analyzed" and thereby rendered harmless. At the same time he desired a more authentic container within which he could begin to experience his wounded soul as a prelude to healing himself.

This dream, too, begins with a variant of a bath but this time in the form of a large fish tank with murky water. Stanley is not ready to immerse himself in the water—he reaches in with a stick (not a hand) and pulls out an archetypal image of the negative mother. Just a little one, the image reassures him, not a truly dangerous octopus that could envelop and smother him.

At this point the dream shifts to a hospital, indicating an equivalance: the capture of the octopus/squid/clam brings Stanley to the mutilated women. They are fished out of Stanley's depths through his capture of the squid. He has analyzed the feminine, indeed understood her right down to her muscular and veinous systems. As the violence done to her by that thorough analytic exploration hits him, he fends off his reaction with a weak rationalization: this is a medical procedure (conceived, no doubt, by Dr. Mengele). We could turn Stanley's rationalization around: his attempt to stick his feelings down is a major element in the ongoing violation of the feminine within himself. (Notice the repetition here of the word "stick" amplifying the meaning of Stanley's use of a "stick" to pull the squid out of the fish tank.)

The little squid, leaping into the woman's womb, is seeking a safe haven and is expressing its affinity with the tormented woman. The negative mother is frightful seen through the eyes of her wounded son (or daughter). From another perspective, she is a deeply wounded woman herself. Stanley's natural wish was to put as much distance between himself and his destructive mother as he could. Emotional healing, however, comes from bringing lost pieces of oneself back together. Just as Sydney needed to redeem the Nazis, Stanley needs to heal this dread feminine aspect, not evade it.

This interpretation is supported by Stanley's association to the membranelike bag containing old clothes and bloody body parts: a gruesome new birth in an amniotic sac. The squid has been transformed into the contents of this bag. We would imagine these contents to be worthless, but apparently they are not: both the pimp and his victim value this sack of apparently ruined pieces of the past. Stanley's conscious attitude seeking to discard the remnants of his dreadful mother complex is corrected by the dream figures. They alert us to the fact that the damage of his history—his old adaptations (clothing) and the pieces of himself that have been amputated and stuffed away—should be preserved, for they can be redeemed. Broken pieces of oneself can be repaired; indeed, they form the essential raw materials for the soul's redemption. The dreadful mother Stanley fled lives on inside him in the form of the injured woman who carries Stanley's soul.

The dream ends with a distressing image which also contains a bit of hope. Through the dream Stanley has tried to defend himself from the urgency of his soul's injury with intellectual distancing defenses. He keeps his hands clean, first in the fish tank and then by pretending the scene he was watching was somehow acceptable. His remote stance, a major inadvertant source and expression of the damaged feminine, ultimately fails, and Stanley finds himself covered with the woman's blood. He *must* experience his inner reality, it will not be evaded, and however excruciating that experience may be, it will also bring the healing he seeks.

Nearly two years later, Stanley began his therapeutic hour with the following dream:

> *My glasses were made of plastic and broke at the bridge. My left thumb got immense — like Pinocchio writ large — maybe a yard long. I thought, "Oh, it's good all this is coming out."*

The therapist, Michael, aware of how Stanley distanced himself from his emotional inner world through intellectual defenses, was struck by the image of Stanley's glasses breaking. He thought of the mythic stories that link inner sight to outer blindness (Oedipus and Tireseus, for example) and he shared those associations with Stanley. Michael also communicated his excitement about the dream, commenting, "That's an interesting dream!"

Stanley seemed taken aback at Michael's interest, apparently unsure *what* it was that had caught his attention. He worked on the dream in his habitual way, associating to the various elements with some freedom, but also staying on track and trying to work out a full interpretation. Within 20 or 25 minutes he had worked out an interpretation that seemed reasonable to Michael: his instinctual side, represented by the image of his thumb (a substitute for a penis), was growing, following the diminution of his dependence on Apollonian seeing and thinking. Unfortunately, this interpretation was worked out and talked about from a totally cerebral, intellectual place. The reference to Pinocchio reflected this lack of feeling: the meaning of life is denied by Stanley's habitual intellectual stance and in some strange way this deletion of feeling amounts to living a lie.

Although Michael made various remarks attempting to move Stanley into a more emotional, embodied relationship to the dream, nothing he said made any difference. He wondered, for example, how

Stanley felt seeing his thumb blow up that way in the dream, but Stanley reported having no feeling. Rather, it reminded him of a time when he watched his seven-year-old son fall off the garage roof: seeing the accident coming, Stanley realized there was nothing he could do to prevent it. Everything had gone into slow motion, with no feeling at all, as he watched the child topple off the edge. Michael said there would have been some feeling if Stanley had had the time to take in what was happening. Stanley agreed but did not open up to his feeling about his blown-up thumb.

As the hour proceeded Stanley became more and more frustrated. He had his interpretation worked out, but it was not satisfying. He felt that Michael "knew" things about the dream he was not saying; he felt teased and withheld from. At last Michael commented that Stanley had a strong feeling there was more to the dream than he had said. Michael said he thought both that Stanley's interpretation was correct and that Stanley's strong feeling should be respected—he was sure there *was* more to the dream than had yet been said although he did not know what that more would prove to be. The idea occurred to Stanley here that he was withholding something from himself and was projecting that withholding stance onto Michael.

"How do I get to the rest," he cried. "I feel like banging on the door of the cave." Michael was reminded of the scene in *The Lord of the Rings* where Gandalf tries every forcing spell he knows to enter the sealed gates of Moria only to discover that the magic word was simply, "Friend" (Tolkien 1965). Michael shared this association with Stanley. He suggested Stanley let himself associate and see what came up rather than trying to force his way in. At this point Stanley took his glasses off and allowed his mind to wander in a more relaxed fashion than before. He came to the thought that therapy worked through his stomach; his stomach knew everything, he speculated. He was changing and growing all the time but his head would be the last part of him to know how or why he had changed or developed. His friends and colleagues had all commented on his increasingly relaxed manner; therapy seemed to be affecting him without his understanding how it was happening. Stanley never wore his glasses in his therapy hours again, and shortly thereafter he began using the couch, something he had not previously felt safe enough to do.

One year later, the new attitude taken up by Stanley in this hour bore fruit in the following dream:

> *It's night, in this large room, like a retreat center/meditation hall. People are sitting on the floor. An area is marked off with lights on the floor: an unraised stage. There are full-length windows leading out to a patio.*

Then African drums and African dancers start up. They are Zulus: painted, tatooed, and scarred. It is all men dancing in the center space. It has an aboriginal quality. There is a really noble, attractive feel to what first seemed primitive. The dancers are filled with power and dignity. I especially liked one man—he was spectacular. At the end of the dance a white man who looks like Rod Steiger, dressed in shimmering, radiant armor appears at the end of the runway. He is encased in a headdress like Ishtar's that covers his entire body. The dancers begin moving toward him. They have a worshipful attitude toward him, he is their totem or icon.

Then it is over. The lights come up. I find the man I'd been especially looking at is 81 years old. My wife comes in. I try to tell her about the dancers but she isn't excited.

This dream takes place in a protected place deep within the psyche. It is night, when darkness cloaks the outer world and dreams emerge most easily; we are in a retreat center, an area explicitly separated from the outer world's bustle. Within this place, established to foster inner exploration (meditation), a formal exhibit is taking place, a spotlighted performance we are supposed to watch but from which we are not cut off. We are on the same level as the action. Stanley's distancing defenses are on the way out, evidenced only at the very end of the dream in his wife's inability to appreciate the experience he tries to share with her.

The scene surrounding Stanley is intensely masculine in nature but the dark, powerful dancers are men filled with reverence for the feminine principle and the Great Mother (Ishtar). They are totally embodied (dancing), dominated by rhythms of the soul, immersed in an experience of being that has no rational value in the other world, a religious experience in which the masculine expresses its profound interdependence with the feminine, the source of life and animation. The feminine is healthy and vital, as far from wounded as we can imagine, the masculine is engaged in a virile, potent partnership with her. As with Sydney's transformative dream, a healthy masculine orientation calls forth a healthy feminine counterpart.

The deep shift in Stanley portended by this dream is further amplified by Rod Steiger's appearance in the role of Ishtar. Ishtar was the Babylonian form of the Great Goddess who preceeded the Father Gods in power. Babylonian scriptures called her the Light of the World, Leader of Hosts, Bestower of Strength, Lady of Victory and Forgiver of Sins, among other things (Walker 1983). She is the Goddess of Goddesses, one of the more warlike versions of the Great Mother. Stanley's primary association to Rod Steiger recalled the movie *No Way to Treat a Lady* in which Steiger plays a man caught in a tremendously destructive mother complex. In the movie he murders one woman after another, each time winning the woman's confidence by playing a different role, dressed in costumes from his theater's large costume collection. (Recall, here, the old clothes from Stanley's first dream.) In this movie Steiger enacts the complex that Stanley entered therapy to heal. But in this dream, Steiger's role reflects the same transformation of that complex captured by the dancing men: rather than hating and fearing the feminine as he did in the movie, Steiger has turned himself over to her service, encasing himself in her body-length headdress. Total submission to the Goddess's worship brings Steiger into his full manhood—he is dressed in shimmering, radiant armor. Strongly grounded in his masculine nature, ungrudgingly honoring the feminine, he is, in turn, the object of the dark men's worship. He is their totem, their ideal.

When this spectacle is over Stanley sees that the man to whom he had been especially drawn is 81 years old. We need to think of this man as an idealized alter ego for Stanley—the dancer with whom Stanley can identify, whom Stanley hopes to grow to resemble. The man's advanced age implies that Stanley has not yet actualized the capacities expressed in the images of the dream. The incompletion of the journey to the dancers' harmonious relationship with the feminine is underscored by the fact that Stanley's wife—the real woman who shares his life—cannot yet understand Stanley's vision. That he has become able to imagine this harmonious, vibrant marriage between the masculine and feminine principles is a tremendous advance, well worth celebrating. But the realization of that marriage in concrete reality will be the task of a lifetime, something he can hope eventually to complete in his very old age.

I have begun my discussion of the nature of the feminine and masculine principles with two cases in an attempt to emphasize that the words "masculine" and "feminine," as I use them throughout this book, do not refer to men and women; they refer to energic patterns of being, both of which are present in all people at all times. Sydney and Stanley each had to struggle with masculine and feminine aspects of themselves and with the relationship between these two sides of their psyches. Our ideas about what is masculine and what is feminine are largely determined by our particular culture but the fact of sorting human experiences into masculine and feminine categories is universally present in all cultures. All people's dreams contain male and female dream figures who are based not on real outer people but on inner tendencies that are experienced as masculine or feminine. While disturbances between these two aspects of oneself need not be central, such disturbances always exist between the male and female sides of an individual. In thinking about healing these disturbances, we must begin with the psyche as it exists, with tendencies that are subjectively labeled masculine and feminine in some friendly or warring relation to each other.

Masculine consciousness—the consciousness with which we are most familiar—rests on splitting the world into opposites. We can imagine hardness because we contrast it with softness, dryness because we know about wetness. Perhaps the most basic set of opposites into which the universe has been split by human consciousness is masculine and feminine. Our species divides itself into two "opposite" (not "neighboring") sexes, male and female, which form completely exclusive categories of roughly equal size. One is either male or female, one can never pass from one group to the other. Even surgeons cannot enable a biological male to experience the central feminine mystery of pregnancy and childbirth. In some way each sex considers the other mysterious; the opposite sex's physical and emotional experience is eternally impenetrable at a core level. Freud was one of a long train of male thinkers to comment on the impossibility of ever understanding women—despite the fact that the great majority of his patients were women! For a woman, of course, it is men who seem intrinsically obscure.

Basing itself on this inherent human experience of the unbridgeable difference between the two sexes, human cultures throughout the world have developed rich and complex sets of ideas and images associated with the qualities "masculine" and "feminine." Each culture's understanding of the masculine and feminine principles is expressed in the images of men and women found in its art, mythology, and folklore. Just as we turned to the dreams of a woman and a man to understand each of their inner images of the feminine and masculine principles, we will turn now to the collective dreams of Western civilization in an attempt to describe our culture's image of the masculine and the feminine.

Let us not forget that these images of feminine and masculine essences have little, if anything, to do with the innate nature of men and women, though they will reflect something of the ways men and women have been conditioned to be within the context of our culture. It is unfortunate that we are saddled with these labels—masculine and feminine—rather than some neutral words like "yin" and "yang" because it is difficult, if not impossible, to avoid getting caught up in identifying with the label that corresponds to one's own sex. Men generally want to be masculine. Because of the ways in which the feminine has been denigrated historically, women are more conflicted about their relationship to the label "feminine" but a woman will almost inevitably assume that "feminine" has something to do with her essential nature.

It is possible that this idea holds a grain of truth, but for our purposes its inaccuracy is far more important. Mythology, folklore, fairy tales, and art the world over have constructed images of "men" and "women" more appropriately understood as stereotypes of masculinity and femininity than as anything realistically reflecting the way men or women are. These stereotypical images of male and female, developed by human cultures through the millenia of human history, are complex, multifaceted, and profound in content. But living human beings would be flattened into two-dimensional cutouts were they to model themselves on either image. Rather than thinking of these images as telling us anything about what men and women are like, we can understand them as outward indications of the kinds of projections each sex makes on the other and the kinds of expectations we hold for ourselves. Inwardly, these images portray the way we sort our innately conflicting unconscious impulses and the way these inner oppositional tendencies relate to each other.

The feminist movement began addressing the various inequities in the social system by seeking access for women to the men's world. Caught in the cultural overvaluation of the masculine, feminist thinkers too often seemed to insist that women could be as good at being men as men could be. This thinking misses the central difficulty toward which feminism is now turning more fully: when either a man or a woman is saddled with a gender-based stereotype, his or her *human*ness suffers. This wounding is more basic than any gender-linked wound could be. Neither the traditional man's role nor the traditional woman's role is desirable when one is trying to become a whole person with access to all of one's potential qualities.

We cannot discard the imagery of human history—our collective character structure, much of which, in any case, is fascinating and beautiful. But we do not want to support the age-old imposition of this sex-linked imagery on real men and women. In an attempt to accomplish this impossibly contradictory task, I will reify the masculine and feminine principles, asking the reader to split them off from flesh-and-blood people who must be seen as human beings first, male and female only secondarily. I will use the sex-linked images of the cultures of the world as two poles of a continuum of possible ways of being, thinking, and behaving. These images, from mythology, folklore, art, religion, and so on, are the cultures' dreams, x-rays of the collective psyche as it has developed over many centuries. In the course of this book I will look at excesses and deficits in common therapeutic approaches, understanding them in relation to this masculine/feminine continuum. To begin, however, let me describe the composite fantasy our Western culture has developed of masculine and feminine, a composite drawn from as many cultural images as possible. Because we are *not* talking about men and women, but rather about a one-sided stereotype, we will call these combined images the Masculine and the Feminine or the masculine and feminine principles. We are talking about a complex inner image that is strongly rooted in the deep unconscious, distorting our perceptions of the material world.

Real men and women, unlike archetypal figures, must operate from and contain both principles all of the time. Over the centuries of human history all possible human traits and attitudes as well as many nonhuman ways of being have been sorted into these two categories. Feeling, for example, is generally associated with the Feminine and thinking with the Masculine. But we all must think and feel; no matter how unequal the weight we give the two activities, no matter how highly we value the intellect and how disparaging we may be about our emotional side, every human being must engage in both activities to some extent. Traditionally, young people's energies are devoted toward developing their sex-allied characteristics (although this has been much less true for girls in recent history). But as we age, if we are to mature at all, we must confront the tremendous limitations imposed on our natures by any attempt to force our beings into categories that limit us to experiencing only one-half of the human condition. Within each individual is a whole universe that embraces all possible states of being, those in the realm of the Masculine and those from the world of the Feminine. As our years unfold, the underlying human drive toward wholeness pushes us increasingly into those areas we neglected in our youth. For many modern women, as well as for men, this means an increasing interest in the feminine sphere, in areas that were rejected in youth as worthless.

We are all familiar with the fact that our culture is patriarchal and discriminates against women. Less often recognized are the ways that cultural bias discriminates against the feminine side of each and every individual. *Human wholeness has been the most important victim of humanity's biases against the Feminine.* Men have suffered from the oppression of their own feminine qualities. Women have raged against men in the outer world, unaware of the ways in which their own inner masculine aspects have oppressed them more brutally and consistently than outer men could imagine.

As psychotherapists our central task involves mending physic splits and restoring inner wholeness; we especially need to include both sides of the psyche, the feminine and the masculine, in our approach to our work. Being children of our own time, this has been impossible for any of us to accomplish, for we, too, have been imbued with the patriarchal biases against our own feminine sides that pervade our culture. Male and female therapists alike need to redeem the unlived elements of their nature, and for women as well as men those unlived elements often prove to belong to the feminine sphere.

If my description of the feminine and masculine principles sounds biased in favor of the feminine, this reflects only my attempt to redress a balance long since lost. Neither principle is adequate on its own; in therapy as in life we need a balance between the two. Snow White and Rapunzel need Prince Charming to rescue them from their excessively feminine enclosures. Hansel's brilliant plans for his and Gretel's safety are inadequate; they must both submit to the witch's dominance, waiting patiently for Gretel's opportunity to present itself. Most of us *have* the Masculine, and what one already has often seems tawdry or at least unappealingly familiar. Working in a man's world, most of us lack the Feminine and so its qualities seem radiantly appealing. Let us not imagine, however, that substituting a domination of the Feminine for the long-standing domination of the Masculine would be an improvement. A balanced partnership is our goal.

The Feminine Principle[1]

Each principle has a static and dynamic aspect. The static Feminine is imaged by the containing womb. It values Being in an organic, undifferentiated form, where all components of the whole are equally valued, all elements dependent on all other elements. This static feminine outlook fosters an impersonal orientation in which the focus is on reproducing the species and continuing the great chain of life, rather than on the individual. We see here Mother Nature at her most prolific and dispassionate, producing hundreds or even thousands of baby sea turtles, for example, in the expectation that tens of them will survive to carry on the species. The commitment to the continuation of life is central, but the commitment to any specific life is nonexistent; there is an unconflicted acceptance of the value and necessity of death as an integral part of life. This orientation is a uterus, personified in human form.

In human cultures this attitude unconsciously colors many groups characterized by intense family relationships. In these groups children are highly cherished but their value is for their membership in the tribe

---

[1]The following discussion of the feminine and masculine principles relies heavily on Ulanov (1971) and Hill (1978).

rather than for their particular personal qualities. The Jewish tradition, for example, fosters an orientation to life that values one's children above all else, but if a deeply loved child marries a non-Jew, the child may be mourned as though dead by his or her parents. If the child does not continue to be Jewish, he or she becomes nonexistent.

The dynamic side of the feminine principle is the basis of play and playfulness, the main element in the creative process. The virgin maiden, for whom all things still seem possible, is the image most aptly associated with this state. The dynamic feminine experience involves messing around, trying things out, moving randomly and without direction, being open to what might come up, letting events affect one, responding to the unexpected. It leads to the creation of new combinations of life's elements, each combination being valued as it arises simply for its existence, not comparatively with other combinations. The central value of the dynamic feminine principle is Eros: the connections between individuals, the relationships that encircle our lives. This side of the feminine principle seems to be completely determined by culture, not linked even imagistically to female biology. But while we can hope to modify a cultural assumption in a way we cannot shift a biological given, we still must begin with what does exist: this kind of energy is ordinarily imaged by our deeper selves in feminine forms.

As the static Feminine is symbolized by the womb, the dynamic Masculine is pictured by the penetrating phallus. This side of the masculine principle values initiative and action directed toward a goal. Here we have the story of the hero with his drive to conquer and to become a differentiated individual. From this place the individual seeks objective analysis, linear and rational thought, causes and effects. Progress is a central goal, and when this masculine attitude has run rampant, untempered by feminine considerations, progress's partner, technology, may be deified. This should not lead us to disregard the tremendous value of dynamic masculine energy. It has brought us the airplane and the printing press in the outer world, and in the inner world, this spirit has enabled us to develop the Western ego through its deep commitment to the uniqueness and value of each individual's personal quest.

The static aspect of the masculine principle is captured in the image of the benevolent king. Here we have the tendency toward laws and organization, the systematizing of knowledge, the codification of rules. Impersonal objectivity is valued, the clear judgments of Logos are sought. Government and the law are grounded in the static masculine sphere. Again, there is not even an imagistic link to male biology. (Let us remember that even where an imagistic link to the male or female sexual organs exists, it is the nature of the sexual organs, not the nature of the people who carry them, that is being described.)

All people contain static and dynamic energy currents associated with both principles. The masculine principle urges us to meet competitive challenges, to seek honors and recognition, and to focus on concrete achievements—to go forth into the world, hoping to slay a dragon. Mythology and folklore offer us a wealth of heroic stories describing this attitude. Wagner's Seigfried offers a prime example of this stereotypical masculine approach to life.

Often myths or fairy tales depict the ways the masculine or feminine principles are incomplete in themselves, needing a connection to the other principle. The *Iliad,* for example, begins with the theft of the Feminine (Helen) from Greece by Troy. The enraged Greek warriors wait endlessly on the beach for favorable winds to take them to Troy. At last Agamemnon sacrifices his daughter, Iphigenia, to the gods to win the winds' cooperation. In order to undertake this masculine task of making war the men must absolutely sever their connection to the Feminine. Although this approach begins the tale that ends in a Greek victory, the tremendous problems stemming from pure masculinity unrelieved by any feminine elements are dealt with in a number of related mythic sagas. When Agamemnon returns from Troy the Feminine takes revenge on him in the person of his wife, Iphigenia's mother, who murders him for his heartlessly goal-oriented behavior. The *Odyssey* tells the tale of Odysseus's return to Greece from Troy; one element in Odysseus's 20-year journey involves his need to become reconnected to the Feminine before he can successfully return to his wife, Penelope. Odysseus must encounter a variety of female figures—Circe, the Sirens, Calypso and finally Nausicaa—before he manages to find a successful way back to civilization where the Masculine and the Feminine must live in harmony with one another.

In direct contrast to the heroic masculine approach, the feminine principle values the noncompetitive creation of things that are appreciated for their own essence regardless of their comparative qualities. The emphasis is on caring for people and for life in all the myriad forms of its manifestation, each more interesting than all the others. One holds each form for its own sake. Rather than seeking to conquer nature or the world, a feminine approach values being in nature and the world, experiencing and savoring one's interdependent enmeshment in the great web of life that encircles the earth. The popular sense of Mother Nature embodies this attitude as do paleolithic images of the Great Goddess such as the Venus of Willendorf (Neumann 1955, plate 1) with her enormous breasts and belly and her strongly emphasized vulva. The Greek goddess Artemis incorporates this aspect of the Feminine, living in the forest with only female companions, almost ferral in her connection to nature and her separation from civilization. A statue of Artemis in Ephesus pictures her with 50 or 100 lactating breasts covering the front of her body, apparently able to nourish countless living creatures endlessly.

A masculine approach disregards relationships, orienting toward accomplishments and power. The worst side effects of this approach can injure individual people, pushing them out of the way of the future, as, for example, the white man pushed the Native Americans aside to make room for the westward expansion of the United States. Historically, this masculine striving for accomplishment has often been invaluable. If a bridge needs building, if a population needs to be innoculated against smallpox, if a desert needs irrigating, the demands of specific individuals may need to be sacrificed for the sake of the project. But where we have been able to see the value of these kinds of masculine accomplishments easily, it has been harder to appreciate the complimentary feminine orientation that puts relationships to others at the center of life. This pure feminine attitude might see the destruction of the Native American cultures as the central event in our nation's history, ignoring the construction of the railroads, the building of the steel mills, the California gold rush—most of our high school history class's content would be irrelevant to a purely feminine assessment of events. This would make no more sense than the traditional masculine attitude, which discounts the destruction of the native cultures.

The core feminine experience is one of being immersed in the living world, one link in an infinite chain. The corresponding masculine position emphasizes one's separateness from the rest of life and values behavior that acts upon the not-me world, effecting it, leaving one's mark on it, dominating and transcending it. Neither approach is superior to the other, both are essential for a full experience of life. Aphrodite embodies the relationship-centered aspect of the feminine mode. The goddess of love and the mother of Eros, she focuses on relationship to the exclusion of all else. She is married to Hephaestus, the physically unattractive god of fire and of the arts, the craftsman of the gods. Aphrodite, who would spend her entire life swimming blissfully in loving relatedness with no goal other than the experiencing of that relatedness, is incomplete alone. She needs Hephaestus, whose craft can accomplish something concrete and lasting in the material world.

At the same time as the essential feminine experience resides in being linked with all life, it also includes a need for space and solitude, for contemplative being that has no product or justification for its existence. But this separation from others is qualitatively different from the masculine separation that seeks to act upon others. Feminine withdrawal seeks aloneness without an outer goal, disconnection for the experience of one's being. When the need is for aloneness, the focus is on the fact of wanting separateness from others rather than on wanting to accomplish something in opposition to others. Interestingly, in our culture, men are more apt to live out this element of the feminine principle than are women. It is more often the man who feels engulfed and needs space to find himself in a love relationship. But if we keep to our culture's expression of the archetype of the Feminine, rather than the experiences of living men or women, we can see that mythology and folklore typically depict this self-involved, self-contained quest for one's unique nature in a woman's form. Think about the princess playing endlessly with her golden ball in the fairy tale of the frog prince, for example. This idyllic experience of wholeness in her aloneness is found through feminine withdrawal. The limitations of this purely feminine state form the basis of the fairy tale's story line: the princess must embrace the Masculine (kiss the frog), which seems disgusting at first glance, in order to become complete.

We can summarize this major differentiation between the Masculine and the Feminine as Doing versus Being. This will be one of the most important polarities in relation to which we will reassess the effective action of psychotherapy.

The feminine principle seeks an embodied relationship to the world, the masculine reaches toward the world of the spirit. Woody Allen's twin obsessions, sex and death, are two central mysteries from the realm of the Great Mother. It is Woman whose body swells with new life, whose organs, hidden and mysterious, bleed in rhythm with the moon, whose breasts produce nourishment for the infant miraculously created out of her own body. Until very recent times childbirth brought women into frequent, intimate contact with death. Where the Feminine accepts the weight of the body, an acceptance that necessarily includes the gruesome ills of the body and its ultimate death, the Masculine seeks to transcend the body and death. Where a feminine viewpoint urges us to emotionally experience our grounding in our physical incarnation, to relax into our being, a masculine approach seeks the immortality of achievements that will live after one's physical death. The danger of the Masculine is depicted in Icarus's fate: in trying to fly too high into the world of the spirit, Icarus tries to leave utterly behind his embodiment in feminine matter, and the consequence is his disastrous fall into the arms of Mother Earth and Death. The danger of the Feminine is pictured in Sleeping Beauty's tale: as she becomes a woman, beginning to bleed at the age of 13, she falls into a deep sleep, into a state of Being that does not include room for any

Doing, a state from which she can be rescued only by the Masculine—Prince Charming.

Unlike masculine consciousness which depends on splitting the world into opposites—on separating elements from their union with each other—feminine consciousness exists in close proximity to the unconscious. The Apollonian, masculine view conceives of coldness in terms of its measured value, compared to a measurement for hotness. A feminine experience begins with the skin rather than the eyes; a temperature quality is felt in the body and is not split within itself. Coldness and hotness are *one* quality in this mode, not two. If hot or cold are contrasted it would be with something different from temperature such as solidity (hardness/softness) or speed (fastness/slowness). But contrasts are more the province of the Masculine than of the Feminine.

If masculine consciousness exists in Apollo's bright light, feminine consciousness develops in the soft light of the moon, or even in the dark. The constant, reliable sun is almost always ruled by a god while the moon, whose monthly rhythms are echoed in the female body, is usually personified as a goddess. Feminine knowledge proceeds in the dark much like the organic process of conception, out of sight, imperfectly imagined by the intellect, announcing its advent through hints and intuitions. In this mode one knows oneself first through one's digestive tract rather than through a mirror, one feels one's shape from the inside out. In Stanley's language, feminine consciousness emerges from the stomach, unlike masculine consciousness which is rooted in the head. Where masculine knowing seeks laserlike clarity that fosters perfection, feminine knowing orients toward a state of wholeness that includes imperfection and that blurs edges and differentiations.

This book is written largely in a masculine mode. It is an attempt to interpret the much neglected contribution of the Feminine to therapeutic work in terms that those of us trained in masculine thinking processes and values can understand. This undoubtably skews my message considerably. A feminine approach would lead, however, to a poem or a story rather than to a coherent, relatively linear discussion.

Feminine consciousness explores ideas, affects, images, and sensations within the inner depths; they seize the individual's attention, drawing him down into his psyche. Masculine consciousness separates the individual from his dark inner labyrinth: the individual reaches in and pulls something out to be examined in the clear light of day. It is like the difference between scuba diving and deep sea fishing.

Masculine consciousness analyzes life from a rational perspective, breaking it down into its component parts, examining each piece, judging it in a directed, disciplined, logical way. Feminine consciousness enters into the experience of any one of life's given elements and swims around in it. A feminine approach considers this bit of life, ponders and meditates on it, bringing together the inner experience with its outer reality, seeking to digest the whole of something, neglecting the masculine expertize which can sort situations out. The feminine concern is with meaning rather than with facts, with an entirety rather than with causative chains of pieces. This kind of understanding implies sitting with a problem, walking around an issue, familiarizing oneself with the territory over and over, until one may imperceptibly outgrow any given way of existence, any particular problem, possibly finding oneself living in a new situation. Neither approach is "better" than the other; different tasks imply different optimal orientations.

The Greek myth of Psyche, the story of a heroine's development rather than a hero's, offers many examples of the softer, circuitous approach the Feminine takes to difficulties. Psyche's first task is to sort an enormous heap of mixed seeds into separate piles. Psyche does not even attempt the hopeless chore, sitting instead "in silent stupefaction, overwhelmed by the vastness of the task" (Neumann 1956, p. 42). As she sits, helpful instinctual forces in the form of ants emerge and sort the seeds for her. When Psyche must gather some wool from the fiercely destructive golden rams of the sun, a helpful reed advises her on how to proceed. She hides in the shade until the early evening when the beasts sleep, following their frenzied activity of the day, and then she gathers wisps of fleece that have been caught on nearby bushes. The accomplishment of this task in Psyche's development contrasts vividly with Jason's approach to the same task in the story of the Argonauts. When he is asked to retrieve the golden fleece, the hero sets off on a lengthy quest involving a whole series of adventures, completing many apparently impossible tasks directly, overcoming obstacles through his strength and cunning. The individual emerges from an experience like Jason's with an increased sense of one's own size, boundaries, autonomous solidity in the world. One comes out of Psyche's encounter with the golden rams with a heightened sense of connection to the world of nature, of relationship to other living creatures.

This feminine experience of immersing oneself in one's situation as a means to becoming conscious of it means that rather than being guided by the mind, the whole personality, down to its animal and vegetable elements, is involving itself in the process. The knowledge—the consciousness—gained through this experience can never be shared directly with another person. This learning comes only from living. Attempts to share what has been gained in the feminine mode will take the form of images, metaphors, parables, paintings, poems, or stories, like the tale of Psyche.

The product of a feminine immersion in life is experiential knowledge. We call this feminine consciousness wisdom. It has been personified in Christian theology as Sophia and in Jewish mysticism as the Shekhina, God's feminine aspect. In Greek mythology, Athena was the goddess of wisdom. Unlike the brilliant analytic thinking of the masculine principle, which produces the knowledge of the intellect, feminine knowing is the intelligence of the heart, even of the stomach, the wisdom of feeling. It comes only with experience and therefore only with age and maturity. Unlike humanity's masculine intelligence that grows with each new generation's contribution, wisdom has not increased in human history. If one seeks wisdom, one begins with Ecclesiastes and Socrates; they are as relevant now as in their own time, for wisdom comes only with years of deeply savored and suffered life. It is a knowledge of oneself and of the world attuned to one person, to a unique incident. It is never guided by universal, abstract truths.

We can see the contrast between masculine judgment and feminine wisdom in the biblical story of Jesus's encounter with the adulteress. He came upon a woman who had been caught in an illicit liaison. The crowd, following the patriarchal law, "Thou shalt not commit adultery," prepared to stone the woman to death. Jesus intervened, saying he who was without sin among them should cast the first stone. Sobered, the lynch mob dispersed. In this story, Jesus is rejecting a masculine approach to the situation, an approach that evaluates this woman's behavior according to the codified, inflexible standards of the static masculine principle. He is urging a shadowy, vague "assessment" of the situation, an assessment determined by a loving immersion in the demands of a unique situation, by a deep empathic resonance with this woman's life. The fact that feminine wisdom is carried in this story by a (relatively androgynous) male figure underlines the fact that wisdom leads to a mutual and harmonious marriage between the Masculine and the Feminine, not to the substitution of feminine domination for masculine. Jesus's attitude is akin to the Native American adage that urges us not to judge another until we have walked a mile in his moccasins.

One way in which the Feminine has been devalued by our culture is that it has been depotentiated: all the life and power has been drained out of it. A soft, frilly pink doll has been left in the place of a vibrant, awesome Mother Goddess. Nowhere is that loss of vitality more clear than in the belief that passivity is feminine and activity is masculine. There is a whole realm of feminine activity, but, as we saw in Psyche's case, it is very different from the direct, phallic activity associated with a masculine approach. Feminine activity is receptive rather than forcing in nature. A masculine approach takes aim at its goal and moves decisively toward it, grappling with obstacles and (at least ideally) overcoming them. A feminine approach is not primarily goal-oriented. The individual harbors hopes and dreams, but rather than going after them in a determined way, a feminine sensibility moves one to submit to the processes of life that are activated at this time. There is a mixture of attentiveness and contemplation as one tries to attune oneself to the current of one's development, to let one's growth process happen, to avoid blocking a journey that is trying to proceed. The ego turns toward the unconscious, letting itself be guided by the organic processes of the psyche, immersing itself in its own depths rather than trying to direct the psyche. Great quantities of energy are called for as one tries to work *on one's own ego* rather than on the outer world, to align one's being with the forces of nature at work in both the inner and the outer worlds. Penelope, hounded by suitors as she awaits Odysseus's return, relied for many years on this patient receptivity, buying time for herself as she wove by day and unravelled her work by night, hoping for the emergence of a more favorable configuration in the world.

This feminine orientation is not simple. It involves a painful recognition of one's smallness, of the fact that one's psyche contains one's ego rather than vice versa. The core attitude is one of openness to the self and of submission to one's fate. There is a recognition and acceptance of the fact that one does not actually have control of one's life and an active relinquishment of the attempt to exert control where none is possible.

This is not a case, however, of simply letting happen what will. The ego as a factor in the equation is intensely active. Much of its activity is directed toward keeping in check its own impulses to struggle against the current of life, but, when the time and situation are favorable, the ego latches on to that strand of life moving in the desired direction. The cat, stalking its prey, provides an image of this feminine activity. She lies in wait, attentively tracking the creature she hopes to snare, apparently "doing nothing" at the same time as all of her being is intensely focused on the web of life, waiting for the emergence of her exact moment in history. How different from the masculine hound, crashing through the brush in fierce pursuit of his prey, flushing the fox out of its lair for the hunters. The cat attempts to capture her prey through perfectly attuning her own being to the life currents of the larger world.

This image of the patiently attentive cat, crouching immobile for long stretches of time, reminds us of the essential differences between a feminine view of time and a masculine sense of it. Masculine time is that marvelous development of the age of technology, time that is exactly and perfectly calibrated: every minute is the same as every other minute, they are each 60 seconds long. Masculine time makes scientific and technical progress possible; it structures much of the rhythm of our lives. Feminine time is qualitative rather than quantitative. Every minute is unique. Each hour may contain 60 minutes, but feminine wisdom emphasizes the fact that some hours are infinitely longer than others: some hours color entire days or even weeks, while other hours make no impact on us at all. Feminine time attunes itself to the cadence of the soul, masculine time orients to the movement of the sun in the outer world. The dancers of Stanley's healing dream were immersed in feminine time, attuned to the rhythms of their souls rather than the progress of the sun.

Feminine time is periodic and rhythmic, it is the time of the Book of Ecclesiastes reminding us that there is a time to be born and a time to die, a time to plant and a time to reap, a time of joy and a time of woe. From a feminine perspective one sees cycles of fertility, growth, birth, withdrawal, decline, and death. Each of these kinds of time is equally valid, equally intrinsic and necessary for the wholeness of life. A feminine perspective recognizes the necessity of death for the continuance of life, and it consequently accepts all the metaphoric deaths that fill our days: the death of a hope, the death of a marriage, the death of a plan.

Our resistance to a feminine orientation is tremendous. We are taught in every setting that we should be in control of our lives and that our lives will proceed in positive directions if we control them properly. We are urged to refuse to give in to depression and despair, to think positively. In the face of the clearest, most consistent evidence, our culture insists upon denying the ubiquitous, inescapable fact of darkness and death and upon maintaining a fiction of the possibility of living happily ever after if we will only manage our lives properly. The consequence of this attitude is not an increasingly widespread incidence of happiness, it is rather a situation in which people feel guilty about their depression and despair, exacerbating their pain by struggling against the legitimate suffering that life involves and that, when submitted to, ultimately brings wisdom. In Chapter 4, I will explore at length the way in which this distorted masculine attempt to dominate life and to exclude the darkness from existence undermines therapeutic work.

In this description of the feminine and masculine principles I have tried to highlight the assets embedded in the lost feminine orientation and the limitations of the culture's dominant masculine approach. The

Feminine is not more valuable than the Masculine, it is simply the missing half that we need to complete ourselves. Our exaltation of the Masculine has wrought wondrous blessings in our lives. We have developed a capacity to think and to plan, to subdue nature and create a quality of life beyond anything we could have even imagined several hundred years ago. But the loss of the Feminine is increasingly injurious to the deeper layers of our lives. The Feminine is not superior to the Masculine, but because it carries what we lack, it may seem more desirable than what we have.

Chapter 2

The Art of Psychotherapy[1]

All historical cultures have valued men more highly than women although contemporary scholarship suggests this was not true of prehistorical human cultures (Eisler 1987). The contemporary Western world is so much less extreme in this regard than previous cultures that we are currently seeing an attempt by women (and their male allies) to acquire equal rights and privileges for both sexes. Despite the very real prejudices that still block them, women today have more opportunities to become all they are capable of being than has ever been true before in the history of humankind.

On the other hand, this same liberated Western culture rejects the feminine principle and idealizes the masculine in ways that go beyond any historical precedent. When the contemporary women's movement began, its foremost goal seemed to be to allow women access to the man's world on an exactly equal footing. Women, too, were to have the right to drive themselves into the ground with overwork and ruthless competition, to leave their children from dawn to dusk, to measure their value by the size of their incomes. No one would ever get stuck bathing a baby or planting a rosebush again. This contrasts dramatically to a culture like India's where actual women were traditionally so devalued that they were expected to leap onto their husbands' funeral pyres. At the same time, Indian culture valued the feminine principle more highly than the masculine values those in the West have been taught to admire. The Indian culture's focus on Being (at the *expense* of Doing) has been denigrated in the West; Westerners note first the ways this focus has prevented material progress to a better life. However, this focus has also been associated with a spiritual depth that Westerners have difficulty comprehending.

Coming out of our culture's one-sided worldview, therapists, like all

[1]Portions of this chapter first appeared in Stevens (1984).

other "normal" members of society, have tried to belong to the valued (masculine) group. We have tried to develop clear diagnostic categories into which we can sort patients; we have insisted that one or another approach is correct in treating one or another of these categories; we have tried to measure the outcomes of our work along quantifiable dimensions; and we have tried to prove our points. Our vision has been skewed in a masculine direction even in our attempts simply to describe what it is that we do: sitting alone with another person for 50 minutes, we may spend 47 of those minutes attentively listening, but when asked what we do to help people, we describe what we do in the 3 (perhaps widely separated) minutes we spent talking. Our understanding of what we do and of what is helpful in what we do has been distorted by a worldview that values rationality, logic, and a stereotyped version of the hard sciences, at the expense of art, emotional meanings, and intuition. In many, many ways this masculine perspective provides an inhospitable attitude for psychotherapy, but rather than shifting our values and our conceptions, we have tried to cram our profession into this mold.

Individual psychotherapy as a formal professional procedure is barely a century old, but it has already splintered into countless factions ranging all the way from behavioral modification to classical psychoanalysis. The *New York Times Magazine* recently reported a survey identifying more than 450 forms of outpatient psychotherapy (August 30, 1987, p. 30). With the passage of time, the span of therapeutic orientations does not seem to be narrowing; rather they are proliferating. Critics of the field maintain that the welter of conflicting points of view indicates a basic flaw in the very idea of trying to effect a person's emotional life through one-on-one talking procedures. Attempts to measure the effectiveness of psychotherapy via the procedures of science, rationality, and logic have not been successful. Various researchers may believe they have definitively demonstrated the efficacy of Freud's talking cure, or at least of some of its variants, but many other psychologists and psychiatrists dispute their findings, insisting on organic or behavioral approaches to the psyche. Honest and intelligent practitioners in this field disagree on the most basic issues in sweeping ways.

On the other hand, people who have had personal therapeutic experiences tend to feel very strongly about them. Sometimes they are angry and feel cheated or abused or exploited by the months or years of time they spent working with a psychodynamic therapist. But often they are grateful to their therapist and feel, subjectively, that the experience was significantly helpful to them. The people in their lives often agree that therapy or analysis helped them. Although most therapists and analysts suffer private crises of faith from time to time, we usually manage somehow to maintain a basic belief in the value of our work, despite the lack of proof and despite our ingrained biases leading us to crave scientific proof of its efficacy.

Sometimes people's problems clearly get worse while in therapy. How can we measure to what extent the therapy is causing the deterioration and to what extent it is slowing or modulating a deteriorating process that cannot be arrested? Surely the psyche, like the body, can suffer from incurable injuries. From the opposite pole, I know of one woman who had a lengthy analytic experience that left her feeling betrayed and abandoned by her analyst at the same time that it transformed her life and her self in positive ways. Although she acknowledges the dramatic positive developments the therapy initiated she does not thank her analyst for the changes; she believes—and her intimate friends certainly agree—that she changed *against* the flow of his energy rather than with it. If this description of her experience is correct, and if we could scientifically measure therapeutic outcomes, would her case be a success or a failure? I believe both she and her former therapist would consider the therapy a failure; but she, her friends, and her family all know she has thrived. The operation was a total failure, but—as a direct result—the patient was reborn. Our masculine impulses toward scientific evaluations of our work are frustrated by the fact that there are no clear measures of success and failure in this work and no ways to control the infinite number of factors operating in any given case.

The Art of Psychotherapy

I could go on at greater length describing the chaos in the therapeutic field when it is viewed from a scientific, masculine perspective, but this small sample should suffice as a backdrop for my point: psychotherapy is closer to the humanities than it is to the sciences. For a long time we have all known that therapy involves art; it is not only science. But therapists have wanted therapy to be a science, because our culture values science unambivalently while often viewing art as a frivolous way to spend one's workweek. We like the certainty of science; we admire its replicable quality. Physicists agree the gravitational constant is 32 feet per second squared; we don't find some physicists insisting that things really fall up, not down.[2] Psychoanalysts are constantly heard disagreeing among themselves, united only in a belief that people actually feel things or want things that ordinary people are sure they would never, ever feel or want.

As a science develops, the viewpoints of its practitioners converge. Unlike depth psychologists whose work leads to increasingly disparate viewpoints, scientific work leads to ever expanding areas of agreement. When scientists disagree on something they collect evidence in the area and study it. In time they demonstrate to each other's satisfaction that one thesis or another is correct. If results cannot be replicated, they are dismissed. As one point of information is explored and agreement on its nature is reached, a new area of discovery is uncovered for exploration. Intense, even violent, disagreements, regarding the nature of the reality being studied may emerge. Intuitive leaps of judgment and wild hunches guide many scientists' efforts. Cutthroat competition may dominate the relationships between various scientists and their laboratories. But the nature of the business is such that truths are ultimately demonstrated either mathematically or empirically and agreement settles over the entire field regarding these demonstrated truths.

The humanities and the arts lie more in the realm of the Feminine and their development is in marked contrast to the development of the hard sciences. As these feminine pursuits unfold, their forms proliferate. Artists have not mastered landscape painting, for example, in such a way that the ultimate landscape has been painted and there is no more to be done in that area. Each artist's talent vis-à-vis landscapes feeds each new artist's vision and helps him create an original approach to the beauty of the natural world. An art would not be developing if its forms converged; we would have, instead, Socialist Realism or some comparable school, drained of the creative juices that make an art grow, that lead each artist to produce a vision of the world uniquely hers, distinct from all other individuals' images. The humanities, those intellectual fields that explore the arts, literature, philosophy, and human culture in general follow a similar, spiraling developmental path. There is no definitive dissertation on Hamlet or Socrates to be written. Each scholar must study others' work and go on to produce his own sense of its meaning.

Although therapists almost universally talk about their work as though it were a science—as though there were a clear-cut right or

---

[2]I am dealing here more with the nonscientist's image of science than with its current reality. Contemporary physics is incorporating more aspects of the Feminine both in its approach to its material and in the theories being constructed regarding the nature of reality.

wrong way to approach suffering individuals—the reality of the field approximates literature more closely than chemistry. Each decade finds new ways of working with emotional disturbances. Some approaches are dropped with the passage of time and others abide, but even those that last and seem stable in form, like classical psychoanalysis, vary greatly from one practitioner to another, even between contemporaries. Surely it would be a very different experience to be the analysand of Ralph Greenson or of Otto Kernberg, of Melanie Klein or of D. W. Winnicott.

Michael Franz Basch, the noted Self Psychologist, addresses this issue of the proliferation of therapeutic viewpoints. In an article in *Contemporary Psychoanalysis* he states his thesis:

> [T]he repeated splintering of our field into various schools was, and is, unnecessary and counterproductive. We are today in a [good] position . . . to establish a unitary theory of psychotherapy . . . . (1987, p. 368)

He then proceeds to suggest that we resolve our differences by accepting his perspective. There is an inherent naïveté in Basch's approach. Arnold Cooper, a psychoanalyst associated with the Columbia Center for Psychoanalytic Training and Research, discussing the paper, is in full agreement "that the time has come for a unification of psychoanalytic points of view" but he "*disagree[s]* concerning the grounds for unification" (1987, p. 384, emphasis added). Cooper suggests we "unify around the compatibility of multiple viewpoints," (ibid.) and while the word "unify" puzzles me, it does seem that we need to find a way to accept and value the many divergences between depth therapists. We need to relinquish the fantasy that one viewpoint is right and all others are wrong. Somehow we need to imagine a way that many contradictory ideas can all be right—without, of course, denying that some ideas are wrong.

In their insistence on scientific status, psychoanalysts first maintained that there would be no difference in the experience of analysis with different analysts. Any competent analyst would make the same intervention at the same point. This primitive idea was rapidly dropped, but some analysts still maintain that working with any competent analyst will have the same result. This idea can never be evaluated experimentally. The same individual cannot work with two analysts at the same time, and no two individuals can ever be matched for the purposes of analytic experiences. The hypothesis can be accepted on faith, but it seems intuitively comparable to the idea that the particular qualities of any good-enough mother will not leave a significant impact on her adult child. Although any two analysts may be equally capable of healing an individual's inner complexes, the impact of a thousand-odd profoundly intimate hours with another person will surely reflect the uniqueness of that other person. The wish to question this simple fact can only come out of a wish to preserve a "scientific" aura around our field, despite the fact that in practice psychotherapy does not behave like a science.

Scientists do not read original documents. Pasteur's discoveries regarding invisible organisms have been incorporated into later scientists' work. Beginning biology students would have no reason to read Pasteur's original papers; they would contain many inaccuracies that have since been corrected. Pasteur's valuable contributions are now included, along with those of later scientists, in textbooks that present them with more thoroughness and depth than Pasteur himself was able to.

This is not true in the humanities, and it is not true in the field of clinical psychology. Plato's truths have not necessarily been absorbed by later philosophers. If one wants to understand Plato's contribution to human culture, one should read him directly. This is more obviously true of the pure arts such as literature or painting or music. Rembrandt's contribution can only be absorbed by contact with his work.

A psychology student must read the great contributors of the past directly. Freud, Jung, Klein, Winnicott, Bion, Kernberg, Kohut. . . . Great psychological innovators have not and cannot incorporate each other's work though they naturally deepen their expertize by reading the work of others and in many important ways they do build on each other's work. But each offers a view of the human soul that is uniquely his or her own, and as later practitioners struggle to develop their own images of the depths of the human psyche, they must absorb each great visionary's vision afresh. If one is able to make an original contribution, it will be some new way of seeing an ancient piece of data, an insight that will be closer in its nature to a poem than to an equation.

The fact that the subject of our investigation is the unconscious is one major determinant of the situation. A masculine, scientific approach depends on the light of day, on amassing data that can be codified, sorted, clarified. The unconscious is no longer unconscious when analyzed in the light of day; we can only explore it in the dark. Our data is inherently unclear and deceptive. Examining the products of the unconscious—slips of the tongue, dreams, jokes, and so on—Freud demonstrated the existence of the unconscious and something about its habitual ways of behaving. But he could not *map* the unconscious, for its nature is uncontainable, infinite, eternally unpredictable and contradictory. We may learn a great deal about the unconscious of the moment from its products, but we can never codify these products in masculine terms. Books purporting to translate dream images, for example, are useless, for they miss the very essence of dream images: the imagery's fluid, shifting implications over time and between dreamers. The nature of our subject matter rejects a masculine approach to its understanding.

Our stubborn attempt to study our field in terms inimical to its nature (because these are the terms valued by our culture) has created a basic misconception regarding the nature of psychotherapy. This profession has been misunderstood not only by the lay public but also by its own practitioners. The field grew out of medicine—which is also, we know, an art as well as a science. But medicine has become more and more scientific as the twentieth century has progressed. Physicians increasingly tend to agree on the issues in their field. This has not happened in the field of psychotherapy, and therapists' wishes to be taken seriously as scientists, have been largely unfulfilled. As therapists we need instead to take ourselves seriously for what we really are. We need to seek the public's acceptance of us as artistic craftspeople rooted in the humanities, and we must educate first ourselves and then the public about the value we, as humanists, have to offer, particularly to the world of the late twentieth century.

We are not simply artists any more than we are simply scientists. We are transitional, moving somewhere between art and science, and our great social contribution (as distinct from the good we may do our individual patients) lies in that transitional status. We live in a world that has lost touch with the feminine values of culture and art—where being, rather than doing, is most valued; where beauty and meaning may be more important than utility, practicality, and cost. If the depth therapy world can recognize and value its own essential nature, perhaps it will be instrumental in helping our increasingly scientific culture to shift its biases, to move toward a more balanced view of life in which cost equations are weighed in relation to meaning as well as to productivity and output.

It is logical and sensible that psychotherapists began by hoping to create a body of scientific knowledge. How appealing an image, to imagine we could diagnose a specific form of depression in the same way a physician diagnoses a specific infection, and to hope to prescribe a particular intervention to cure that depression in the same way an antibiotic eradicates the bacterium that is debilitating an infected body. There would be, as we shall see, grave moral and emotional problems with this image even if it were practically possible. But since we continue to make no progress in the direction of achieving this state—since we seem, by many measures, to be moving ever further from the attainment of this kind of certainty—why, then, do we continue to cling to the illusion of becoming more and more scientific? What has stopped psychotherapists from saying that what we are doing is delicate, creative work, that each project (case) is a unique challenge which demands, certainly, our professional skill and expertise, but which also calls for the commitment of our whole psyches, most crucially our unconscious depths? The outcome of a case rests more broadly on intuition, empathy, and lucky (or unlucky) *unconsciously* guided movements than it does on thought-out, demonstrably effective interventions. In the real world therapists frequently say something first and figure out why they chose that intervention retrospectively. Our work is not replicable: no two practitioners would ever behave in exactly the same way, and although two therapists may be equally effective in some overall sense, they will never affect people identically.

This is a situation in which an emotional bias has clouded psychologists' viewpoints: our culture values the rational materialism of science and discounts the ephemeral, unquantifiable values of the humanities. Therefore we will insist on scientific status for all kinds of things, including our clinical work, which actually lies farther from the crystalline world of pure mathematics than it does from the insubstantial, shifting realms of poetry. This distorted evaluation may be fruitfully understood as resting on the basic split in our worldview that denigrates the feminine principle and idealizes the masculine.

Drive Theory versus Object Relations Approaches

Freud's own theories contained two major approaches: "drive theory," his central orthodox construction; and, rooted in his understanding of the transference and in his theories about the oedipal complex, a second strand which led to that vast proliferation of analytic approaches contained under the umbrella "object relations."[3] These divergent, innovative modes share an openness to the Feminine that orthodox psychoanalysis lacks.

Freud's early thinking bears some striking resemblances to later object relations approaches, but at the time of his father's death in 1896, Freud abandoned this early interpersonal theory of neurosis—the seduction theory—that he had been constructing. Marie Balmary, a French psychoanalyst, has written an arresting analysis of the internal pressures that forced Freud to renounce the insights he had gained

---

[3]Much of the following description of the divergence between drive theory and object relations theories is based on Greenberg and Mitchell (1983). See also Guntrip (1971) and Breger (1981).

in order to protect his inner image of his father (1982). There has been much further discussion on this point recently. For my purposes here, it is enough to say it is hard to imagine a modern psychoanalyst maintaining that 10 or 12 or 15 of his patients, all of whom believe they were sexually molested by their fathers, have simply "imagined" the occurrences, translating latent fantasies into objective memories. In the absence of strong evidence to the contrary, average, expectable analysts accept their patients' memories as roughly accurate. Recognizing the impact of the real outer world need not imply a lack of appreciation for the reality and power of the inner world.

Freud and his followers all maintain that orthodox psychoanalytic metapsychology rests on his rejection of the seduction theory and on his construction, in its place, of a drive/structural model of the psyche. This model maintains that two bodily drives, ultimately identified as sexual and aggressive in nature, form the entire basis of the psyche. The psyche is a secondary phenomenon, growing out of the conflict between the body's drives and the material world's frustration of those drives. All psychic structure develops out of the clash between these two physical realities. The unfortunate psychoanalytic use of the word "object" originated with this conception: an object is not a person or even a part-person such as a breast; it is a target for an instinctual drive. It is the drive that is clear; the object is fortuitous and replaceable.

A core assumption of this model, which follows from the centrality of the drives, is that the individual is a closed psychic system, an entity that can be studied by an outside observer without being unduly affected by the observer. The observer (the therapist) becomes a target for the patient's drives, but the therapist's individuality will not ordinarily have any striking impact on those drives, which will proceed inexorably on their own instinctual course.

This orientation is profoundly masculine in nature—rational, clear, distinct. It provides a superb foundation for a scientific approach to analytic work in that it allows the subject ("I") to study a separate object ("you") in the same way I can study frogs or stars or lichen. This early approach attempted to avoid one of the terrible difficulties of depth psychological work: the fact that analysts, no matter how "well analyzed" they may be, have infinite and independent unconsciouses of their own that become involved with their patients and with their patients' unconsciouses in unpredictable and even unfathomable ways. The object of our study (the psyche) is also the instrument of our study. Certainly by the 1960s all analysts, orthodox or revolutionary, were struggling in one way or another with this inherent difficulty of the therapeutic situation.

The drive/structural model suggests a particular conception of relationships. Freud derived all issues of closeness and distance—of intimacy—not from interpersonal or affiliative urges, but from the vicissitudes of the sexual and aggressive instincts. "[W]ithin the drive model the goodness or badness of relationships is fully determined by the nature of the drive quantity with which they are cathected" (Greenberg and Mitchell 1983, p. 296).

The inhuman character of this therapy is epitomized by Freud's 1905 analysis of Dora's response to Herr K.'s sexual assault. When Dora was 14 years old, Herr K., a friend and contemporary of her father's, suddenly and unexpectedly grabbed her and kissed her forcefully on the lips.

> This was surely just the situation to call up a distinct feeling of sexual excitement in a girl of fourteen who had never before been approached. But Dora had at that moment a violent feeling of disgust . . . . In this scene . . . the behavior of [Dora] was already entirely and completely hysterical. I should without question consider a person hysterical in whom an occasion for sexual excitement elicited feelings that were preponderantly or exclusively unpleasurable . . . . (Freud 1963, p. 43–44)

The assumed primacy of the budding biological urges over any interpersonal affective considerations is obvious. Many psychoanalysts who consider themselves classical Freudians have criticized this particularly extreme expression of drive theory—drive theory driven to an implacable conclusion. I include it not to imply that many contemporary psychoanalysts would support Freud's assessment to Dora's reaction to Herr K.'s assault, but rather to highlight the ultimate breakdown of drive theory untempered by other considerations.

Orthodox psychoanalysis evaluates all psychological theories against the measure of their adherence to or divergence from drive theory. Instinctual drives, and drives alone, set the psychic apparatus in motion and form the bridge between the body and the psyche. To the degree that Jung, Adler, Fairbairn, Sullivan, and Kohut, among many others, have sought other—or at least additional—principles to explain human motivation, they have been rejected by the orthodox establishment. While those theorists who have rejected drive theory are a more diverse group than its loyalists, we can see something of the essence of their divergence from Freud in the following contrast between the views of Freud and Jung.

In 1921 Freud attempted to explain the origin of erotic human love.

> It was possible to calculate with certainty upon the revival of the need which had just expired [i.e, after orgasm]; and this must no doubt have been the first motive for directing a lasting cathexis upon the sexual object and for "loving it" in the passionless inter-

> vals as well. (From *Group Psychology and the Analysis of the Ego*, quoted in Greenberg and Mitchell 1983, p. 42)

Contrast this with Jung's assertion, in the first of his *Two Essays on Analytical Psychology*, that neurotic complexes are indeed rooted in unconscious conflicts concerning "love" but that "love" implies far more than simply sex.

> Freud's sexual theory [he maintains] . . .commits the imprudence of trying to lay hold of unconfinable Eros with the crude terminology of sex. (1943, par. 33)

Eros, the god who inspired relatedness to others, who works through the heart rather than the genitals, and who raises issues of intimacy rather than of lust, is a central figure for an object relations orientation. This orientation is more feminine than masculine and it begins with the central value of the feminine principles, relatedness.

Whereas drive theorists hypothesize a bodily-based drive that seeks an object on which to discharge itself, object relations theorists begin with the psyche as a primary reality, not developing simply in reaction to the bodily frustrations of life. They hypothesize one or another variants of an affiliative drive, grounded in the psyche, not the body. This instinctual search for attachment and intimacy uses biological urges as a bridge to various forms of connectedness and separateness. Genital and pregenital zones of bodily pleasure are available to individuals to be used in the service of creating and maintaining relationships with others and with themselves. Here drive theory is stood directly on its head; relationships with others, not instinctual drives, are seen as the fundamental building blocks of psychological life. Creating and re-creating patterns of relatedness replace drive discharge as the central human motivational force. Satisfying emotional contact with others has supplanted physical pleasure as the core drive. Physical drives serve interpersonal needs rather than vice versa.

The British School (Klein, Fairbairn, Winnicott, and Guntrip), the American Interpersonalists (Sullivan, Fromm, Horney, Thompson, and Fromm-Reichmann), Jung, and Kohut were all object relations thinkers. All of them rejected drive theory as a fundamentally wrong approach to human motivation although the directness with which each of these thinkers rejected drive theory varied. Many of them considered drive theory's mechanical, narrowly biological orientation pernicious. They all saw the individual's relationships with inner and outer objects as the central area of psychoanalytic interest. They believed the human individual, in interaction with others, to be the crucial object for our attention.

D. W. Winnicott

My work relies heavily on the contributions of D. W. Winnicott. In America, after many years of relative neglect, Winnicott is gaining influence in psychological circles. In many ways his orientation comes out of a feminine center, which may explain why some depth psychologists have been reluctant to take him as seriously as he deserves. He spoke in ordinary language, refusing for the most part to use metapsychological jargon. He typically described clinical situations in which he allowed things to happen rather than situations in which he made things happen. He focused on providing a "facilitating environment" for patients, being more concerned with what he called "nursing care" and "handling" than with "treatment."

Winnicott frequently described depth therapeutic work as involving "holding" and "interpretation." Even in the area of interpretation, Winnicott was revolutionary. Although he did maintain he was not rejecting the traditional psychoanalytic approach of interpreting instincts and defenses, his papers and case examples almost never illustrate an interpretation of that traditional nature. His interpretations begin with his patients' psyches, not with their bodily instincts; he addresses people first in relationship with others, and only secondarily vis-à-vis their bodily drives. Although he certainly recognized that an individual could be gripped by an instinctual drive, he maintained that an id drive impinging on the individual was as much outside the individual (infant) as was any other impinging experience. Winnicott was interested in a self, a person, seeking contact with others. His image of health involved instinctual drives used by the individual to express relatedness with others. "We differ from Freud," Winnicott maintained. "He was for curing symptoms. We are concerned with living persons, whole living and loving" (quoted in Guntrip 1975, p. 151).

But Winnicott's most radical contribution to the theory of technique lay in his focus on the "holding" aspect of the therapeutic process. The vast majority of the psychiatric literature has dealt with interpretation. Holding—which we might compare with cherishing or polishing, a central element in mothering behavior—has been almost entirely neglected. Winnicott spoke extensively about holding; he introduced it as a major area of study.

This book is about the holding—the nursing—that occupies the majority of time in any effective therapeutic venture. Although both holding and interpretation are needed, of the two holding seems more often primary to me; interpretations cannot be heard unless the holding is working and the holding will do some good all on its own, even if interpretations are never effectively made. Once one recognizes the extent and importance of this side of the work, one is astonished at the lack of attention that has been paid to it. This lack rests almost entirely on the fact that holding is a primary expression of the devalued feminine principle. This book attempts to redress the lack of attention paid to psychotherapy's nursing functions.

C. G. Jung

Part of my attempt to reassess the therapeutic process from a feminine perspective will involve some examination of the ideas of C. G. Jung. One major element in the divergence between Jung and Freud lies in the fact that Jung oriented, in major ways, from a feminine perspective while Freud was firmly rooted in the masculine, scientific outlook of the Enlightenment. Jung's work is considerably less known than Winnicott's because he functioned far outside mainstream psychoanalytic circles. Much of his writing is quite esoteric in nature, relevant only tangentially for clinical work. But the ways in which he did address the clinical encounter strikingly anticipate later analytic developments and offer profound insights, rooted in the feminine principle, into the nature of the healing process. Let me briefly sketch some Jungian attitudes toward therapeutic work that grow out of a feminine orientation and offer a much needed balance to the masculine biases of our field.

Where much of the therapeutic world has aimed at "curing" patients of their "illnesses," Jung talked mainly about individuation and wholeness. He did not ignore emotional illness, and he frequently expressed the idea that Freud's approach was of great value in dealing with emotional illnesses, but Jung's own interest was in working with people who were trying to become all of themselves in creative, vital ways. Often, perhaps always, the suffering individuals who seek therapeutic help fall into both categories: they are caught in disturbed complexes that leave them emotionally "ill," and they are yearning to become truer versions of their potential selves than had theretofore been possible. There is much overlap between these two difficulties, but there is also some distinction between them. Where Freud focused on the former, Jung turned to the latter and he therefore offers us not a substitute for the approach Freud initiated, but a valuable addition to it.

In practice, Jungian work has suffered from a relative neglect of the illnesses that block people's development. This relative weakness in Jung's legacy also reflects one of his strengths; this inattention to curing illnesses also expresses itself as an attempt to help people find room within themselves for their inadequacies and wounds. Rather than trying to help patients overcome the dark, imperfect aspects of themselves, Jung sought to help them integrate their shadow sides. As James Hillman (1975) puts it, the psyche's pathology brings pathos to life. Although mainstream therapeutic approaches also recognize the imperfectibility of human nature, it has been hard for many therapists, caught in our culture's masculine quest for perfection, to accept the ways that therapeutic "success" must encompass human failure—limitations, death, inadequacies, and so on. Through his connection with the Feminine, Jung found a way to accept the dark side of our natures with peace and even joy, believing that a wholeness that could encompass our darkest aspects would radiate light.

Jung suggested a dramatically unusual view of the individual's relationship to difficulties and to life in general. Most traditional analytic approaches ask the person to become conscious of subterranean machinations and to take charge of oneself and of one's life. A heroic, masculine stance is called for vis-à-vis the inner and outer assaults of life. While Jungians certainly orient toward consciousness, the entire Jungian literature is permeated with a constant attempt to eschew a heroic attitude either toward oneself or toward the outer world. We are invited to take an attitude of humility toward life and to recognize that in relation to our inner selves as well as to the outer world, *we are not in charge*. However unpleasant that recognition, however existentially distressing, the wisdom that comes with maturity consistently supports the inescapable fact of our smallness in a vast inner world. Jung wanted people to become constructively related to their larger selves, to the unconscious depths that *are* largely in charge, believing that out of a positive connection to the inner world, the individual could modulate the expression of that inner reality into socially and personally constructive, appropriate forms in the outer world. The Jungian attitude tends to be humble rather than dominant, feminine rather than masculine.

Nowhere is Jung's unique contribution more vividly operative than in his work on religion, the quintessential expression of the irrational depths of the human psyche. Freud rejected religion as an illusion and hoped that at least conscious individuals would leave it behind and view the world rationally. Jung never defended religious beliefs as rational or realistic—he never maintained their objective truth. But, unlike Freud, his interest vis-à-vis religion was not in eradicating it. Accepting religion as intrinsic to the human psyche, Jung wanted to understand its psychological role in the deepest reaches of the human mind. As he explored this role, via his theory of archetypes, he found the meaning of religious beliefs to be multifaceted and complex, far beyond our trite intellectual stereotype that defines religious beliefs as wish-fulfilling denials of death.

Jung's courage in exploring this traditionally feminine realm of religion, an area much despised by contemporary masculine consciousness, should be respected. Like Winnicott after him, Jung was interested in revivifying the human capacity for illusion while maintaining the legacy of the Enlightenment which allows us to recognize illusion for what it is rather than imagining that our spiritually enriching capacities for fantasy reflect objective outer realities. Where Freud hoped that reason would triumph over the irrational reaches of the soul, Jung hoped that reason would accept a partnership with the spooks and demons—the gods—who emerge from deep inside our selves and who dominate so much of our existences.

Implications for Clinical Work

The two theoretical models I have described—drive theory and object relations theories—imply different senses of the psyche's healing processes and, consequently, compel different technical approaches to the analytic situation. In the drive model, the drives are fixed, and healing comes from bringing them under the control of the ego. In this heroic, masculine approach one strives to replace unconscious defense with conscious choice. Interpretations that make the unconscious conscious are consequently the core intervention. Heinz Hartmann follows out drive theory's implications most implacably: the impact of psychoanalysis derives solely from insight, which modifies the judging apparatus of the ego. The transference relationship is not a real object relationship, and the reliving of the past has no value outside the intellectual insight it produces. There is no place for experiential effects of the analytic process, which is never conceived of in relational terms (in Greenberg and Mitchell 1983, p. 265).

This focus on insight as the healing factor has been carried over, unexamined, into the work of many object relations therapists, although it is actually inconsistent with a relational model. The crucial issues in an approach based on the psyche's attachment needs is not insight, mediated by correct interpretations, but rather the quality of the transference-countertransference relationship that the therapist and patient construct together. In this model, a "correct" interpretation is helpful because it expresses a deep conscious and unconscious resonance between therapist and patient. And in this sentence, "correct" is not necessarily synonymous with "accurate" (a tricky concept in any case); "correct" means usable, valuable, soothing or nourishing to the individual's true self.

Where the drive model seeks to tame eternally fixed instincts, object relations models focus on patterns of relationships that are unquestionably capable of change. The drive model sees the therapist as an object for the patient's drives, separate from the patient and able to interpret the patient's drives objectively. The relational model conceives of the therapist and patient as a unit reenacting the patient's past relationships—in some modified form. This new relationship then modifies the patient's internal images of relationships. The psyche's structure begins as a mirror of the individual's initial attachments; the psyche re-creates these infantile relationships in the transference; the resulting interpersonal patterns are modified by the therapist's noncooperation in the patient's complexes; the modifications are then internalized by the patient in new psychic structures, which manifest in new transference patterns. By participating in the patient's patterns, the analyst affects the form of those patterns. In this model, there is no such thing as a neutral analyst interpreting drives and defenses. There is rather an interpersonal field involving both participants. The observer and the observed form a relational dyad, an interpenetrating, living organism from which a single psychic system can never be clearly extricated.

Jung took this feminine position to an extreme, rejecting even the attempt to discuss technique, insisting that it is "the personality of the doctor himself [that is the] curative or harmful factor . . ." (1931, par. 172). For Jung, the personality of the doctor is

> infinitely more important for the outcome of the treatment than what the doctor says and thinks . . . . For two personalities to meet is like mixing two different chemical substances: if there is any combination at all, both are transformed (ibid., par. 163).

The therapist " 'takes over' the sufferings of his patient and shares them with him" (1946, par. 358); the therapy is not working, he maintained, until the patient has become an emotional problem to his therapist. Winnicott emphasized this same inextricable interdependence in his famous statement denying the possibility of conceiving of an infant apart from the mother-infant unit. Michael Balint, a colleague of Winnicott's, describes the two individuals in the analytic consulting room as becoming all tangled up with each other in what is, at its height, a "harmonious, interpenetrating mix-up" (Balint 1968, p. 136). In this interpersonal model, change flows from experience, not from cognitive interpretations. The goal of the work is feminine wisdom; masculine insight is not the central curative factor, it is a by-product of shifts in the psyche's underlying structure.

From this survey of my subject, I turn now to a deeper exploration of each of its elements. Chapter 3, "The Archetypal Foundation of the Therapeutic Process," presents evidence from six major analytic thinkers, representing a wide range of theoretical orientations, demonstrating the existence of a consistent underlying pattern in successful therapeutic work. If we can become aware of the nature of this pattern, we may facilitate its emergence and more effectively nurture its development. Chapters 4 and 5 examine in more detail the role of the feminine and masculine principles in therapeutic work. Chapter 4 in particular, "Psychotherapy Grounded in the Feminine Principle," presents the major arguments of this book. In Chapter 6, "An Archetypal Perspective," I describe Jung's essential contribution to depth psychology: his archetypal perspective provides a foundation for my work and offers us a channel to expand our vision and deepen our reach. Chapter 7, "Two Clinical Examples," offers a tangible discussion of the restorative effect of a feminine approach to psychological disturbance. In Chapter 8, I attempt a brief look at the limitations of a feminine approach and survey one particular situation that highlights those limitations—the clinical predicament in which the therapist dislikes the patient.

Chapter 3

The Archetypal Foundation of the Therapeutic Process[1]

I have described two broad strands of psychoanalytic thinking, drive theory and object relations theory. Archetypal theory is a particular object relations approach that developed separately from the main analytic community as a result of the 1912 break between Freud and Jung. In Chapter 6, I will explore Jung's concept of archetypes more rigorously in an attempt to discover how an archetypal perspective can enrich clinical work. Here I will use the word "archetype" loosely to mean a broad pattern of human behavior that the psyche (as distinct from the ego) will naturally evolve to deal with the existential demands which have marked the human condition for time immemorial. Jung coined the term "archetype" to describe the innate foundations of the psyche and postulated that these inborn potentialities structure one's developing inner object relations.

My hypothesis in this chapter is that psychological healing follows an inherent pattern which emerges from the depths of the psyche. Just as an expert physician facilitates the body's own healing capacities rather than introducing health from without, so a successful therapeutic venture enables the distressed patient to tap into the healthy potential stored in implicate form within his own unconscious. Viewing the work of therapy from an archetypal perspective, the therapist tries to understand, first and foremost, where the patient's life force is heading. In what direction are her native energies trying to move her? In what direction are they pushing the analytic work?

This effort does not imply talking about archetypes with the patient. The stereotypical Jungian analyst is an older man with a (Swiss) German accent amplifying his patient's dreams with mythic stories and motifs. The fact that archetypal images are being discussed does not mean the analyst is taking an archetypal perspective on the analytic

---

[1]This chapter is a revised version of Sullivan (1987a) expanded with a section of Stevens (1986).

process; this stereotypical Jungian analyst is trying to attend to the content of the archetypal layer of the patient's psyche. His attention is not turned to the analytic process at all. When the therapist takes an archetypal perspective on the therapeutic process, he tries to see the thrust of the psyche's own healing instincts and to align himself with that thrust. He does not attempt to channel the psyche's growth according to ego-based conceptions about how the psyche does or should grow. An archetypal perspective on therapeutic work tells us the patient's psyche itself is the primary healer.

As we can see, this implies that being a Jungian does not mean the analyst does, or even can, take an archetypal perspective on the work. It is possible to block the psyche's path by means of a Jungian theory regarding what direction the patient ought to take, even if the theory is based on a mythological parallel to the individual's situation. Jungians often analyze the individual patient from an archetypal perspective: the patient is caught in the archetype of the puer, or the trickster, or the senex, for example, and therefore needs to develop in this or that direction. Non-Jungians diagnose their patients more traditionally—in ways that I experience as even more dehumanizing and pathologizing. But for our purposes here, a traditional diagnosis such as "borderline personality with strong obsessional features" is no different from a Jungian formulation. Each calls up an image of a wise therapist in control of the situation, understanding what is out of joint in the patient's psyche and what needs to be done to correct the trouble. Regardless of the language, this attitude is contrary to an archetypally grounded perspective in which the therapist begins by centering herself firmly in her awesome lack of knowing and turning toward the deep unconscious which does know what needs to be done. An increasing number of non-Jungian analysts are investigating both the archetypal processes that analysis mobilizes and the archetypal layer of the psyche—without, however, using those terms.

An archetypal perspective suggests that all psychotherapy—any depth therapeutic endeavor—follows a natural gradient which we can at least theoretically identify. If we can delineate this innate form of psychological healing, we can hope to align ourselves with it. I will begin my search for this essential form by surveying a number of analytic writers who have directly or indirectly addressed the nature of this pattern. I believe I can demonstrate that a variety of Jungian and non-Jungian analysts have described the same basic structure for the work. The analysts whose work I will try to correlate on this topic are C. G. Jung, Donald Sandner, Sylvia Brinton Perera, Michael Balint, D. W. Winnicott, and Heinz Kohut.

Joseph Campbell: The Monomyth

As a backdrop to the exploration of these clinicians, Campbell's description of the skeletal structure of the universal hero myth is worthy of mention. He suggests that all hero (or heroine) myths follow the same pattern. The hero, leaving his ordinary world, descends into the underworld where he confronts hostile and helpful forces in a variety of forms. After any number of preparatory adventures, the hero undertakes his ultimate ordeal and gains his reward. Whatever concrete form that reward may take, it symbolizes "an expansion of consciousness and therewith of being" (Campbell 1949, p. 246). The final stage of this universal myth deals with the return of the hero to the ordinary world where the treasures of the underworld rejuvenate life (ibid., p. 245–246).

Jungians use this mythic pattern as a template for the individuation process. Through the course of life, one makes any number of minor descents to the underworld and several major ones. Any night's descent into sleep/unconsciousness and the retrieval of a dream may be seen as sketching in the bare outline of the monomyth. Life's major crises and initiations also conform to this general pattern. The more deeply they are experienced, the more clearly we see the congruence between the drama of the myth and the individual's life. A depth analysis is a major initiatory experience for which the monomyth is an excellent template. I hope to describe how an analyst–patient dyad will subjectively experience the monomyth's various elements as they unfold in the course of a therapeutic venture.

C. G. Jung: *The Psychology of the Transference*

Jung's monograph on the transference uses a particular set of alchemical engravings to describe "the 'classical' form of transference and its phenomenology" (Jung 1946, Foreword, p. 164). The question Jung is addressing corresponds closely to mine: What is the universal form that guides the development of any particular person's therapeutic experience?

In order to understand Jung's description of the archetypal dimension of the analytic encounter, we need to get some sense of the meaning of his alchemical work. Although the medieval alchemists were trying to transform base metals into gold, their writings make clear that something much less straightforward was also taking place. A typical alchemical recipe might tell the worker to mix the *menstrum* of a whore with the fiery spirit of Mars; take this mixture (the instructions might continue) and bury it in the deepest, darkest sea until it becomes dry and, by desiccation, sandy and black. These peculiar kinds of instructions have no possible concrete relevance. We have no way of knowing what percentage of the alchemists might have guessed that their work was *psycho*logical rather than logical. Without our modern psychological concepts, they certainly could not explain what they were doing, but some of them probably suspected that the base substances they were trying to transform were aspects of their own selves. The alchemist was projecting his unconscious into the matter he was using in his laboratory, seeing his own inner growth process in the various changes and developments the substances in his beaker were going through. The result was alchemy's fantastical, complex imagery.

It was Jung's particular insight to recognize this imagery as a metaphorical description of the same phenomena that we psychologists try to discuss cognitively. Like the modern analysand, the medieval alchemist was trying, probably unconsciously, to heal his injured psyche. The despised and rejected elements of his soul—what Freudians would call his repressed unconscious and Jungians his shadow, and what an alchemist or a contemporary dreamer might image as "the *menstrum* of a whore"—these unconscious elements were to be redeemed, changed into gold. Alchemical recipes are therapeutic formulae, descriptions of how to change the psyche and of how the psyche changes. Alchemy's arresting imagery may reflect simply psychotic hallucinations, or its symbolic significance may have been grasped in some inarticulate fashion, at least by some workers. But in either case, its value for us remains the same: alchemical imagery captures the archetypal experience of psychological development. It is a symbolic system that was never organized in any orthodox fashion the way a religion is organized, and it stays much closer to the immediate individual experience of growth than a more coherent mythic system does. We may use its imagery as a metaphorical guide to the consistent ways human beings develop.

Jung took a series of ten medieval alchemical pictures—the *Rosarium*—as the basis for the description of the development of the transference bond. The engravings depict the alchemists' emotional experiences as they immersed themselves in the study of the imagery being produced and projected by their unconsciouses. Their work—their dedicated focus on the products of their psyches—exactly parallels a contemporary patient's work, his immersion in the products of his psyche. Alchemical imagery potently captures the modern patient's emotional experience of deep therapeutic work. We will refer to this imagery throughout the book as an underlying thread to guide us in appreciating the unfolding of the transference-countertransference relationship.

Figure 1. *The Mercurial Fountain*

The central image in Jung's work is the *coniunctio*. The series shows a king and queen meeting, fully dressed in court clothing, standing rather far apart. In the next image they are still quite separate, but now they face each other, naked. As the series proceeds, they lower themselves into a bath where they have sexual intercourse. The product of this union is one person with two heads lying dead in the bath which now resembles a tomb. Their soul leaves the body and rises heavenward; from heaven, a healing moisture waters the dead body, and the soul returns to reanimate the corpse. The last picture shows the king and queen, now a unified hermaphrodite, risen from the tomb, reborn. The base matter of the psyche has been transformed into a new entity that comfortably contains all the possible tendencies the human condition can encompass. This potential wholeness is symbolized by the union of the most fundamental pair of opposites into which we divide our species—male and female.

These pictures capture both the relationship between patient and therapist and the relationship between the patient and her psyche. The therapeutic process that occurs within the patient is mirrored in the

Figure 2. *King and Queen*

transference; the unfolding of the transference reflects the patient's inner development. Following Jung, I will translate this picture story into a description of the natural progress of the therapeutic endeavor.

Therapist and patient meet each other with the intention of exploring the patient's suffering, his unique pain contained in the endlessly flowing fountain of humanity's eternal suffering (figure 1, The Mercurial Fountain). Knowing very little about each other, therapist and patient make a commitment to one another (figure 2, King and Queen) and relax their guards. They come to know each other as undefendedly and authentically as possible (figure 3, The Naked Truth). They immerse themselves in the patient's suffering (figure 4, The Bath), gingerly at first, then more and more deeply until the distinction between the two individuals is lost (figure 5, The Conjunction). This union is possible—or unavoidable—precisely because the patient's suffering reverberates with humanity's and thus with the therapist's as well. "Doctor and patient . . . find themselves in a relationship founded on mutual unconsciousness" (Jung 1946, par. 364). An experience of "unconscious identity" (ibid., par. 376) arises between them.

Figure 3. *The Naked Truth*

Jung says of this stage that the two participants "have gone back to the chaotic beginnings" (ibid., par. 457). A therapeutic regression is in progress.

The result of this union, this loss of interpersonal and intrapsychic boundaries, is a state labelled "Death" (figure 6), a word that captures the adult ego's experience of a deep regression and merger. This picture and the next, "The Ascent of the Soul" (figure 7), in which the soul ascends to heaven leaving behind the lifeless body, depict the depths of disorientation and despair which any successful treatment must navigate. Depression is an inherent part of life. If the patient's presenting complaint involves depression, the work will, of course, be imbued with it. If the patient is not depressed to begin with, he or she will become depressed as manic defenses give way and the pain that existence necessarily involves is faced. A descent to the underworld will be experienced at least partly as a depression.

If the patient is able to reach the nadir of her pain, however, and comes to accept it, something new may appear out of her own depths.

Figure 4. *Immersion in the Bath*

Figure 5. *The Conjunction*

A healing moisture washes away the blackness (figure 8, Purification); the patient's patience is rewarded with hope (figure 9, Return of the Soul), and with some measure of resolution (figure 10, The New Birth). Neither the therapist nor the patient has *done* anything, but something has *happened*. We can think of this as the result of the patient working through his complexes, provided we remember that "working through" is an intellectualized term for "suffering." When the individ-

Figure 6. *Death*

Figure 7. *The Ascent of the Soul*

ual "accept[s] the conflict just as it is, with all the suffering this inevitably entails" (ibid., par. 392) the conflict will resolve itself and allow the individual to move on.

In translating these alchemical pictures into a modern depth psychotherapeutic form, we must remember that in a given case, the

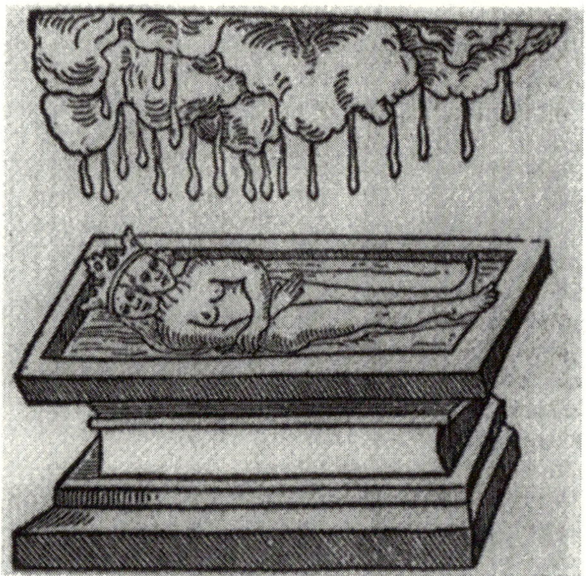

Figure 8. *Purification*

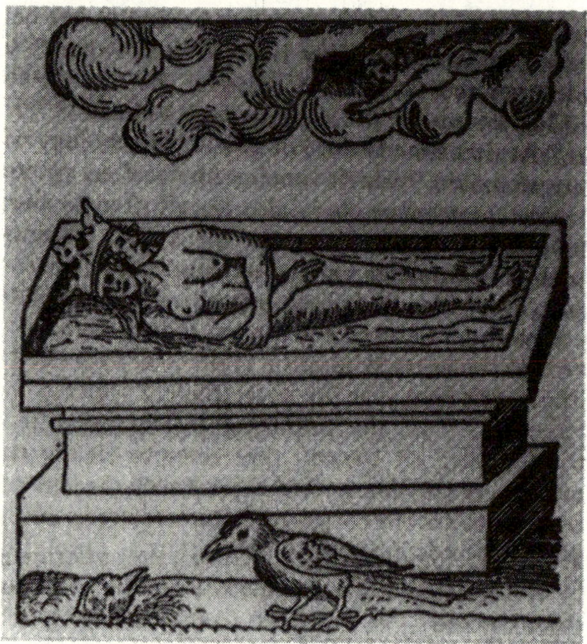

Figure 9. *The Return of the Soul*

Figure 10. *The New Birth*

order, duration, and intensity of the stages will vary (ibid., p. 322). The general sequence in which states of intense suffering are relieved by hopeful developments in the individual's inner and outer life (figures 6–10) repeats itself many times, always in the atmosphere of figure 5, the *coniunctio*. Whether one is in the *nigredo* (the blackness) or the *albedo* (the whitening or purification) is always a question of degree. Eventually the transference more or less wears itself out. This particular descent resolves itself, and the analysis as an interpersonal event is over, although the intrapsychic *opus* continues throughout one's life.

Donald Sandner: Patterns of Symbolic Healing

In looking for the archetypal pattern that underlies psychoanalysis, we are struck by the fact that analysis is a new procedure, and as any involved analysand will attest, it fosters an emotional experience that seems unique. Does analytic work nevertheless have roots in human history – are we looking at an intensified form of a procedure that has a past?

The most obvious forerunner of analysis would be the symbolic healing practices of primitive societies—the work of medicine men and shamans who, like modern psychotherapists, seek to cure the ills of the soul. Donald Sandner, a Jungian analyst who has studied primitive healing practices extensively, has outlined a structural pattern that all symbolic healing practices follow and a set of experiences through which symbolic healers commonly take their patients (Sandner 1979). Like Jung's alchemical imagery, Sandner's stages parallel Campbell's description of the universal monomyth.

Sandner differentiates symbolic and scientific healing: scientific healing (that is, modern medicine) attempts concretely to cure the patient, while a symbolic healing procedure such as analysis "explains, or at least provides a context for, the sufferings of [the patient]" (Sandner 1979, p. 11). The "cure" proceeding from this attempt may be much less tangible than the cure mediated by penicillin. Jung does not even strive for cure, focusing instead on wholeness. The results of a successful analysis are similar in some ways to those of primitive healing ceremonies: the patient "feels better"; the process "helps some." There is still pain and suffering, but it becomes tolerable, meaningful, and even enriching instead of tormenting and chaotic.

Sandner suggests that symbolic healing practices move through five stages:

1. Purification—of the doctor and the patient and perhaps of the space within which the healing rituals are to be held.
2. Presentation or evocation—in which the relevant symbolic images are presented in visual or audible forms and are invested with the numinous power that underlies them.
3. Identification—both the doctor and the patient become identified with the powers that have been evoked. "The medicine man symbolically becomes the supernatural power, and at the same time may take into himself the evil or bad part of the patient that is causing the sickness" (1979, p. 21).
4. Transformation—the healer "wins the battle, banishes the disease, expels the evil, counteracts the sorcery, or recovers the soul" (ibid., p. 21).
5. Release—the healer and the healed are ritually returned to their ordinary lives, divested of the numinous symbolic power with which they have been imbued during the ceremony.

In trying to imagine how this pattern might manifest itself in analytic work, we must ask first what the "relevant symbolic images" might be that are evoked in the second stage and that dominate the remainder of the work. In primitive healing practices these symbols are presented in visual or audible forms, forms the culture has developed and passed on from one generation to another. As Jung indicates in *The Psychology of the Transference*, underlying depth psychological treatment is the image of the *coniunctio*, symbolizing the individual's union with his deeper self. Depth psychotherapy constellates this symbol in invisible and inaudible emotional forms. We call these invisible emotional forms "the transference relationship"; the analyst and the patient live the symbol out, and the analysis consists in large measure in studying the various transformations of the symbol embodied in their relationship. Alternatively, we could say that analysis consists of a quest for the symbol initially presented in invisible form. Via a long-term experience of incarnating the symbol, its image may become manifest in a dream or vision.

The invisible nature of the symbol is a function of the fact that analysis, unlike primitive symbolic healing practices, is a completely individual affair. The analyst is concerned with a particular person's descent and union with himself, with finding the specific images that capture his unique marriage with his self; the medicine man attempts to guide every person's descent into the tribe's collective pattern.

We can now see how Sandner's stages guide modern psychotherapy. Purification involves the establishment of the analytic contract and frame. A container is created, set apart from the ordinary world. The alchemists enjoined the worker to make sure the alchemical *vas* was hermetically sealed lest any part of the wholeness they sought be lost. Between the second and third pictures of the *Rosarium* we see this purification in the shift in the connection between the king and queen. In the second picture, when the king and queen first meet, they symbolize their connection by joining their left hands and connecting on their right sides by jointly holding the end of a flowering branch over which hovers the Holy Ghost. Jung suggests that the left-handed connection indicates the secretly incestuous nature of their bond. In the third picture their left-handed connection has changed, and they hold the flowering branch with *both* hands, indicating that their attachment in all areas now proceeds through the Holy Ghost. The boundaries of their container have been firmly established: impure instinctual behavior is banished from the work, the experience will be exclusively spiritual/symbolic in nature.

At some point after the container has been established, the transference clicks into place, and we have moved into the second stage of presentation or evocation. On a personal level, the analyst embodies the patient's particular original objects; on an archetypal level, the same instinctual psychological energies that initially bound the infant-patient to his parents now bind him to his analyst. As the intensity and power of the bond grows, we move more deeply into stage three, identification. Willingly or otherwise, the analyst must "take into himself the evil or bad part of the patient that is causing the sickness," and he must carry these projections through Sandner's stage of transformation—the stage of "working through." As the patient's inner self realigns itself in a stronger, more harmonious pattern, the final stage of release or termination is navigated. This stage, in which the power of the transference is reabsorbed by the patient, is often lengthy and difficult and it is never really complete. Analysts, like parents, cannot become true peers, but when enough movement in that direction takes place, the analyst and patient can be freed from their interpenetrating connection, allowing the patient to leave and go on with his life.

In addition to describing the cross-cultural stages of symbolic healing practices, Sandner describes the four central principles of the Navajo healing ceremonies, principles he suggests may be basic to healing in other cultures as well. These four elements—principles inherent in Campbell's universal hero myth—are:

1. Return to origins.
2. Confrontation and manipulation of evil.
3. Death and rebirth.
4. Restoration of the universe (ibid., p. 4).

In analysis, the four elements overlap and interpenetrate. The return to the origins—the hero's descent—is experienced as a therapeutic regression. The patient feels infantile and dependent on the therapist. Substantial time and energy are ordinarily spent exploring the particular forms the patient's childhood suffering took. On an archetypal level, the patient is descending into her unconscious, immersing herself in the alchemical bath. Consciously or unconsciously, the descent is experienced as a merger with the analyst comparable to the infant's merger with her mother.

In the primitive healing ceremonies Sandner examines, the elements of the work are collective rather than individual in nature, so the patient is returned to the origins of his *tribe* via his culture's mythology. Discussing this common healing procedure, Mercea Eliade says, "We get the impression that for archaic societies life cannot be *repaired*, it can only be *re-created* by a return to sources" (quoted in Sandner, p. 111, italics in original). A similar situation exists in analysis. Sandner describes the primitive's experience of this return to the origins of his tribe: "[T]he presentation of the origin myth . . . allow[s] the patient to

Table A *Comparison of Campbell's Monomyth, Jung's Images, and Sandner's Stages*

<table>
<tr><th>Campbell's Monomyth</th><th colspan="2">Jung's Images*</th><th>Sandner's Stages</th><th colspan="2">Sandner's Principles</th></tr>
<tr><td>Preparation for the Journey</td><td colspan="2">The Mercurial Fountain
The King and Queen
The Naked Truth</td><td>Purification</td><td colspan="2"></td></tr>
<tr><td>Descent of the Hero</td><td rowspan="3">The Conjunction</td><td>The Bath</td><td>Presentation
or
Evocation</td><td rowspan="4">Death and Rebirth</td><td>Return to Origins</td></tr>
<tr><td>Encounters with Underworld Forces</td><td>Death
Ascent of the Soul</td><td>Identification</td><td>Confrontation and Manipulaion of Evil</td></tr>
<tr><td>A Successful Ultimate Ordeal</td><td>Purification
The Return of the Soul</td><td>Transformation</td><td></td></tr>
<tr><td>Return to the Upper World</td><td colspan="2">The New Birth</td><td>Release</td><td>Restoration of the Universe</td></tr>
</table>

*from *Psychology of the Transference*.

identify with those symbolic forces which once created the world, and by entering into them to re-create himself in a state of health and wholeness" (ibid.). In analysis the patient returns to his individual origins and connects with the archetypal forces within himself that once—in infancy—created his world. Out of this experience he is able to re-create himself.

Sandner's second element, the confrontation with and manipulation of evil, is pictured in Campbell's monomyth as various encounters between the hero and negative underworld forces. In analysis, the patient confronts and deals with the question of human evil in the regressed state induced by his return to his origins. The parents' evil is uncovered, evil the patient has heretofore arranged to not notice, and the patient's rage emerges. Through the experience of rage and other negative emotions directed at all the people who can be blamed for this distress, the patient begins to face his own evil (for example, his rage) and come to terms with it.

The entire analysis is experienced as a death and rebirth. The descent into the unconscious and its attendant emotional regression to the individual's origins feels like a death. The confrontation with evil occurs in this disoriented, abnormal state. The renewal that eventually emerges is a rebirth that leads to and supports a new ordering of the individual's life, both inside and out, a restoration of the universe carrying him ultimately to the end of the analysis. The parallels between Sandner's stages and principles, Jung's alchemical images, and Campbell's monomyth are outlined in Table A.

Sylvia Brinton Perera: *Descent to the Goddess*

Sylvia Brinton Perera's monograph uses the myth of Inanna as a template for feminine development, amplifying the myth with clinical examples. By examining feminine development *in the context of analysis*, she offers us a sense of what an analyst with a patient of either sex might experience as the archetypal pattern underlying human development unfolds in a late-twentieth-century consulting room.

Inanna, the Sumerian goddess of heaven and earth, journeys to the underworld, the goddess Ereshkigal's realm, and demands admission. She is brought naked into Ereshkigal's inner sanctum. Here her soul is judged, and Ereshkigal kills her. She is hung on a peg where her body turns into rotting meat.

When Inanna fails to return, her aide organizes a rescue. The great father gods refuse to help, but Enki, the god of water and wisdom, is responsive. He creates two mourners from the dirt stuck under his fingernails, and they slip into the underworld unseen by its guardians, carrying with them the food and water of life. Penetrating to Ereshkigal's throne, the mourners find the dark goddess consumed by her own pain. They empathize with her compassionately and, her suffering relieved by their empathy, she rewards them by returning Inanna's corpse.

After the mourners revivify Inanna, she returns to the upper world charged with the task of finding a substitute to take her place. She comes upon her primary consort, Dumuzi, who sits enjoying himself on his throne, unaware of her absence. Sacrificing the one she has loved best in this world, Inanna fixes on Dumuzi the same eyes of death that Ereshkigal had fixed on her and condemns him to take her place in the land of the dead. We have here a female hero whose story corresponds in form to Campbell's monomyth.

As a template for the analytic process, the myth presents the movement of the work toward its core as a disrobing: at each of the underworld's seven gates, one article of Inanna's clothing is removed until she enters the central chamber naked. Perera suggests that a similar process occurs in analysis as the adaptive defenses that protect and hide the patient's essential nature peel slowly away. The central experience of the work is one of unravelling. Subjectively, a journey to the underworld—to the world beneath our conscious, adult world—is a passage to childhood, the ground on which we have built our adult selves. The deeper the layers we are compelled to explore, the more infantile the experience becomes. The patient's return to his preverbal core is frightening for the therapist as well as the patient, but the myth reassures us of the experience's ultimate value. During Inanna's descent, the earth is barren and appears to have died. We must tolerate the patient's loss of competence—especially within the hour, but also at times in the context of his life—if we are to hold him through this regression into rebirth.

Only when the therapist feels secure can the patient allow the process to continue. As the regression deepens, the analysand suffers "the dismembering dissolution of her own old identity" (Perera 1981, p. 53) in a powerful depression. Rather than seeking a cure for this depression, Ereshkigal "demands death, complete destruction of differentiations and the felt sense of individuality, and total transformation. She demands a terrible empathy, one that surrenders, waits upon and groans with her" (ibid., pp. 26–27). Patient and therapist are called upon to worship the Black Madonna, the Death Mother, the Old Crone. To the extent one can revere her, her poisonous side can turn to the service of life.

Similarly, the analysand must learn Enki's view of the raw material of the work: the dirt caught under his fingernails. This worthless initial stuff, the menstrum of a whore, the psychological garbage out of which healing ultimately emerges, is the patient's

> unpremeditated, raw, basic reactiveness . . . the small, potent, autonomous flickers of emotion, the gripping, vibrant, and painful concrete details, the compelling fantasies . . . the autonomous [that is, archetypal] psyche as it is revealed in the small, personal, here-and-now, affect-laden facts . . . the despised slag of life's processes. (ibid., p. 69)

In what is always a difficult and painful development, the patient's attitude toward the infantile aspects of himself must shift from rejection and disgust to acceptance and respect.

In a variation on this theme, Enki's mourners affirm Ereshkigal's suffering rather than trying to smooth over the negative aspects of existence. Like these mourners, the therapist's task is to

> trust the life force even when it sounds its misery. Complaining is one voice of the dark goddess . . . . It does not, first and foremost, seek alleviation, but simply to state the existence of things as they are felt to be to a sensitive and vulnerable being. (ibid., p. 70)

In facilitating the regressive unfolding that affords the patient the opportunity to experience the full range of his aliveness—his vibrancy, miserable and ecstatic in turns—both patient and therapist are called upon to take a receptive feminine stance that conflicts with the heroic ideals with which we have been indoctrinated. Inanna undertakes her journey to witness the funeral of Gugulana, the Great Bull of Heaven. The dominating will embodied in the Great Bull is the heroic attitude that must die for individuation/analysis to proceed. Inanna, our universal analysand, must submit to a transformative process that works upon her, that she cannot control, that manifests itself in the rotting of her body (her familiar ego/self). This is the alchemical *putreficatio*, which the patient experiences as terrible suffering that must somehow be both endured and worshipped, for it is part of God's (Ereshkigal's) order. Suffering grounds the patient in life.

Just as the patient must accept the death of the hero, so the therapist must let go and submit to the therapeutic process rather than trying to run it. We must recognize our helplessness and focus not on how to *do* the work but on how to *let* the work happen, how to restrain our impulses to block the process, how to find the courage to sit still to receive the emotional experiences that a descent of any significance unleashes. We are called upon to accept a far humbler (and more difficult) role than that for which our academic training prepared us. We must witness rather than guide, enter into the patient's pain rather than cure it. We must accept the disorienting participation mystique generated in the therapeutic container and relinquish our Apollonian, analytic separateness that allows us to imagine we understand and guide the therapeutic experience. We must be willing to be confused and lost if we are to accompany someone into chaotic, uncharted areas of his soul.

When Ereshkigal's deadly negativity is resisted, it becomes fixed, demanding an opportunity to exist in the material world; accepted, it leads to rebirth. But what is the nature of that rebirth? We can be sure the cure will not be the one imagined by the old ego; that ego denied the demands of Ereshkigal, while the reborn initiate has learned, to some extent, to honor life's darkness as well as its light. Inanna is surrounded by demons when she first emerges from the underworld; the "cured" patient no longer seeks a happily-ever-after ending. There may be those in the patient's life who are not thrilled with her transformation, for the reborn individual is one who "can be obnoxious, but she speaks her own word, and looks deep inside to find it" (ibid., p. 41). The patient, losing her old adaptation to collective norms, will be clumsy and difficult as she struggles to integrate the dark forces—Ereshkigal's eyes of death—that she has contacted. She will *not* meet society's expectations but will be her own true self: not a static self, but a developing individual who can be unpleasant as well as nice. She will be less amenable than before, but more vital, more real, and more exciting to know.

Roughly half way through our survey of analytic descriptions of the archetypal layer of the therapeutic process, I wish to note the central role that regression has played in each of the theorist's conceptions. Jung's patient-therapist pair immersed themselves in an alchemical bath and returned "to the chaotic beginnings" (Jung 1956, par. 457). Sandner's patient gave himself over to the transference experience—identified with the symbol—and returned to his origins. Perera's analysand descended into her preverbal depths. As we study these three Jungians' work, the emerging pattern of analysis centers on a regressive experience. The death and rebirth of the therapeutic process occur for the patient in an infantile, disoriented state. In a letter to Jung, John Perry asked if the birth of the self necessarily involves a return to the personal infantile complexes. Jung replied that in general "patients revive their infantile reminiscences . . . it is an unavoidable mechanism . . . a teleological attempt to grow up again" (Jung 1984, p. 123).

Perera's experience-based work has been helpful in sketching what might happen in the clinical situation as the archetypal process mapped out by Jung and Sandner unfolds. Non-Jungians have worked extensively in this area—the manifestation of the archetype in reality. Less able to imagine the archetype as such, they have been more fascinated than Jungians with the forms of its concrete emergence in the analytic process. As we turn to neo-Freudian work, we shall look through the clinical reality toward its archetypal foundation. Where Jung and Sandner described the archetypal basis of the work and left us largely to intuit what it might be like to live out the archetype, the neo-Freudians help us more firmly grasp how Jung's "chaotic beginnings" will feel for the analyst–patient couple immersed together in the bath.

Michael Balint: *The Basic Fault*

Unlike Winnicott or Kohut whose work I shall look at later, Michael Balint did not offer a major perspective on the nature of the psyche, but he explored at length both the potentialities and the dangers of the deep regression that occurs in a successful analysis. He describes what I would consider the universal (that is, archetypal) human wound that fuels all analytic work: the analysand's initial environment in some way failed, consistently over time, to meet his needs adequately. Out of this initial failure arose a basic fault: a pattern of adapting to an inadequate environment that enabled him to cope at the cost of distorting his essential nature. To the extent an analysis is successful it will enable the patient "to go back to the pre-traumatic period . . . to relive the trauma . . . in order that he may mobilize his 'fixated' libido and find new possibilities [for life]" (Balint 1968, p. 82). The patient regresses in order to make a "new beginning" (ibid., pp. 131–132).

The analyst knows the patient has reached the level of the basic fault (often called the preoedipal level) when words no longer serve their ordinary purpose of communicating content. Interpretations are experienced as "an attack, a demand, a base insinuation . . . [or] as something highly pleasing and gratifying, exciting and soothing, or as a seduction . . . [The analyst's every] gesture . . . assume[s] an importance far beyond anything that could be realistically intended" (ibid., p. 18). Subjectively the analyst knows the patient has regressed to this formative layer when he begins to feel a wish to rescue the patient—to make his environment treat him properly, to provide him with the love and concern his parents failed to offer (ibid., p. 184). When the analyst feels a yearning to bypass the analytic task of *experiencing* the patient's suffering, he knows they have reached a point where interpretations are no longer a useful tool in the work.

How, then, is the therapist to work? Balint suggests the therapeutic task at this stage is to create and maintain an object relationship that can hold the regressed patient. Whereas an effective interpretation will lead to insight, "the creation of a proper relationship results in a 'feeling'; while 'insight' correlates with seeing, 'feeling' correlates with touching" (ibid., p. 161). The therapist must touch the patient at the level of the soul. The analyst must be a "primary object" for the patient, consenting

> to sustain and carry the patient like the earth or the water sustains and carries a man who entrusts his weight to them . . . . [T]he analyst . . . must prove more or less indestructible, must not insist on maintaining harsh boundaries, but must allow the development of a kind of mix-up between the patient and himself. (ibid., p. 145)

Out of this "*unio mystica*, . . . [this] harmonious interpenetrating mix-up," the patient's true self can be born (ibid., p. 74).

Balint meticulously sorts through the dangers that a therapeutic regression may unleash: the infinitely spiraling demands for one special gratification after another, culminating at its worst in a psychotic reaction when the analyst's limits must eventually be faced. He suggests we differentiate between regressive demands that seek to gratify the individual's cravings and those that ask the analyst to witness the depths of the patient's needs. When the patient's demands fall into the latter category, or, I would add, *when the therapist is able to remain centered in his willingness to witness but not to gratify*, an object relationship may be established within which the patient can experience his regressive needs fully by letting go of his adapted false ego and centering himself in the true self waiting to be born.

Like Perera, Balint urges us to recognize the value of the patient's complaining rather than attempting to soothe the complaints away (ibid., p. 108–09). He tries to "tolerate" the patient's pain, to "bear with it," to accept the experiences of darkness and death that emerge as the patient's psyche slowly unravels in the therapeutic container (ibid., p. 184). Like Jung, Balint focuses on the value of "entering into" the patient's suffering as the key healing factor rather than attempting to operate on her from the outside.

Balint's therapeutic goal is Jungian in nature. He does not hope to cure but to "enable the patient to experience a kind of regret or mourning about . . . the unalterable fact of a defect or fault in [him]self which . . . has cast its shadow over [his] whole life, and the unfortunate effects of which can never fully be made good" (ibid., p. 183). The goal is wholeness, not perfection.

D. W. Winnicott

Balint and Winnicott were mutually influenced colleagues. Balint suggested that by regressing to the site of one's primary wound, the individual could reconnect with his "true self." This conception of a true self and a false, caretaker self is Winnicott's (1960). The false self shields the true self from the impinging toxic environment. To the extent that the individual lives out of a false self, his life is based on complying with the demands of external reality, and the result is a sense of futility, a pervasive doubt about the value of living. Cut off from life by the false self, the true self cannot develop, but its existence may be preserved, along with the hope that some day a more nourishing environment will present itself within which it may emerge and begin to grow.

Winnicott's image of an effective analysis centers on providing the patient with that adequately nourishing environment. As he comes to trust the analyst's reliability and good-enough-ness, the patient regresses to *need*, to that infantile level where the split between the true and false selves began to entrench itself. At that level, the patient reconnects with his true self and redevelops a new maturity based on creative living rather than on complying with the demands of the outer world.

The true self, which can live creatively, is both the beginning and the goal of the work. (We see in this paradox one example of Winnicott's delightfully alchemical approach.) Psychotherapy consists of a search for the self, and "it is only in being creative that the individual discovers the self" (Winnicott 1971b, p. 54). In the experience of playing, which is the basis of all creativity, the individual discovers his existence as a center of initiative rather than a reaction to outer impingements. The spontaneous, playful gesture that originates only in the true self becomes the thread leading the patient to his self.

> Psychotherapy takes place in the overlap of two areas of playing, that of the patient and that of the therapist . . . . Psychotherapy has to do with two people playing together . . . . [It is] a highly specialized form of playing in the service of communication with oneself and others. . . . When a patient cannot play the therapist must attend to this major symptom before interpreting fragments of behavior. . . . Playing is itself a therapy . . . a creative experience. (ibid., pp. 38, 41, 47, and 50)

We might remember here the description (in Chapter 1, p. 18) of the dynamic aspect of the feminine principle which focuses on playing and creativity in exactly Winnicott's sense. "Playing" is not at all equivalent to "fun." Although in many contexts play may be fun, in psychotherapy it ordinarily is not. Think about a child in play therapy, playing through some dreadful trauma in his life—his brother's death, his father's brutality, his mother's abuse—over and over. This child is in pain, working that pain through by repeatedly experiencing varying aspects of it in play, mastering it in the sense of finding a level of inner strength adequate to contain it. The adult patient also plays his pain out repeatedly, most typically through free association. Images, memories, affective states are like toys in a playroom, used to paint or sculpt the state of the soul repeatedly, again mastering pain by finding ways to live with it. Play is the expression of a state of mind, a state Janet described as an *abaisement du niveau mentale* (a loosening of mental controls). It reflects an inner openness to one's self, a voluntary relinquishment of control.

In Jungian terms, Winnicott's orientation toward play is a suggestion that we treat the analytic interaction as an exercise in active imagination, a technique Jung originally invented to deal with his own emotional crisis precipitated by his break with Freud. In this technique the individual attempts to enter what Winnicott might have called a transitional space, between the level of conscious ego dominance and the level of dreaming. One tries to let go of control and to see what the psyche will do on its own; at the same time, one's waking ego is present, both watching developments and interacting with them.

One might begin by imagining a person or creature from a recent dream, asking it questions, trying to enter into its emotional state, seeing where it wants to go. One might paint or sculpt a dream image, or play with paint or clay hoping to see what will emerge from the medium as the ego is set aside. Gestalt therapist use this technique in a more extraverted way, urging the patient to imagine himself as a dream figure and then to act out a relationship between his ego and the figure. Jung describes active imagination as a procedure in which "an unconscious *a priori* precipitates itself into plastic form . . ." (Jung 1954a, par. 402). By experiencing in the material world the "unconscious *a priori*"—the dream figure in our example above—one encounters the tangible reality of the unconscious psyche.

Rather than encouraging the patient to attempt this focused playing on her own, Winnicott invites her to deintegrate in the consulting room and to surprise both herself and her analyst with the spontaneous, creative movement that emerges from her depths. Gradually allowing herself to fall backwards in time into a state of unintegrated formlessness, the patient opens the way for a creative gesture to emerge from her true self, and the analyst has the opportunity to mirror this creative movement. If it is seen and reflected back, it can be integrated by the conscious personality. The patient's free associations provide the raw material, comparable to a dream, with which to work. The therapist takes over much of the conscious ego's role, trying to see what the patient's psyche is trying to create and to reflect that back. The unplanned mutual experience that develops is the "plastic form," the sensuous creation that makes the self real.

Winnicott suggests that a normal infantile developmental process can be constellated anew in the analytic situation. Navigating this process heals the crippling that resulted from the ways the individual's initial environment blocked his authentic unfolding:

> When I look I am seen, so I exist.
> I can now afford to look and see.
> I now look creatively and what I apperceive I also perceive. (Winnicott 1971b, p. 114)

Winnicott explicitly states that psychotherapy involves re-doing development (ibid., p. 137). The crucial element the analyst offers is a specialized setting within which the patient may allow himself to descend into "a non-purposive state" (ibid., p. 55). The patient gradually hands over to the analyst the caretaking functions of his false self, allowing himself to live out of his breathtakingly vulnerable center, his true self.

Interpretive work is of minimal significance. "[T]he significant moment is that at which [the patient] *surprises himself or herself*" (ibid., p. 51, italics in original). Winnicott voices "a plea to every therapist to allow for the patient's capacity to play . . . to be creative in the analytic work. The patient's creativity can be only too easily stolen by a therapist who knows too much" (ibid., p. 57).

> Psychotherapy is not making clever and apt interpretations; by and large it is a long-term giving the patient back what the patient brings. . . . [I]f I do this well enough the patient will find his or her own self and will be able to exist and to feel real. . . .
>
> But I would not like to give the impression that I think this task of reflecting what the patient brings is easy. It is not easy, it is emotionally exhausting. (ibid., p. 117)

Winnicott offers a lovely image of the essence of the regressive experience on which therapy is based. All the clinicians discussed in this chapter see analysis as recapitulating development. Winnicott is especially adept at describing how the tiny interactions of each analytical moment work to bring the patient back to the center from which he started, the point where he can find his self.

Heinz Kohut

Heinz Kohut founded a new branch of psychoanalysis, Self Psychology. Unbeknownst to himself, this neo-Freudian became involved in an attempt to describe the archetypal patterns underlying the analytic encounter. A thinker of considerable influence in American Jungian institutes, his work on the self meshes with and complements Jungian thinking about the self in striking ways.

The basis of Kohut's ultimate break with Freud was similar to Jung's: both men rejected Freud's libido theory. Using different terminological systems, both Kohut and Jung turned their attention to the individual's wholeness—to the self—and both men postulated that issues of selfhood, not drives, are paramount in human motivation. Jung described the central human attempt as the urge to individuation, the drive to become the whole person one is innately meant to be. Kohut believed successful analysis would enable the patient "to devote himself to the realization of the nuclear program laid down in the center of his self" (Kohut 1984, p. 152). Where Jung focused on the intrapsychic ramifications of the drive to individuate, Kohut studied the manifestations of that quest in the analytic situation. His relative comfort with entanglement (relative to Jung, at least, and perhaps to analysts in general) enabled him to penetrate deeply into the analysand's personal experience of the archetypal core.

He postulated a universal transference pattern within which the patient experiences the therapist as a "selfobject," as an extension of the patient's own being. Kohut identified three varieties of this experience, each revolving around a particular set of defects in the self. Each form heals the injuries of the ego-self axis (Edinger 1972) from a different angle.

One pole of Kohut's self involves the individual's creative ambitions. To the extent the patient's psyche focuses on healing the self from the vantage point of the creative pole, the patient will develop a "mirror transference" to the analyst. She will need and demand unbroken mirroring from her therapist/selfobject who, by seeing the patient as an intact unit with a consistent wellspring of initiative emanating from her center, can enable the patient to connect with that wellspring and to actualize an increasing proportion of her creative energies.

The other pole of Kohut's self involves ideals. When the patient's psyche is trying to heal the self via attending to the wounds of this pole, an "idealizing transference" emerges. In this pattern the therapist is seen, perhaps unconsciously, as omnipotent and omniscient. The patient unconsciously merges with the therapist and enters into his godlike state, introjecting the therapist's idealized strength and solidity and transforming them into psychic structure. In Kleinian language, the patient eats and then digests the therapist.

Between the poles of ambitions and ideals lies the area of the individual's native talents and capacities. Work in this area causes a "twinship transference" to develop. The patient imagines that she and her selfobject/therapist are identical. The healing potential of this experience is rooted in the need to be a human being among other human beings. (The disorder this experience soothes is described in Kafka's "Metamorphosis.") A mirror transference helps the patient overcome depersonalized and dissociated defenses, to believe in the reality of her subjective emotional experience because she can feel the therapist resonating sympathetically to it. A twinship transference, on the other hand, enables someone who feels real to feel human, to know that she belongs to the group, the clan, the race, that she is a valued member of the family.

These three varieties of selfobject transferences are universal—archetypal—rather than personal in nature. Kohut is not concerned with the way the patient reexperiences idiosyncratic original objects. Instead he focuses on the instinctual energies that initially fueled the individual's attachment to her original objects and describes the way they reemerge and shape her new attachment to her analyst. The energies of Kohut's focus are *psychologically* rather than *biologically* instinctual in nature. Where Freud began with the body and postulated the psyche as a secondary phenomenon, Kohut, like Jung and other object relations thinkers, postulated the psyche as the primary reality of the work.

Regardless of which particular form of the transference is operating at any moment (for in practice all three are always operating to one extent or another), Kohut describes a consistent underlying pattern for analytic work. Somehow the patient has managed to keep alive some hope that a satisfactory, empathic selfobject exists despite the ways in which her parents failed to fill that function. The patient's hope is activated by the inherent nature of the psychotherapeutic situation, in which the patient experiences herself as "the focus of the empathically listening analyst" (ibid., p. 202). If the analyst does not interfere too much, "selfobject transferences arise spontaneously and without any active encouragement from the side of the analyst" (ibid., p. 201). Given the space in which to operate, the patient will regress to the site of her original childhood traumata and will attempt to redo her development. "[T]he progression of the therapeutic process . . . essentially repeats (though not in all details) the steps of normal childhood maturation" (ibid., p. 186).

Kohut suggests a particular conception of the healing process in this central stage of the treatment, where the analyst holds the regressed patient through her dark night of the soul. Time and again, the analyst's imperfectly empathic behavior disturbs the selfobject transference. Each time, the analyst optimally responds to the patient's distress by understanding it, by recognizing (often with the patient's help) how her equilibrium was upset and, when the patient's self becomes strong enough to tolerate it, by tying the upset to its genetic roots in the patient's childhood. Each time this process occurs, a potential trauma is transformed into a structure-building experience which Kohut calls "transmuting internalization" and which I described earlier as the patient eating and digesting the therapist. As these experiences accumulate over the years of analysis, the patient's self grows in strength and integrity. Her dependence on the analyst as an archaic selfobject lessens as she becomes increasingly able to find mature selfobjects in her outer life, and the analysis comes to a natural end.

"Transmuting internalizations" is Kohut's particular fantasy of how the growth process works. It is a useful one in that it provides a container to hold the therapist through the process that must be allowed to unfold in its own way. The fantasy functions as a rationale for the therapist's continuing support of the patient and the process, until the process more or less completes itself and the patient emerges from it a more solid and authentic adult than the one who entered treatment. Whether one accepts or rejects this fantasy is peripheral to our interest. Kohut has described a pattern for psychotherapy that, regardless of *how* it works, meshes well with the other descriptions of this pattern that we have examined.

Discussion

I have looked at the work of Jungian analysts, of British Object Relations analysts, and of the founder of American Self Psychology. While we must assume that these three groups of clinicians had some familiarity with each other, they almost never cite each other's work. We may therefore also assume that each school's work is relatively independent. Before underlining the striking similarity in the vision of analysis *qua* analysis that their work reveals, I wish to deal with an area of ambiguity.

Perhaps because they do have available the concept of archetypes, the Jungians are comfortable suggesting that the patterns of analysis they describe are universal. Both Balint and Winnicott hedge on this issue, and it was only at the very end of his career that Kohut allowed himself to assert that his work was about mankind, not about a particular diagnostic segment of humanity. It is always clear in reading these analysts and their followers that their interest was in those patients who immersed themselves in a deeply healing regressive experience, but they maintain they are talking about "patients *in a certain classification category*" (Winnicott 1971b, p. 86, italics in original). Other patients presumably live out a different analytical pattern. Contemporary depth psychological work increasingly centers on patients in this classification category, the category called "borderline" in America and "schizoid" in Britain. The split that Winnicott and Balint postulate (fuzzily and in passing) between "borderline" cases and true neurotics is now made quite vehemently by such leading theoreticians of borderline pathology as James Masterson.

I believe this division itself is an important example of borderline pathology, of splitting. To quote Winnicott's description of the borderline case, it is

> the kind of case in which the core of the patient's disturbance is psychotic, but the patient has enough psychoneurotic organization always to be able to present psychoneurosis or psychosomatic disorder when the central psychotic anxiety threatens to break through in crude form. (ibid., p. 87)

In my very ordinary outpatient practice, among my close friends and family, in my intimate dealings with colleagues, and certainly in my exploration of myself, I have yet to find a human being to whom this description does not apply. I do not wish to suggest that there are not profound differences in ego strength between people; in their abilities to experience and contain the underlying psychotic anxieties. But I do believe that the psyche always contains a borderline layer where islands of madness emerge and recede in inchoate forms. Whose dreamscape does not include the madwoman locked in the attic, the rabid dog, the homicidal maniac, the suicidal anorexic? The psychotherapist's ability to experience this psychotic layer of oneself and to allow his or her patients to bring it into their analyses is often a sign of ego strength, not fragility.

Talking about this kind of case (which I would call "nonpsychotic human beings"), Winnicott continues:

> [T]he psychoanalyst may collude for years with the patient's need to be psychoneurotic (as opposed to mad). . . . The analysis goes well, and everyone is pleased. The only drawback is that the analysis never ends. It can be terminated, and the patient may even mobilize a psychoneurotic false self for the purpose of finishing and expressing gratitude. But . . . there has been no change in the underlying (psychotic) state and . . . the analyst and the patient have succeeded in colluding to bring about a failure. (ibid., p. 87)

In very different ways, these six major thinkers offer congruent pictures of the psychic place where healing occurs: a place of deep regression or descent, where the primary process holds sway, and unreasonable, infantile emotional experiences are the norm. Bit by bit, the patient sheds his defenses, his character armor, held in the secure container created by his relationship with the analyst. He regresses to his wounded center where the archetypal forces ruling his existence are experienced as directly as possible. The defensive fantasy human beings construct, in which the individual is imagined in control of his psyche, is dropped. A recognition emerges that the psyche contains and dominates the ego which must, willingly or otherwise, follow the dictates of its human nature. The individual is reborn, centered in the self rather than the ego. From this place he constructs a new maturational line along which he navigates a second journey to adulthood. Where his first development was distorted by various wounding splits that alienated him from his self, in this second development he is able to integrate his many ego skills more authentically with his true nature.

In different ways, all six thinkers emphasize the fact that this regressive experience involves a deep and disorienting merger between analyst and patient. Jung's *coniunctio* grows out of a state of participation mystique between the two individuals. He compares the transference experience to a chemical combination that alters both the analyst and the analysand. "It is inevitable that the doctor should be influenced . . . and even that his nervous health should suffer. He quite literally 'takes over' the sufferings of his patient and shares them with him" (Jung 1946, par. 358). Sandner's shaman "symbolically becomes the supernatural power," embodying the patient's unconscious psyche. The patient finds his depths in the other (Sandner 1979, p. 21). Perera discusses the therapeutic merger at length: "On the deep levels of the transference-countertransference . . . two individuals share one psychic reality . . . [I]t is often hard to discern what affect or image belongs to whom" (Perera 1981, p. 60). Balint describes this crucial loss of boundaries as a "harmonious interpenetrating mix-up" and surveys some of the terms other Freudian analysts have used in referring to it (Balint 1968, p. 168):

Anna Freud: the need-satisfying object
Heinz Hartmann: the average expectable environment
W. R. Bion: the container and the contained
Margaret Little: the basic unit
M. Masud R. Khan: the protective shield
R. Spitz: mediator of the environment
Margaret Mahler: extra-uterine matrix

Some terms are more descriptive than others, but all call up an image of two individuals losing their edges and mingling with each other at the level of the soul. Winnicott, as Balint notes, coined images of this merger prolifically: the good-enough analyst/mother, the environment analyst/mother, primary maternal preoccupation, the facilitating environment. Kohut's core concept of selfobjects emphasizes in its spelling as well as its definition the merger on which successful therapy rests.

In Jungian circles, a regressive experience is sometimes contrasted with an archetypal one, a distinction I suggest is fundamentally flawed. An immediate experience of the archetype can occur only in regressed states; a regressed state inherently immerses one in archetypal contents. In infancy we are in direct contact with the archetypes, swimming around in the great sea of the collective unconscious. As we shed the complicated defensive shields that make us adults, we experience these primary energies again. We may talk about them as adults, but if we are to experience even the most spiritualized aspect of the living numen which *is* the archetype, we must come, like Inanna, "crouched and stripped bare" (Perera 1981, p. 9), in all our smallness before the greatness of the forces from which we come. Paradoxically, we find the archetypal layer of the psyche in our most deeply personal and private self.

The words "infantile" and "regressive" as I use them here do not always imply a return to one's *personal* childhood. When it works, analysis allows the patient to burrow down into increasingly primary layers of his psyche, layers that are *archetypally* infantile. The journey to these root places is regressive in that it involves a return to earlier modes of thinking and feeling, to infantile ways of processing the world. The historical reality that surrounded the individual when he *lived* in those layers of his mind will be reactivated to the extent that that reality is currently alive within his psyche. As one explores one's childhood world, experiencing it with an adult's resources rather than through the helplessness of infancy, that world becomes less emotionally dominating and the individual becomes increasingly able to experience the primitive layers of his psyche in their own natural form, undistorted by experiences with his particular original objects. On the other hand, one can never completely work through formative experiences; the personal parental situation will always lend some coloration to these fundamental layers of the soul, and even in a very deep analysis some work is left undone, large chunks of personal infantile experience which come up to be explored in later, and inevitably deeper, analyses.

The Jungian world has been divided along an axis that has been called the London–Zurich split. Where the London school can be seen as placing the transference at the center of the work, Zurich Jungians put the dream at the center. The image of analysis I offer here might represent a step toward reconciling those positions, for it would be a misunderstanding of my view to imagine that I think the analysis of the transference is the central element in the work. I suggest rather that the analysand's *experience of the living reality of his psyche* is the crucial therapeutic agent. In analysis, that experience occurs in the interpersonal container called "the transference relationship," and it is therefore natural to expect that relationship to capture a significant amount of the participants' attention. It is the experience itself, however, not its analysis, that has the paramount impact, for in this powerful affective encounter the self becomes tangibly real.

Outside of analysis, the individual may experience the reality of her psyche in her dreams or in her life. Unfortunately, many people, lacking either a vision of existence that values suffering or an intimate relationship to support them in their suffering, are afraid to wake up. Their lives are spent mainly looking for pastimes and diversions, for interesting, exciting experiences that will distract them from the grief with which their authentic inner lives are saturated. They may develop the capacity to experience their dreams and their lives only via the intensification of aliveness the analytic relationship provides. As Jung put it, the heat of the "strong compulsive tie" of the transference bond enables the individual to "rediscover the force of [his inner, archetypal world]" (Jung 1946, par. 466).

In analysis, the content of the conversation between patient and analyst is of secondary importance. The nature of the object relationship between them is the primary issue, for this is the medium within which the reality of the patient's psyche may become manifest, where his volatile inner world can become as real as the couch or chair that holds his material body. For some people, at some points in the work, talking about that object relationship can destroy its nourishing potential, especially if the discussion tends toward analyzing the bond. Similarly, talking about a dream may undermine the person's potential living connection to that part of his psyche the dream is portraying—especially if the dream is analyzed rather than played with. What matters is the essence of the underlying process between the two individuals, not the manifest content of their exchange. The regressive unravelling may be partially, perhaps even largely, unconscious, but it is that dissolution of distorting adult structures and the subsequent development of new, more supple and authentic ones, that form the core of the work.

Chapter 4

Psychotherapy Grounded in the Feminine Principle

All psychotherapists—social workers and psychologists as well as psychiatrists—are initially trained according to a medical model. We are taught to diagnose the patient, to devise a treatment plan, and then to implement it in order to cure the patient of illness. Much, perhaps most, of the psychotherapeutic literature echoes our academic training. For example, the current interest in differentiating borderline and neurotic individuals is matched by an extensive literature on the different therapeutic approaches one must take to a patient, depending on the category into which he falls.[1] Whether we look at the literature on short-term intervention with families or the literature on psychoanalysis or all the counseling/psychotherapy literature in between, we find a wealth of thinking on what should be done to whom: who is "analyzable" and who is not; should a given case be treated with "supportive psychotherapy" or "psychoanalytically oriented psychotherapy"; is this case short term or long term; should the patient be seen alone or with significant others.

Such thinking is deeply masculine in nature, completely oriented toward Doing rather than Being. It is predicated on separation and expertise, on viewing the patient from a distance in the bright light of the sun, and on knowing (ideally) all there is to be known about the patient's illness and the "healthy" human condition into which he must be re-formed.

The heart of this active approach is the interpretation. An interpretation—an explanation, a construction—is given by the therapist to the patient in an attempt to put something—consciousness, health, understanding—into him. The patient is given something by the therapist, the therapist does something to the patient. It is virtually unheard of in the analytic world to question the centrality of the analyst giving interpretations to the patient. The classical psychoanalytic stand

---

[1]Editor's note: In this chapter, the hypothetical therapist is female and the hypothetical patient is male. In Chapter 5, this is reversed.

is that there is *no* legitimate therapeutic activity *except* interpretation. That making interpretations is the best therapeutic activity conceivable is a nearly universal position. Other analyst behavior (questions, mirroring, self-revelations, and so on) may be allowed, but only because the patient is too disturbed to withstand the deprivation of a purely interpretive approach.

Interpretations are additionally assumed to be insights the therapist gives the patient. Very little attention is paid in the literature to interpretations patients devise for themselves, although any sensitive clinician knows that many of the interpretations in a therapeutic experience are made by the patient. (This is not to deny the fact that the therapist may have had the insight before the patient articulates it.) Similarly, insights the patient develops and shares about the therapist's actual personality and problems as they are revealed in the work are relatively neglected in the literature, although here, too, if we are open to it, we will receive a wealth of self-awareness from simply hearing what our patients tell us about ourselves (Searles 1979). From a classical perspective, the patient's job is to free associate, the therapist's is to make sense of the associations and feed them back to the patient as interpretations. The consistent and overwhelming bias in the field invites the therapist to put consciousness and health into the patient from outside.

Thus, Heinrich Racker, who labels interpretations "the analyst's principle activity" (1968, p. 2), describes his sense of the progress analysis has made in the years since Freud:

> While . . . the analyst of the past had to listen during hours, and sometimes for weeks, to the patient's associations before being able to give him an adequate interpretation, nowadays the analyst usually grasps much sooner what the patient needs to know and is capable of using profitably, so that the analyst can interpret, in general, many times in each session. . . . In the past we were like the two paupers in the Jewish joke, who could change their shirts only once a week. At present we are already like the rich merchant who changes his shirt every day. . . . And in the future we shall perhaps be—following the same joke—like the banker Rothschild, who continuously takes his shirt off and puts on a new one, takes off and puts on without interruption. (Racker 1968, pp. 21–22)

Unfortunately, Racker does not seem to get the point of the joke; although his understanding of the analytic process is superb, he consistently orients toward the interpretive product as the healing factor, assuming, therefore, that the more frequently interpretations are given and received, the quicker and deeper the healing will be.

A Feminine Approach

A feminine approach to the therapeutic work begins in an altogether different place, a place of not-knowing, of experiencing, focused on Being rather than Doing. We all face the same essential problems throughout our lives: what we could call problems of intimacy, of closeness and distance from others, of the need to be our own separate selves at the same time as we attach to and unite with other human beings. Each person works out the insoluble strains and paradoxes of our innately oppositional needs for closeness and distance in his or her own way. To begin our acquaintance with the patient in the realm of Being means we begin in the dark, by the light of the moon. We do not know how this person will work out the terrible dilemmas of human existence until *he shows us* his path.

This receptive approach believes everything the patient needs is inside his own psyche; the issue is to mobilize and actualize the patient's own health rather than to cure him. Somehow the therapist must facilitate a process that is already trying to happen. She must coax out a developmental line, feed and water the seeds of the patient's growth that lie hidden in the depths of his soul, smoothing the path for their growth into the light of day. Instead of trying to act on the patient, the attempt is to receive from him what his psyche is trying to produce. Much of the effort goes into trying to efface oneself, to create enough space in the room for the patient to take on whatever shape and size he needs to assume at the moment. This is in no way a passive stance, it is an actively receptive one. The therapist is not flaccidly inactive, she is trying to welcome the patient's wholeness into the room; she deeply wants to be with the patient, but she wants to *be* with the patient, not to *do* something to him.

The culturally dominant bias toward activity urges us to be *different* with each of our patients, based supposedly on the precise differential diagnosis we have formulated. A less brilliant but wiser approach invites us to be *the same* with each patient. We are consistently called upon to be our own authentic self in each encounter with a fellow suffering soul. We must attend religiously to the patient in every way: to his conscious experiences with us and in his outer life, to his dreams and fantasies, to the unconscious communications embedded in the manifest content of his material. At the same time, we must focus a similarly intense gaze on our own inner experiences and outer behavior while with the patient (especially if some unplanned behavior slips out of us): our feelings and thoughts, fantasies, memories, and lapses of attention. Out of this stew of data we hope that something coherent will emerge to make sense of each hour.

In this model the therapist's central role is to be the avid champion of the reality of the psyche. The patient's experience, perceptions, ideas, and assessments are never seen as distorted, for they can only be "distorted" when measured against a supposedly objective, outer reality. As expressions of the individual's inner reality, they are exactly correct and must be cherished in their precise current state. The therapist's authentic interest in their current state gives the patient the courage to experience and express what really comes into his mind in its raw form. In fact, the therapist will be most interested in associations that are *not* consonant with the outer reality, not because these associations are "pathological" but because they most clearly reflect the individual's inner reality. One finds the patient's most authentic individuality by following the patient's crazy ideas, not by trying to modify or amputate his craziness.

The therapist is called upon to understand and immerse herself in the world of the patient, rather than to relocate the patient in the "objective" (that is, the therapist's) world. The outer world, insofar as it is objective, needs no additional spokespeople. It makes its presence known insistently, unremittingly. It is the inner reality that is easily lost.

In an ordinary outpatient practice, the universal problem is the patient's loss of his inner reality. This loss has occurred because unless another person will see one's inner world and share it, the subjective nature of that inner world isolates one. The patient disowns his inner reality because no one else has been able to see it. He strives to share whatever existence offers some hope of companionship. Human alienation from the inner world varies in degree, but disconnection is universal for no parent can be perfectly attuned to the infant's experience. The individual is cut off from his own experience to the degree his parents failed to share it. The individual abandons his own world in an attempt to join his parents in *their* world. Unfortunately, disavowal of the true self inevitably leaves one cut off even from one's own companionship, isolated in an inherently unreal world, having become an unreal person. The patient's health—his wholeness—depends on repossessing his true inner state and on finding a way to create a secure space for it in the outer world. These steps, in turn, depend on his therapist's unswerving commitment to the reality and primacy of his inner state.

We could say that the issue is to force the outer world to make space for the individual's authentic being more than to accommodate his authenticity to the outer reality. It is necessary to accommodate, of course, but we must each find an inner bedrock that we cannot yield or shift if we are to develop into substantial individuals. Accommodating to the demands of the outer world is much easier than finding that solid core within ourselves. Distortions of the soul manifested as the emotional disorders that bring people into therapy occur because their true natures have been abandoned, not because they have been asserted.

The outer world asserts itself as a reality that cannot be ignored, but, in more subtle ways, the inner world does too. Emotional disorders reflect the individual's disordered relationship to his inner reality, but they are also attempts by the individual's reality to become real. A symptom is always a double thing, reflecting the individual's lack of wholeness and attempting at the same time to complete him. Compulsive handwashing, for example, images the person's driven self-destructive effort to purge some unwanted (unclean) part of his soul while also asserting the hopelessness of that task: undesirable elements reappear continuously, sullying the individual's perfection everywhere he goes. The therapist's task is not to point out the objective reality—that the patient's hands are not in reality dirty. Her job is to help the individual reorient inwardly, to find the actual dirt that *is* contaminating him and to take a welcoming rather than a rejecting attitude toward that dirt. In this example, the therapist would begin her work by accepting this dirty symptom, compulsive handwashing, which the therapist herself wishes she could wash away. If the therapist speaks for the reality of the psyche and devotes her energies to making space for *that* reality in the consulting room, the objective, outer reality will speak up for itself, and an accommodation between the two will grow naturally out of the interaction that can emerge between equals.

Devoting herself consistently to this task of recognizing and validating the patient's inner reality requires considerable faith on the therapist's part. She is called upon first to have faith in the reality of the psyche. This is actually contemporary terminology for what historically would be called "the existence of the (not necessarily immortal) soul," and it is obvious that our contemporary culture is not favorably disposed to faith in the soul; consciously it is largely opposed to any kind of faith beyond the crudest, most literal levels of organized religions.

Second, the therapist must rely upon faith in the value of the analytic process, and this, too, is often difficult. Although rarely acknowledged in the literature, there is a tremendous amount of failure in this work. Even skillful, experienced clinicians fail with some patients, and even the most successful analysis contains elements of failure and incompletion. The objective pressures undermining our faith in the therapeutic process are powerful. Each success is a charm to cling to as we struggle to retain our faith in the process. Those of us who have had our own subjectively successful therapeutic experiences are fortunate, for these are potent charms to possess.

But faith in the therapeutic process ultimately lies beyond our concrete positive experiences, just as religious faith cannot rest on daily, immediate experiences of God's presence. We are regularly confronted, in our patients and in ourselves, with hopeless, insoluble problems. W. R. Bion, the Kleinian analyst, refers to "the catastrophe of childhood," poetically capturing the fact that the traumas normal people are called upon to integrate in infancy and childhood are truly intolerable. This is also the shadow side of Winnicott's phrase, "the good-enough mother." The glass is half full but it is also half empty. When we have our faith it is clear that Winnicott's "ordinary devoted mother" is indeed good enough; when we lose it, we find ourselves face-to-face with the ways in which the ordinary devoted mother is *not* good enough.

Fairy tales and myths depict this reality for us. There is a hopeless situation (the maiden's hand has been cut off, the child is in the clutches of a wicked stepmother, the children are abandoned in the middle of the dark forest). There is an impossible task to perform (climb a glass mountain, recover something from the underworld, steal a treasure from under the wicked giant's nose). The solution is invariably based on magic, on powers people do not "really" possess, the reality of which must be taken on faith. Depth transformation depends upon such faith. It is the same faith that, in previous eras, people focused on God, a god who resided "out there," in the sky, perhaps. In analysis we must recover that faith, but this time in a god who exists inside our own psyche, a magical transformative power that can overcome the grievous wounding—the fairy tale's hopeless situation—that ordinary devoted parents affect on their children in an ordinary civilized world. It is this inner transformative power that can accomplish the tale's impossible task.

Somehow our faith must encompass the reality of despair and carry us through the hopeless dry periods that recur more or less frequently in deep therapeutic work. Perera, who speaks eloquently of that despair in *Descent to the Goddess*, offers the myth of Inanna as a reassuring talisman to cling to when despair threatens to inundate our faith. Inanna hung on a peg in the underworld, dead, a side of rotting meat, for three days. Christ on the cross called out in despair, "My God, my God, why hast thou forsaken me?" When a medieval Christian saint was asked how to cope with a loss of faith, she replied that in despair one must devote oneself assiduously to prayer, praying for its return.

We must somehow take on faith the fact that faith is stronger than despair, and we must believe this even though we all know of instances in which it was not the case. When we lose our faith, we must simply go on doing the work of analysis as though it were in our possession, waiting, perhaps for a good while, for its return. In Jung's alchemical pictures the return or emergence of faith is imaged in the healing moisture that rains gently down on the dried-up corpse, revivifying it.

The analyst's faith permeates her attitude toward the work, an attitude previous ages would have called "religious." Her spiritual attitude serves the patient as a model, offering a cast of mind he can introject toward his own soul. This attitude puts the work of becoming real, of actualizing one's self, at the very center of one's life. It implies that this task of individuating has the highest value. This is in no way a selfish attitude. It demands, in fact, that we let go of our selfish investment in our ego and give in to the demands of the self, the greater personality, which naturally weighs the needs of one's ego against the needs of other egos, impartially. Issues of power or material gain are secondary to interior issues of becoming one's true self. The work of analysis will be transformative to the extent that therapist and patient can hold this attitude of religious devotion to their work.

In Chapter 3, describing Winnicott's approach to the work, I likened his use of the analytic space to Jung's technique of active imagination. With each patient the analyst is trying to feel out what the patient's psyche wants to do with the hour: some part of the self is working to become real, to create itself out of its own depths. The therapist is called upon to fill a role in the patient's inner drama and, always, to witness the tangible existence of an element in the self that has been imperfectly actualized until now. In Winnicott's poetic and poignant formulation,

> I am seen, so I exist. (1971b, p. 114).

As the patient experiences the therapist witnessing his existence as a unique human being, he begins to feel his essence, his shape in the world. In the sense that every imaginal experience is different, the therapist will be different with each patient, but this is not the kind of difference traditional approaches, orienting toward differential diagnoses, suggest. In this humbler mode of not-knowing, the essential posture of openness to the mutual unconscious constellated between therapist and patient is consistent, hour after hour, with every patient, borderline, narcissistic, neurotic, or simply human.

From this receptive perspective, emotional illness is not the result of sickness within the psyche. An orientation based on dominance and expertise sees psychic health as synonymous with the absence of emotional illness, and thus it strives for cure. An approach that seeks the fecund compost of wholeness rather than the aridity of perfection begins by recognizing that illness and death are intrinsic elements in life, in the psyche, indeed, in every experience. Psychic health is not founded on eradicating illness and woundedness. On the contrary, it depends on containing these states.

We have devised many euphemisms for our inner wounds—we have problems in living, for example. It is certainly true we have problems in living, and it does seem more humane to normalize our inner agonies in this way than to describe our injuries with the pejorative labels of the *Diagnostic and Statistical Manual (DSM)*. But the psyche itself, in its uncensored communications (dreams) is more blunt. I am a doctor or a patient, a nurse or a visitor on a cancer ward; a child has been wounded or killed in an auto crash; deformed animals, bleeding victims of revolutions and wars, frighteningly ill living creatures of all varieties file across the nighttime stage, imaging one major dimension of the normal person's subjective experience of a normal human life. The therapeutic issue parallels the task of living: how can we create a space for the individual's crippled elements, his madness, to be welcomed and lovingly contained?

If we, as therapists, can cherish the patient in all his gory messiness, perhaps he, too, will find some way to love his dreadfully imperfect self. Perhaps he will find a way—not to perfection or cure, for perfection is incompatible with life, but to wholeness. We need to find an attitude that can accept the patient as he is now, not trying to hurry him along to a higher stage of development or to a healthier version of existence. In fact, he will move to a more intact state only if we accept him in his present state, in all his dreadful pain. As long as we reject his chaos, seeking to "improve" the state of his psyche, his psyche is left with its desperate, frantic need to be seen and accepted now, as is, and his neurotic complexes will insistantly force their way into every corner of his life, dominating his existence. If we can cherish him in his current imperfect state he will settle into it, experiencing his subjective reality and believing in his own being. From this place, his psyche can begin to develop and grow, to heal.

A woman in her early 30's who lived in one of the most subjectively painful worlds I have ever shared, came upon a fatally ill little girl in one of her dreams. Curled up in the corner of a shack with a dirt floor, huddled on a bundle of rags, the child was covered with sores that announced the final stages of disease. The patient's powerful initial response was to want nothing to do with the child: she was dying, the situation was hopeless. I suggested she consider bringing the girl home with her and nursing her through her death. The patient imagined easing the child's pain as much as she was able, bringing her tea and toast and holding her hand. This imaginal attempt opened the door to a pocket of pain and grief the patient had never shared with anyone before, including herself, because no one had ever before been interested in being with her if "nothing" was going to come of it. It initiated a change in her attitude toward her own suffering that allowed her to begin to take more and more extensive parts of her self into her self experience, to become more and more the person she was meant to be.

Paradoxically, this attitude within which she accepted the hopelessness of her own wounded condition led to healing beyond anything the image of the fatally ill child might have suggested. We might say, interpretively, that the hopeless nature of the child's illness was a function of the patient's flight from the task of caring for her regardless of her prognosis. Or we might remember that we are all dying, all of the time. Insofar as we absorb that fact and cherish each of Mother Nature's living creatures at the present moment in its life span, the greatest possible share of its potential may be realized.

Therapy is successful not when it ends in cure but when it leaves the patient able to continue growing on his own, when he has learned how to work with his inner pain in vital and satisfying ways. We each need to learn how to make our way on our own through the labyrinth of the psyche, to face the fatal or incurable illnesses that run through the fabric of our lives, to find and hold all of our selves in our self experiences.

This is not actually the task for which people initially seek help; they hope for a cure. Therapy is most deeply successful when the patient has let go of striving for perfection and has taken on the job of being a whole person instead—a job that will ultimately be infinitely richer and more satisfying, but that is also much more difficult and challenging.

The receptive Being that the feminine principle values is strenuously resisted, in analysis as in life, because Being involves suffering while Doing offers at least the illusion that suffering may one day be overcome. I do not wish to imply that Doing is not valuable, in analysis as well as in life. Much suffering can be overcome, and a vital involvement in life implies activity aimed at enriching and improving it. But considerable suffering must be endured. Our secular culture offers no containers to hold people through painful experiences, nor does it value experiencing the depths of the darker side of life. In general we begin our therapeutic journeys hoping to be cured of unhappiness, with woefully inadequate capacities to suffer the suffering that will deepen us and lead us to wholeness.

Jung called neurosis the avoidance of legitimate suffering. In our attempts to help our patients untangle their neurotic patterns, our fundamental task is to provide a container within which they find it possible to face increasing quantities of legitimate suffering. The suffering that a full experience of life inherently carries lies behind the neurotic patterns that cause such unnecessary torment in their attempt to stave off more authentic pain. We dread the pain of our separateness and isolation, of our dependence and interconnectedness, of the inevitable limits of others' caring and love, of death and loss, of our weakness and imperfection. The neurotic patterns that torment us also shield us from more meaningful and more deeply searing realities.

Regression and Merger

Let us try to imagine how the therapist can help the patient accomplish the initially unwelcome task of experiencing his whole life rather than amputating its dark side. In Chapter 3, I described a pattern of healing that is archetypally determined: the patient regresses to the level at which his primary distorting complexes began to solidify. He merges in with his selfobject/therapist in the same way he merged in with his original parental objects. Out of that merger he absorbs enough nourishment to begin life again, to sort his psyche out from a larger, containing one, and gradually to develop into a separate unique person. The central healing factor is the patient's primary experience of his own psyche, an experience that is never complete because no ego can ever be large enough to contain all of the suffering or joy that life carries. The major contribution the therapist makes toward fostering this healing experience lies in her ability to offer the patient an expanded container within which he can experience himself. The therapist's devoted attention and concern provide this container. The process may be conceptualized in a variety of ways:

- The patient merges in with the therapist and shares her greater ego strength.
- The therapist's empathy cushions the patient and enhances his ability to stand the real pain of his inner situation.
- The therapist's presence as an empathic ally allows the patient to identify with his own position in his life's drama. In identifying with himself, the patient begins to suffer the pain of his life instead of aligning himself with the people (generally parents) who initiated his suffering by being less than perfectly available to him. Insofar as the patient has identified with the big people in his life, rather than with his own little self, he will feel guilty about his neediness. By taking on his own "excessive" feelings about his deprivation, he comes to the existential grief about his human condition that true living must encompass.

But regardless of *how* it is conceptualized—and my list in no way covers the range of possibilities—the therapist's companionship, her willingness to enter into the patient's aliveness and share it with him, does enable the patient to develop a steadily increasing ability to experience that aliveness in all its height and depth, brightness and blackness, joy and pain. Out of this mutual process of empathic sharing and emotional accompaniment, interpretations and insight evolve. But the insight is more fruitfully understood as a product of the psyche's healing than as its cause. The major healing elements are regression and merger. Both are unacceptable to the dominant therapeutic approaches that value order, boundaries, control, and understanding, all of which are demolished by regression and merger.

The profession's attitude toward these two core processes is not simply negative, it is ambivalent. Freud's position on regression continues to color many clinicians' attitudes: regression to preoedipal levels of development is seen as a defensive flight from the difficulties of three-person relationships. At the same time, *some* regression in the clinical situation is almost universally recognized as inevitable and even desirable. Analysts and analytically oriented therapists welcome the patient's submission to the transference experience, an experience inherently imbued with regression. But the fear of regression is everywhere. This patient's regressive longings for merger are labeled defensive, a refusal to experience his abandonment panic, that patient is regressing "too much" and needs to be brought back to a "realistic" level of dependency on the therapist.

The fear of regression is well-founded. If we recognize the reality of the psyche, we immediately see that *uncontained* regression can lead to disaster, to a shattering of an adult competence that, however fragile, unrooted, and emotionally false, would seem preferable to a total disintegration of the personality, especially when the individual's financial resources will not support the extraordinary level of psychological attention a reintegration might require. But it is *uncontained* regression that poses a danger. Winnicott suggests that the "danger does not lie in the regression but in the analyst's unreadiness to meet the regression and the dependence which belongs to it" (1958, p. 261). When the psyche itself is pressing for a regression, almost invariably against the person's conscious wishes, the therapist should be very suspicious indeed of contrary assessments of the situation made by her own puny ego. If the course which the patient is taking is determined by his deeper psyche, rather than by his ego, the therapist ought to try to allow that course to unfold. Perhaps the therapist should seek consultation—not in an attempt to find out how to manage the unfolding process, but to find support for herself for allowing it.

The second element in an archetypally determined healing process is a therapeutic merger, and the profession's attitude toward merger is at least as ambivalent as toward regression. On some level, all human beings seek union with others, perhaps out of a wish to return to the bliss of the womb, perhaps as an expression of a literal death instinct, a drive toward the peace of nonbeing. Whatever its ultimate root, it is a universal lure and for that reason alone, it is universally feared. To allow an interpersonal merger to occur—to foster what Michael Balint (1968) called a "harmonious, interpenetrating mix-up" is to take a receptive stance, accepting the forces from the depths that push the work in this consciously frightening direction, rather than opposing these inchoate, deeply precognitive energies with our rational constructs and assessments. Out of this therapeutic merger, *two* new selves will ultimately arise and both of the old selves fear the annihilation that will precede rebirth. It will not be possible ever to say who created what out of the merger, to give credit to either participant, therapist or patient, for the experience and its result is a mutual one that depends on both individuals accepting a submissive stance vis-à-vis the demands of the psychological process that sweeps them both along. Each person's "I" is lost, and since most of us have devoted a great deal of energy to creating that precious "I," we find it hard to let it go.

One place we can see this fearful attitude toward merger is in the literature on empathy. In general, empathy is conceived of as resting on the therapist's trial identifications with the patient. Complex cognitive formulations have been devised to explain the empathic process. The tone of this literature implies that empathy is a good thing and that identifications (mergers) with the patient are therefore desirable, but the feeling is that one should merge *briefly*, melting into the other only for as long as one must in order to acquire the needed empathic perspective. One should then leap quickly out of the other's skin into a position of separateness and distance. Separateness and distance are assumed to be healthier, more mature, and more desirable than a state of merger. Merged experiences are frequently described, for example, as defensive against the terrible facts of separation and death; I have not found anything about the ways in which experiences of separation are used defensively against the terrifying facts of merger and union, but this perspective is equally valid and forms the basis of schizoid defenses.

In the ordinary course of events, the therapeutic merger is unconscious for both therapist and patient. Each individual feels like a separate person and imagines that the skin boundary matches a psychic boundary between oneself and the other. The hidden merger can be detected subtly in the ways the two participants begin to think alike, to share each other's values. Phenomenologically a merger can be seen in the common dream images where a significant person in the dreamer's outer life appears as an alter ego for the dreamer, living an experience of the dreamer's depths while the dreamer watches or lives out a different attitude. When a therapist dreams about a patient in this way, she knows the therapeutic merger is powerfully operative in her own psyche as well as the patient's. In my work as a therapist, and in evaluating the therapeutic work of my consultees, I take this dream configuration as indicative of the fact that the therapeutic process has reached sufficient depth to offer hope of real transformation for the patient. It may, of course, indicate any variety of difficulty in the work, but it also assures me that the work itself has gathered enough energy and power to effect both participants in profound ways.

In the therapeutic container, whether the therapist dreams of the patient or not, the patient's experiences of merger reflect a very real state, not an imaginary one; a loss of interpersonal boundaries actually occurs in any intimate relationship. There are many experiences of merger that we have been taught to dismiss as coincidental and meaningless because we have no rational way to explain them yet, but such experiences are frequent, and even the most rigorously scientific academic circles are beginning to acknowledge them. The very concept of projective identification rests on an implicit assumption of merger between two individuals' unconscious selves, a merger that cannot be logically explained at this point in the development of our knowledge of psychology. The following are some examples.

- To help an especially regressed patient through the summer vacation, I allowed her to choose a miniature from the collection in my office to function as a transitional object through our separation. Although it was clearly a loan rather than a gift, I forgot about it for nearly eight months, and neither she nor I mentioned it. One morning, driving to work, for no reason that I could consciously discern, I remembered the tiny statue and began to consider how to open up the topic and ask for its return. That afternoon the patient began her hour by talking about the statue and the various factors that had been keeping her from returning it.

- In many analytic institutes, one qualifies as an analyst by completing an analysis with a patient who knows, from the first, that he or she is a control patient. In my particular institute, each candidate chooses someone from his or her general practice to write up for certification. While some candidates choose to tell their patients they are being used in this way, many do not. The frequency with which the consciously ignorant patient images the situation in a dream is astonishing. I gave up the attempt to write about one of my patients when he dreamed that he and I were being tested, together, by a panel of senior analysts in an office which, as he described it, sounded very much like my consultant's office.

- When one of my children was going through a difficult period, one of my patients dreamed almost the entire situation with such accuracy that I felt compelled to tell her what was happening in my private life. It seemed crazy-making to leave her with the conscious belief that the dream was rooted primarily in *her* psyche when it was clear to me that it reflected her sensitivity to *my* psyche's dilemma.
- A friend of mine who has had three personal analysts confided to me recently that in each analysis she had dreamed about her analysts' homes in the weeks immediately preceding vacations and that they had each told her the dream imagery did, in actual fact, reflect their houses.
- Pregnant therapists not infrequently find that patients dream about their pregnancies before the patient has any conscious awareness of the situation. I know of one case in which the patient accurately dreamed her therapist was pregnant before the therapist had missed her period (Barmack 1986); in another case, a patient spontaneously asked her therapist if she was pregnant on the day the therapist's period should have arrived (Marjorie Nathanson, Ph.D., personal communication).

My examples feature dreams in prominent roles because I am a Jungian therapist and work a great deal with dreams. My patients know of my interest, of course, and the dream is therefore an ideal vehicle for communicating information that the patient does not know he has. Robert Langs, a non-Jungian with no particular interest in dreams, has done a great deal of work on the unconscious messages encoded in patients' manifestly unrelated material. He demonstrates that listening to the hour as a commentary on the therapeutic work leads therapists to "discover that their patients know far more about them than they want to realize or can tolerate" (1978, p. 370).

A group of Jungian analysts in Berlin have been studying the analytic process, examining process accounts of their work with their analysands, accompanied by process accounts of their own inner associations while attending to their patients. Acknowledging that they have no explanation for their findings, they found an "astonishing . . . correspondence between the analyst's and the patient's chains of associations" (Dieckmann 1975, p. 26). In one example, the analyst found himself picturing a rose on three separate occasions in the hour. Although the study group managed to construct several cognitive explanations for this imagery, he was left feeling somewhat dissatisfied—it was too theoretical to be compelling. At the beginning of the next session the patient reported that during the previous hour he had not mentioned that he was obsessively fascinated through the hour by an image of his inner life as a barren plane: "On this scorched earth, stretching as far as the eye could see there grew just one rose" (ibid., p. 28).

To describe this situation as a therapeutic merger is simply to state the fact; *how* people apprehend so much unconscious material about each other is unclear, but that we do is incontrovertible. Our fantasies of separation, our insistence that our skins constitute an impermeable boundary for our unique selves, is a defense against recognizing these facts of intimacy. This interpersonal merger is highlighted by the conditions of the therapeutic situation, but it exists in all close relationships. The terrible reality of separation and death must certainly be faced, but the awesome and terrifying facts of union and merger must also be acknowledged.

Diagnosis

Let me return now to the first major element in the medical model of psychotherapy I am rejecting: diagnosis. There is something so eminently reasonable about the idea that we should begin each case with a diagnosis, and it is certainly true that some people are healthier, stronger, better functioning, or better adapted than others. Unfortunately, although we can all agree on this, there seems little else that we can agree on. When a pediatrician says a child has rubella, virtually all other pediatricians will concur in that diagnosis. When a medical diagnosis is unclear, coherent guidelines exist for demonstrating that a given diagnostician's hunch is right or wrong.

There is nothing comparable in the field of psychology. Skilled clinicians, even when they share the same theoretical outlook, will see any given case in wildly varying ways. I personally know of two cases in which very senior analysts referred a patient they had worked with for some years to other highly respected analysts of the opposite sex. In both cases, the second analyst believed the patient was much more disturbed than the initial analyst had believed. In one case, I believed the referring analyst's assessment was more accurate than the recipient's, and in the other case I believed the recipient was seeing significant pathology that had been overlooked by the first analyst. There were no antibodies to search for or bacteria to culture, no x-rays or biopsies to turn to for definitive decisions.

In a widely publicized custody case (Baby M), attorneys for both parents called a number of mental health experts to testify on each parent's emotional state. One of the more blackly humorous elements in the debate had to do with whether or not the biological mother "had" mixed personality disorder. After two or three experts had disagreed on this point, her lawyer called to the stand the psychiatrist who had *written* the *DSM* III, who then testified that she did not have it. One might imagine that, having written the book, he would know, but his supposed expertise did not daunt several of his eminent colleagues who continued to maintain the mother did have the "disease" in question.

The basic problem is that we cannot point to any personality characteristic as indicative of a given diagnosis because all human beings share all possible ways of functioning. The various diagnoses listed in the *Diagnostic and Statistical Manual* are always a question of degree. Splitting defenses, for example, which are supposedly indicative of a borderline personality structure, are not "bad" tendencies we need to eliminate in order to "cure" the patient. Splitting defenses are primitive, in the sense they appear very early in the individual's life in an attempt to cope with the intolerable demands of existence. They are primitive likewise in the sense that they are less effective, ultimately, than some later defenses will prove to be. But they are never outgrown and left behind. Given ordinary levels of intolerable stress—levels we all come up against at least every few weeks—we all split. And at those stress levels, "primitive" defenses may be optimal. Facing the immediate assault of the moment, they can preserve one's equilibrium until more sophisticated modes of working with the stress can be marshalled.

Another way to put this is to think about splitting as the basic mechanism of Klein's paranoid-schizoid position. There is a deeply cherished fantasy floating around the therapy world that "we" (referring to one's identity group of the moment) have attained the depressive position (or resolved the oedipal complex or whatever our current yardstick may be for measuring psychic health). "We" have transcended the infantile need for good objects and bad objects, we have achieved the capacity to relate to a whole object, an ambivalent object rather than an idealized or diabolized one.

This is nonsense. All human beings split. We all have good objects and bad ones. Even years and years of marriage or friendship cannot strip all our projections from our partners and leave them exposed to an absolutely objective gaze. And who, indeed, would strive for such relationships, free of every distorting affective tinge. "We," like all other human beings, are imperfect, wounded, even inadequate beings, struggling, like Job, to make our way through the very difficult task of living a life.

All human beings actually use all defenses: hysterical, obsessive, borderline, narcissistic, and even psychotic in nature. We all distort reality to one degree or another, and disagreements about a diagnosis rest partly on the varying assessments that are made of how much the patient is distorting and of how much distortion is "normal." W. R. Bion suggested that Klein's two positions, the paranoid-schizoid position and the depressive position, are not psychological states one lives in; they are rather psychological states one travels back and forth between, each having a valid place in a healthy life. In the paranoid-schizoid position, things fall apart and fragment; in the depressive position, they come together again. Healthy living—creativity and joy—depends on maintaining a fluid attitude toward reality, allowing things to fall apart and come together again repeatedly, bringing "vitality to that which is ancient, old and orthodox by re-creating it after destroying it" (D. W. Winnicott, quoted in Greenberg and Mitchell 1983, p. 189).

Traditional diagnostic approaches categorize people by the issues with which they are struggling or by their defensive styles. For example, if the patient fears engulfment, he is a borderline personality; if he fears fragmentation, he has a narcissistic personality disorder; hysterical, obsessive, or borderline defenses indicate their respective diagnostic categories. A core assumption is that such issues and defensive styles can be ranked on a continuum of healthiest to sickest. In the real consulting room, however, ego strength may greatly vary from person to person within any diagnostic category. One hysterical personality will dissociate and effectively disappear under what seem to be fairly mild levels of stress, and another hysterical personality will find the capacity to bear and integrate situations of intense stress. An individual who is dealing with borderline issues and who uses borderline defenses may be much stronger psychologically than a given obsessive compulsive neurotic. The ultimate test of the patient's solidity and therefore of his real psychic health is not his diagnostic category; it is the strength of his ego.

I do believe we might constructively think about a borderline personality that is different from a more neurotic personality but that this is a constructive differentiation only if we are clearly not talking about health, competence, or adaptation. We are simply talking about apples and oranges. Howard Levene (1982) notes that 80 percent of the people diagnosed borderline are under 35 years old and that two-thirds of them are women. What happens to these borderline individuals in their 40's, he asks. Where do they go? He suggests it is actually *the structure of emotion* that has been discovered and described by Kernberg, Masterson, Rinsley, and others, pointing out that women (in our culture) and younger people are much more emotional than men and older people. "In the presence of critical, hostile, angry or withdrawing objects, I, too, feel depressed, rageful, panicky, helpless, hopeless, empty, void, inadequate, guilty, etc.," states Levene (p. 26). As one might expect, he found that his friends, when asked, confessed to similar experiences. Shaken by strong emotions, we all experience borderline states.

We might think of the borderline personality as someone who has easy access to the borderline layer of the psyche where the borders between self and other, personal and archetypal, emotion and reason blur, where one's aliveness originates in a chaotic, swirling *massa confusa.* The neurotic individual is someone who is strongly defended against this layer of the self. The neurotic may appear to function better than the borderline, but this is at least partly owing to the neat and tidy living that is afforded by keeping a firm lid on emotion and stamping out one's vitality. To the extent that this is the underlying situation, it seems most unfortunate to label the neurotic individual healthier than the borderline who is struggling, perhaps with difficulty, with all of his living being. I do not want to suggest that a borderline personality is healthier than a neurotic one. Either adaptation may be flexible and vital or maladaptive. A borderline organization becomes maladaptive flamboyantly and creates chaotic situations. Maladaptive neurotic patterns tend to be rigid, oppressive, and stultifying. The latter are not necessarily preferable.

In any case, it is widely agreed that a significant number of people who are diagnosed borderline are high functioning people. As Winnicott puts it, "many of the patients I am referring to are valuable people who cannot afford to break down in the sense of going to a mental hospital," although that would be one clear way to find the inner distress with which they are struggling to connect (1971b, p. 178). In Chapter 7, I analyze James Masterson's work with Lynn, an extremely well functioning woman whom he calls borderline from a pejorative perspective and who I would agree is borderline from this descriptive perspective. From this nonjudgmental viewpoint, however, a borderline orientation, though more difficult to handle than a neurotic one, has much to recommend it, and we would no more want to "cure" someone of his borderline capacities than we would want to lobotomize him. We would, of course, be very interested in supporting any movement he might make toward strengthening his ego if he were the kind of borderline person whose ego sometimes fragments under the pressures erupting from the depths of his psyche.

Even more important prognostically than the strength of the individual's ego is something diagnosis completely ignores: the strength or intensity of the individual psyche's self-healing impulsion. It is ignored partly because it can be assessed only in the process of the treatment. There is no way to predict it in advance, and its strength may change over time in the same person. One cannot say how far a given individual is going to go in analysis, how deeply into his soul he will descend, until he does it. Prognostically, the healing impulse is central—but we cannot say anything about it prognostically because we know nothing about it in advance.

This self-healing impulse is also ignored diagnostically because there does not seem to be anything we can do to affect it. Any experienced clinician has had the experience of a relatively unsatisfying analysis with a more or less healthy patient; many of us have also seen quite disturbed patients whose inner life is transformed in the therapeutic work—and I do mean transformed, not simply improved or patched up. *I Never Promised You a Rose Garden* tells one story of a transformative therapeutic venture; Margaret Little's account of her analysis (1985) is another. Less illustrious therapists than Freida Fromm-Reichman or D. W. Winnicott, ordinary, anonymous therapists who have had the courage to allow patients to bring their craziness into the work, have also found that falling apart often leads to a new and more solid synthesis.

The first issue is the therapist's availability to receive profoundly disturbing material, and the second is the patient's willingness and capacity to deal with that material. In an appalling number of instances, the therapist blocks the patient's attempts to talk about his deeper issues (Langs 1980). As a consultant or reader, removed from the interpersonal fray and therefore relatively free of blind spots, one can be moved nearly to tears by a patient's persistent unconscious efforts to interest his therapist in doing the work that needs to be done.

But when the therapist is open to the demands of the work, the patient's drive to health is called into question, and there are tremendous variations in that drive having nothing apparent to do with the severity of the patient's pathology. In the physical world, we know that one individual recovers rapidly from a given illness, while a second lingers in convalescence for a lengthy period or even suffers permanent disability. We must recognize and accept that people's inner psychological healing capacities vary as well. At the same time we must recognize and accept the fact that it is this inner drive to health that makes the crucial difference in how far a person will go in his individuation. We each make some kind of compromise with life, facing some issues while sealing off others. We all have our blind spots, regardless of the depth of our analyses and the excellence of our training. Where one person is compelled by relentless inner pressures to face core issues and to wrest consciousness of his suffering from what seems to be the depths of hell, another individual will be content to know as little of himself as possible, discharging inner tensions in self-destructive interpersonal patterns or addictive behaviors that, if they are not *too* extreme, are truly normal.

An acquaintance of mine in his early 20's suffered an acute schizophrenic break. I referred him to an analyst who had considerable expertise in working with psychotic episodes and who told Adam he believed he could help him work through his situation successfully. Another associate of Adam's urged him to see a different psychiatrist, and Adam tried him, too. The second doctor told him he "had" schizophrenia and that it was incurable. Why did Adam choose to work with the second doctor, to medicate his inner distress? There were no apparent outer pressures; something inside his own soul urged him to let things be, to come to terms with what eventually became a crippling, chronic condition of inadequacy rather than attempting the heroic undertaking a schizophrenic difficulty demands if it is to be healed. One doctor is hopeful and another despairing: how strange and also how common to make a relatively comfortable peace with despair and avoid risking the pain and torment of hope and disappointment, longing, frustration, and deprivation that an interpersonally contained inner journey inevitably involves.

Not only do individuals have different capacities for the depth work psychological transformation requires, an individual's drive and ability may change quite radically over time. I worked for eight years with an insubstantial young man who was borderline in the sense that he spent nearly all his time on the border between the outer and the inner world, neither here nor there, in an undefined state where he felt safe from criticism since he had not yet chosen to exist. Although we made some progress in all those years, I was basically relieved when he decided to terminate, feeling his potential for growth was severely limited and that he would never offer much substance with which to work.

Two years later he returned to treatment. I was as close to unwilling to work with him as I ever get and made strenuous attempts to refer him to another therapist (a man being the obvious possibility). He made equally strenuous efforts to force his way back into my practice. Finally bowing to what seemed inevitable, I accepted him back. In the ensuing months, I was amazed to find that his interest in grappling with his inner suffering had somehow increased by several orders of magnitude. The sudden death of a cousin, close to him only in age, had brought home the fact that his life was a finite proposition and he wished to live his life fully and to become all he could be. His willingness and ability to suffer the pain involved in that attempt had increased dramatically. We worked together for six extremely rich, productive years in which I felt grateful for the privilege of accompanying his journey and greatly humbled regarding my capacity to predict who is going to do what in treatment. R. D. Laing reports a similar case of an insubstantial woman whose treatment seemed hopelessly empty and devoid of impact. She abruptly developed a strong commitment to her development as a result, apparently, of seeing a powerful movie.

If the therapist cannot say much about the patient's capacity to grow, at least she hopes to be knowledgeable about the direction in which the patient needs to go. But planning the patient's course for him is even more fraught than is assessing his developmental capacity. When one knows where the patient needs to go, one has identified with an archetype, the archetype of the healer. It behooves us to keep firmly in mind the story of Phaethon's disastrous attempt to drive the chariot of the sun across the sky; his story reminds us of the obligation to *dis*identify with the archetype, to remember our infinitesimal status in the great world of the human psyche.[1] The inner healer I have called the impulsion to growth, consciousness, and wholeness functions in all of us. We must try to be open to the patient's own direction, to the attempts his psyche is making to repair itself. We must try to provide an optimally facilitating environment for that repair. But we must not get confused and think it is our job to heal the patient, for that fantasy is equivalent to playing god. At this stage of our knowledge, attempts to *do* things to people to heal them are apt to be about as helpful as the medieval attempts to restore the body's balance through bloodletting.

Perhaps as our knowledge develops we shall find additional ways to intervene actively in people's psychological struggles, but it is also possible that as our knowledge develops we shall come to understand more thoroughly exactly why one human being cannot heal another's emotional wounds. A nonheroic stance of great humility in the face of the inevitability of human suffering is called for by the intrinsic nature of the human condition.

Jung was not alone in his focus on an individuation process. Winnicott and Kohut come immediately to mind as two neo-Freudians who shared his sense of an inborn self or soul that strives toward actualiza-

---

[1]See Chapter 6 for a more extensive discussion of this point.

tion for the entire lifetime of the individual. Orienting toward the patient's individuation process is diametrically opposed to diagnosing and curing. If we wish to know exactly who this individual is, we do not try to reshape him to fit some "normal" mold. We endeavor instead to make space for the emergence of his authentic individuality. The only thing we know at the start is that his essential selfhood will *not* be normal; it will be peculiar and eccentric in one way or another.

Any therapist will be aware of the neurotic complexes that are blocking the patient's development—the legacy of childhood family patterns that interfere with becoming one's own true self. However, if the therapist puts her energies into assisting the patient's individuation process rather than toward a "cure," she will not see the resolution of the patient's neurotic blockages as an end; the resolution of crippling parental complexes is rather a beginning of a state of becoming that lasts for the rest of the patient's life. Exactly where in that process the analysis will formally terminate will depend on the vicissitudes of the transference relationship rather than on the resolution of the patient's outer symptoms.

When the focus is on individuation, the therapist will not know *how* the patient will resolve neurotic blockages. The singular and unexpected way the patient works through his complexes will be a major element in the creation or discovery of his own uniqueness. Rather than imagining she "knows" what direction the patient needs to grow in, the therapist believes the form of the patient's journey will express the nature of the patient's self. The therapist's interest is in seeing how the patient does it, not in directing the patient in how to do it. Instead of thinking about the material the therapist knows the patient needs to get to in order to "make progress," the therapist will attend to the patient's unfolding associations, waiting to be surprised by some unexpected twist in the pattern of human growth.

Often the analyst, who may be much older and perhaps wiser than the patient, really does know a good deal about the general direction the patient needs to grow in, even if she does not know exactly how that path is going to jog around each corner. The therapist may make interpretations in the service of guiding the patient's general development, hoping to hurry things along a bit. But a process-oriented viewpoint asks us to pause a moment and to question the value of getting there faster. The goal of life, or at least its endpoint, is death; there is no reason to rush headlong to get there. As an analyst I often think that people "get there" fastest when they go along as slowly as possible. So often the manic, driven patient is a bit late to the appointments. The point of analysis, like the point of life, is the experience itself, not the endpoint. When the analyst tries to skip a tiny bit of the process, offering the patient an interpretation in the hopes of making a leap forward, she may be cheating the patient of a morsel of the experience of grappling with his inner process in his own way, of wresting his own understanding from his depths, of building up a tiny fraction more emotional muscle than he started with.

One unfortunate aspect of an approach orienting toward an endpoint—toward cure which can, at least in theory, be reached, rather than toward wholeness, which is inherently never completely attainable—is this tendency to focus on content rather than process. As long as one looks predominantly at the product—insight—of the process, one imagines that some topics are important to talk about and others are not. Focusing the patient's attention becomes an important therapeutic task. Irrelevant topics are seen as resistances when the patient's associations turn toward them. Thus, at a rather crude level, the therapist may assume that when the patient is discussing the conflicts and strains of his marriage, something important is happening, but when he is talking about developments in his garden and difficulties surrounding the upkeep of his house, he is resisting the therapeutic work. At a more sophisticated level, attempts to talk about the strains of his marriage may be seen as resistances to talking about the strains of the transference relationship. Both assessments, however, rest on the same misconception that leads Racker to focus on increasing the quantity of interpretations: the product, the content of the hour, is confused with the essential meaning and value of the hour.

The interpersonal experience of the therapy is touching the patient deep inside his soul, and it is there, in the dark, that important changes are occurring, not in the problem-solving content of the hour. His irrelevant and repetitious discussion of the neighbor's dog's persistent habit of fouling his perfectly tended lawn may image many crucial psychological realities to which the therapist ought seriously (repeatedly) to attend—the patient's hopeless inner attempt to attain perfection or the way the therapist keeps dumping her personal garbage into the patient's field. The therapist's capacity to hear this level of the patient's communications may or may not lead to an interpretation. Perhaps the therapist's attitude will shift, perhaps her empathic resonance will increase and will express itself in inner vibrations or in nearly inaudible murmurs or even in the rhythm of her breathing. Just as the therapist picks up her patient's authentic inner reality by its vibrations in her own unconscious, so the patient picks up his therapist's empathic or disconnected state through preverbal, unconscious channels. When the therapist can attune herself to the message the patient's psyche is trying to convey, the patient will be psychologically held simply by the fact of the therapist's attunement and some healing will come of this soothing experience regardless of whether or not the experience is consciously articulated by either participant.

Although I am suggesting that traditional diagnostic attempts are destructive to the therapeutic process, I certainly do not believe we ought to abandon the attempt to understand our patients. What is called for is a different kind of understanding, one based on empathy, grounded in closeness, identification, and merger. We need to understand people from the inside rather than from the outside. Traditional diagnostic attempts give the therapist a piece of expertise she can teach to another. She has investigated the situation and analyzed it; she can explain to her colleagues, her students, or at least to her patient how the patient works—what is wrong with him and what needs to be changed to make him right.

An empathic understanding is quite different. It allows the patient to teach the therapist something. By immersing herself in the patient's self-state, the therapist becomes able to imagine a new way of being, an experience of aliveness that is slightly different from anything she could have imagined before. Rather than bringing her skills to bear on the patient, she allows the patient to effect her in deeply private places and to change her. The therapist is then in a position to tell the patient what she has learned from him, to reflect the patient's inner state back to him. The patient, seeing that he is seen, can feel secure enough to see himself.

> I am seen, so I exist. (Winnicott 1971b, p. 114).

The contradiction in these two approaches to understanding is most fruitfully understood as a difference in the relative dominance of masculine and feminine qualities. All understanding involves identifying with and merging into the other at the same time that it involves thinking about the other from a distance, comparing him with previous human specimens one has encountered and making educated guesses about his nature. An empathic approach that leaves no space for reflection from a distance about the patient may create a wide-eyed naïveté about the patient's depths that is of no service to anyone. But in general, we shall have infinitely more to offer our patients if we begin by letting them surprise us and teach us about themselves rather than by trying to nail down exactly how they tick.

The Strain of Containing the Work

I want to close this chapter with a discussion of the strain created by turning toward Being rather than Doing. In addition to the fact that one cannot puff oneself up with proofs of one's potency unless one does things that leave an impact on others, the experience of being with another may create terrible pressures within the therapist. Winnicott comments that the job of reflecting back to the patient what he brings "is not easy, it is emotionally exhausting" (1971b, p. 36). This in itself is true, for reflecting back to the patient his inner state requires that the analyst share it, and sharing the depths of another's suffering exercises one's entire being.

But there is a level of strain beyond this that arises when one is called upon to contain a patient's projective identifications. This strain is typically discharged by the therapist via interpreting the situation to the patient. Let me give first a simple example in which I successfully managed this containment, and then a more extensive example in which the material needing to be contained exceeded both my limits and the patient's.

Cara

Cara had been using the couch for her twice weekly therapy for some time, but having recently begun to connect with some fairly primitive layers of herself, she had become frightened. For several weeks she had been sitting up in what I (silently) took to be a resistance to the flow of the work—an attempt to slow things down, to modulate a pace by which she felt endangered.

In one particular hour, the fifth or sixth sitting-up hour, Cara began by talking, first indirectly and then increasingly straightforwardly, about primitive fantasies about her poisonous self. She was afraid I would be injured by contact with her, that I would in some way be infected with badness. From there she went quite easily into feelings she was having about being in the first trimester of a pregnancy. She was afraid her infertile friends would envy her as she had envied pregnant women during the six long months she had tried to conceive. She was afraid, in fact, that her colleagues and students might envy her, even that men in general or her husband in particular would envy her. I asked if she was afraid that I would envy her.

I had gone too far. Suddenly the entire tone of the session shifted dramatically. "Oh, no," said Cara. "You have your two children. I think you're *happy* for me being pregnant." The shift to "reality" was so abrupt as to throw me off balance and I replied, jokingly, "How nice of me!" But I quickly recovered, realizing that she needed to preserve me as an all-good object, that the idea of me as a whole person, with all kinds of murky depths of my own, terrified her, and I assured her that I was indeed happy for her. (Which I was, although I *did* also envy her current state, for she was incarnating the archetype of the Mother, immersed in the living numen of feminine creativity! At some level everyone must envy any pregnant woman.) This was the end of the hour.

In the next hour, Cara returned to the couch, and in the following hour, she tied her return to the couch to a subjectively felt increasing readiness to sink into painful or frightening aspects of her self and of her life. She said her increased readiness was a response to feeling safer with me as a result of my assuring her of my happiness for her in her pregnancy. She had felt my happiness for her was genuine, she said. She began to talk about coming more often than twice a week.

There are undoubtably many ways to conceptualize this sequence. I am suggesting here that one way to think about what happened is that I contained a variety of distressing feelings—my own feelings and Cara's—and that that containment enabled her to feel safer in my office and to move, on her own, to a deeper level of openness to herself in the work. Had I tried to interpret her resistance, had I confronted Cara with the superficial level to which she had retreated regarding her image of me, I would have actually fed her resistance, not her constructive growth process. My willingness to support Cara's progress at her own natural pace made it safe for her to proceed.

Aaron

Aaron was a man in his middle 30's, successful in his work, who had reason to hope to achieve real eminence by the time he reached his 50's. Much of his self-worth was invested in this hope. Although he came from an affluent family, his childhood had included more than its share of loss: a sister, seven years his senior, had been killed accidentally when he was 14, and his mother had become severely depressed. Aaron had been her primary emotional support, for the father was a remote, cold man. Aaron had coped with the demands of the situation by intensifying the manic defenses on which his character structure rested. Neither his grief at the loss of the sister, who had been a major mothering figure through his childhood, nor his rage at the utterly unreasonable demands that burdened him for six or seven years after the tragedy, had been felt at the time.

We worked well together for nearly four years, and his capacity to experience the darker side of life had grown considerably, when another tragedy struck. Aaron was hit by a drunk driver and was permanently disabled in a way that made continuing his career impossible. He tried to focus on the good things in his life—his wife and children, the probability of making a new career for himself as a teacher in a related field, the fact of his financial comfort. But his loss of professional hopes added to the physical impairment represented a huge narcissistic blow and triggered an eruption of all his old buried rage and grief, leaving his sense of self-worth a shambles.

Aaron went through a period of six to eight weeks of intense depression and rage. It *was* intense depression; on the other hand, I had seen worse, and it seemed inconceivable to me that Aaron would not come up against a harsher ordeal in his own psyche in trying to assimilate the physical mutilation he had sustained. But the magnitude of the depression frightened him, undoubtably partly because he could sense how much more was in store. After about six weeks he reconstituted, calling up powerful manic defenses and displacing his distress into the transference situation.

As Aaron's manic defenses took over his life, his rage centered on me. Like most analysts, I expect patients to pay for hours they miss, but I have not felt right about making this a blanket rule, and I give people two weeks' worth of cancellations each year. Aaron was coming three times a week, so that meant he could cancel up to six hours for any reason without being charged for them in the course of the year. I actually had to charge him for two hours he cancelled for medical appointments, which to Aaron meant that I was absolutely without human feeling for him. Although it seemed possible for us to get through the next year without his being charged for any of the many medical appointments he would need, it would be possible only if he were willing to coordinate his vacations with mine—something he had never wanted to do—and if he consistently tried to schedule medical appointments around his hours with me. The idea of making these efforts enraged him. He said he was unwilling to try to protect our hours from his medical schedule because only if *I* made special concessions for him could he believe I was concerned about him. He seemed unable to notice his blunt demand that my commitment to him, rather than his to his analysis, form the foundation for our work.

His life became better and better; he was coping *superbly* with this crisis. He was investigating three approaches to his disability at once, and it was clear it would not represent a long-term problem. He was excited, indeed, ecstatic, about himself and his life and wanted me to be excited for him. At any moment when distressed feelings threatened to break through, his manic defenses came whooshing in, and the rest of the hour would be a triumphant monologue regarding all the difficult issues he was expertly juggling. Increasingly, the monologues ended with an enraged demand that I cooperate with him in setting a date for cutting down the frequency of his visits preparatory to leaving therapy. I certainly never challenged his mania, but my inability actually to share it enraged him. He was doing so well, he was so centered, and so whole: it was clearly time to end therapy, preferably yesterday. He proposed termination in the spirit of how very well he was doing, and he talked at length about the resolution of all the feelings of inadequacy with which he used to struggle. As a passing piece of minor data, he would mention the fact that I was an unfeeling, frigid woman with no appreciation for what he was going through—indeed, never having been disabled myself, there was no way I ever *could* understand his situation.

This period lasted for five months. For most of that time, everything I said enraged him, including even the most strenuous attempts to exactly mirror what he was saying. I *never* got anything right. Attempts to *add* any insight into what was happening (to interpret anything) were disastrous and I quickly learned I needed to give up hope of enlarging his perspective.

The strain was enormous: I could see that a deeply buried pocket of excruciating pain had been tapped and that Aaron was unconsciously terrified by the intensity of the affects exploding inside him. Whether we want to call this an encapsulated psychosis or not, Aaron unconsciously feared that the feelings erupting inside him would shatter his psychological integrity just as the accident had shattered his physical integrity. He was desperately trying to pack all his chaotic feelings into my office and leave them there. Sitting with Aaron generated a large proportion of his disowned affective state in me. During our hours and for hours afterwards, I felt fragmented and jagged, rageful and wild. For days at a time, my work with Aaron dominated my consciousness; in some ways it became the center of my life. He disparaged me beyond anything I had ever experienced before; I felt assaulted, wrung out. He accused me of seeing him as a financial slot in my day; grinding my teeth, I thought there was *nothing* he could pay me to compensate for the beating I was taking at his hands. Any chance word from my lips was seized upon as indicative of severe countertransference problems that necessitated his immediate termination. But silence, of course, was not acceptable either, demonstrating as it did my coldness, my technical removal from our relationship, even my sadistic attempt to play with him like a cat with a mouse. I did once lose my temper and raise my voice. Here was definite proof of the sadism at which my silence had hinted! For hours I was subjected to intermittent lectures and rages about all the reasons therapists are never supposed to get angry at their patients.

It seemed clear that Aaron *was* going to terminate unless he could get some perspective on what was going on. Unless he could see that his feelings about me were seriously exaggerated, it seemed inevitable that he would break his connection with me. He needed to take on as *his* the frenzy that possessed him and give up seeing it as a reasonable response to my monstrous nature. But the last thing he was willing to take on was his frenzy. He even talked about his tendency in the past to get rather "speedy" when emotionally pressured and about how proud he was of the fact that that was not happening now: in this crisis, he was moving efficiently and effectively to deal with all the issues that needed attention while remaining solidly centered. Even if I had not become an utterly bad object for him, no interpretation that challenged his manic defenses could have been tolerated, no matter how mild. And, since I had become The Bad Object, he could not hear any interpretation; every comment, right down to "hello," was dissected and found wanting, for its tone of voice, if not for its content.

I was left with one single possible approach: an attempt to contain the wild frenzy he was generating in me. I knew theoretically the intolerable strain I felt could only represent a diluted version of the strain he was under. If I were to take seriously the theoretical position I have been laying out in this book, I should not have to interpret what was going on to him. At an unconscious level we were merged—he was certainly having no trouble passing his fragmented chaos on to me! If I could manage that chaos, contain it, live with it and continue to function well as a therapist, perhaps he could borrow back that capacity via the same route he had taken in handing it over to me. In many hours I sat behind him, grinding my teeth and rolling my eyes, repeating to myself over and over, "I can't do this, I can't contain this, I'm going to discharge at him with an interpretation." For it was clear to me that to try to tell him what was going on would be an attempt to discharge the tension I was suffering. The only hopeful intervention was an empathic sharing of his pain and to do that I needed to set my own pain aside—to contain it.

When I was able to do so and when Aaron's own inner capacity to contain *his* pain was functioning well, some progress could be made. Aaron remembered he had had deeply positive feelings about me for many years. At some point, it occurred to him that our relationship had been so central to him, for so long, that he was perhaps focusing some of the distress of his objectively terrible outer situation on me—"the way husbands and wives sometimes blame each other for their troubles." At times, Aaron allowed himself to experience more of his realistic distress and to hear my comments as sympathetic rather than as attempts to force him to wallow in despair. When an hour worked well, he slowed down and took in increasing layers of his condition.

Sometimes Aaron could feel my caring and concern, but the other side was always present for him, too. Our alliance, in addition to affecting me deeply, was also a business relationship, and Aaron felt devalued by this. At times my empathic responses enabled him to know I appreciated him, but the great loss of self-esteem triggered by his physical impairment overwhelmed his ability to feel valued, for it devastated his ability to feel valuable.

I felt I was doing the hardest work of my career in these hours; I remembered two difficult cases: an overtly psychotic girl who mutilated herself, and a severely suicidal woman. Both had been trying, for in each case the patient's life had always been immediately on the line. Aaron had never been in any such danger, but our alliance had been shattered. I had never before experienced such pressure to carry a patient's illness for him with no appreciation on his part—with no awareness on his part—of my burden. It was a vivid example of therapist and patient sharing one psyche in the depths of the work. It highlighted the fact that it is not what the therapist *says* that matters, it is who the therapist *is* in the deepest and broadest sense. This was a situation in which attempts to describe accurately to Aaron what was happening were instances of countertransference acting-out. I was called upon in these months to immerse myself in an utterly feminine orientation, to *be* to the nearly complete exclusion of *doing*, and it was the hardest thing I have ever had to do.

Ultimately, it failed. Insofar as I failed, it was my inability simply to *be* that tripped me up. I could not completely stop myself from trying to *give* Aaron insight that he could not bear to have. I knew he needed somehow to see his rage at me as something of a distortion. I was unable to accept the fact that he could not bear to see this for it would have opened him up to a level of inner pain he could not yet tolerate. Perhaps if I could have borne more pain, Aaron could have stayed with the therapeutic process. But it seems unlikely. His ability to contain his grief was apparently exceeded by the torrent of adversity crashing down on him, and he needed the manic defenses of his youth to protect his intact nature even if these defenses temporarily blocked his development.

My use of this case as an example is unusual, for it came to an unsuccessful conclusion. Many readers will undoubtably see many points in the story at which I could have said "X" or done "Y" constructively. I am aware of various errors of omission and commission. But I have come to think Aaron was actually right in believing he needed to terminate therapy. When he works out a new basis for his self-esteem, he will be able to let go of his manic defenses enough to return—perhaps to me, more probably to another therapist. At the crisis point I have described, he apparently needed to seal things off rather than to open them up. He had made great gains in our work in his authentic connection to himself, gains he ragefully insisted I not forget. They will not be lost, and the fact they are incomplete does not devalue them.

In any case, my use of an unsuccessful therapeutic experience to illustrate the intensity of the demands analytic work makes on the therapist has a certain appropriateness. There is a great deal of failure in this work, and it is almost completely unacknowledged in the literature. Even Robert Langs, the quintessential masculine seeker of perfection, has begun to focus on questions like, "Why patients reject properly conducted therapies" (i.e., why good therapists fail) and "Why/How deviant-frame therapy succeeds" (i.e., why/how people grow swimmingly in flawed situations). We must acknowledge failure or incompletion as an inevitable experience instead of imagining that if we could only do it RIGHT, the work would always work.

As my own focus was shifting, some years ago, from a masculine stance in my work to a more feminine one, I had a dream:

> *I am talking with my stepfather, a dream figure who resembles my analyst. I am finishing high school and preparing to go to college where I hope to study nursing. I want to go to Barnyard (sic) College, which is run by the Sisters of Mercy and Hope. My stepfather, whom I deeply love and whose approval I intensely seek, tells me I'm too smart to be a nurse, I should go to medical school and become a doctor. With some faint tremors of regret I agree to go to Harvard Medical School.*

Reflecting on the dream I experienced much more than faint tremors of regret. It was vividly clear to me I wanted to be a nurse, not a doctor: I wanted to accompany people in pain, to dress their wounds and hold their hands through their long dark nights. I did not want to operate on people and leave them to recover or die in other people's care, to medicate them or even to diagnose them preparatory to prescribing a healing regimen—which other people, notably nurses, would carry out. I wanted to study at Barnyard College, the home of the animals, where I could immerse myself in the instincts of the body, where Mercy and Hope make their home, somehow surviving recurring contact with failure and death. It is indeed difficult to reject the power and prestige of a masculine outlook, to choose to reject the most eminent institution of them all, Harvard Medical School, if one actually has the choice. But what I had to do seemed clear, and I believe our field, depth psychology, also needs to turn radically toward the Feminine, away from power, activity, and success, towards love and acceptance of life as it really is rather than as we wish it were.

Chapter 5

The Role of the Masculine

While I am trying in this book, to describe psychotherapy *grounded* in the feminine principle, I do not mean to imply that the masculine principle is negligible or even secondary in importance. Although a given task may require primarily one or the other orientation, creative living demands that the individual be comfortable in relationship to both principles. Therapeutic work is effective to the extent that it is steeped in both patient's and therapist's creative living.

An optimal marriage is one between equals. I have emphasized the feminine principle so vigorously because it has been so devalued and neglected in our understanding of life and, consequently, of the therapeutic process. I believe the best therapeutic work is *centered* in feminine relatedness, because the heart of any therapeutic venture is found there: the relatedness that develops between the two individuals, between the patient and her self, between each of the adults in the consulting room and the patient's infantile core.

But many things go on in analytic work besides this essential experience of the patient's infantile self. There is usually much work to be done—often years of work—before the infantile psyche becomes consciously available for direct contact. And even when that exquisitely vulnerable place has been reached, the issue of protecting the nursing mother/infant pair is crucial. Just as that role traditionally falls to the father in an ordinary nuclear family, so in analysis that task devolves on the therapist's masculine side.

Talking about marriage as a psychological relationship, Jung offered the image of a container and a contained. He suggested that either partner could function in either role for the other. Bion used this same metaphor of container and contained for the mother/infant couple, suggesting that the mother must take into her own psyche the infant's indigestible emotions and process them—detoxify them—before returning them to the baby. Both men extended their imagistic sense of primary relationship into the therapeutic experience. Bion suggested that a major element in the therapist's role is the functioning as a receptor for the patient's projective identifications, just as this activity comprises a major aspect of the mother's role. The therapist must process the patient's beta elements—chaotic, meaningless bits of psychic matter—turning them into alpha elements with coherent linkages to the warp and woof of her greater psyche. The therapist's psyche takes in and contains the patient's. Jung spoke of therapy as occurring in a *temenos*, a sacred, magic circle. Using the language and imagery of medieval alchemy, he described the therapeutic relationship as an alchemical *vas bene clausum*, a well-sealed vessel. In this metaphor, the therapeutic relationship or process contains both therapist and patient. Robert Langs has extended this intuitive apprehension of psychotherapy occurring inside a symbolic container in very concrete cognitive formulations regarding the therapeutic frame (see especially, Langs 1979).

The feminine energy and work I described in Chapter 4 depend on a boundary. The traditional mother/infant couple can relax into each other, lose themselves in a fluid mutual merger, because the father provides a safe hold for them. He maintains a home and brings in the material nourishment needed from the outer world. In the analytic situation, the therapist is called upon to fill both roles, the mother and father, in turn. The therapist/patient pair can merge into each other only if they can rely on the boundaries of the therapeutic container to hold them. If a relaxation of the skin boundary will lead to one's psyche leaking out, unimpeded, melting or puddling into infinity, one will not (and should not) risk it.

Similar considerations apply to the patient's need to regress. The patient can lay aside her adult competences when she knows the therapist will safely hold her, protecting the temporarily relinquished adult strengths and supplying them when needed until the patient is once again ready to take them up. As Langs demonstrates repeatedly, one important element of this safe hold is the therapist's protection of the frame.

The Fixed Frame

The first aspect of the frame is its fixed—rigid, unchanging—aspect. Langs suggests the following essential elements of the fixed frame: meeting in the same place, for a constant fee, at a regularly scheduled and largely inflexible time, in a set position (normally face to face or on the couch). There should be a clear policy regarding cancellations, and guarantees of confidentiality and of privacy. Some of these elements are simple and rarely deviated from; others require exploration.

Most therapists have one office and meet the patient only there. When a therapist has more than one office, he may meet the same patient in both places. My experience with this situation is limited to two cases, but in both, switching offices had a disorienting effect on the patient and limited her ability to do regressive work. Perhaps issues of convenience will compel alternating offices, but, when possible, it should be avoided.

In one of my two cases, the therapist met the patient for an emergency appointment on a weekend and asked her to come to his office at his home rather than to their usual meeting place. Although she agreed and felt consciously appreciative at the time, she later came to feel it as a major abandonment. She was frantic and distraught following an abortion and felt the therapist had been unconsciously sadistic in bringing her into his home, forcing her to step over an overturned tricycle in the garden. But even without this thoughtless added element, it seemed to her in retrospect that he had issued an ambivalent message in both agreeing to see her and refusing to drive the 10 minutes to his regular office. He was inviting her into his private life, available to her as a friend, but not perhaps as a therapist. This became an image, for her, of his more major later abandonments.

In the second case, a patient who was wavering about the depth of her involvement in the work found herself scheduled to see her therapist on Mondays in one office and on Thursdays in another when he changed her geographic location on one of those days. The offices were equidistant from the patient's home, so the shift was not physically inconvenient for her, but she was never able to settle securely into the second office. The shift in location proved—perhaps synchronistically rather than causally—to coincide with the beginning of a lengthy termination phase in her work. While many other factors were operating, she felt afterward that the process of working in one place on Mondays and another on Thursdays would never have been viable for her and that she would have had to change her appointments to meet in one constant place if she had wanted to continue and deepen the regressive work she had been doing. Some people, less sensitive to their physical surroundings, might find meeting in two places less difficult.

Similarly, variations in patients' reactions to a consulting room located in the therapist's home undoubtedly exist. To the extent that a patient feels the presence of the therapist's family and private life, some elements of the patient's potential transference will be suppressed. To the extent the therapist is able to open his life and family to the patient's imaginative exploration (and potential hostile attack), such suppression will be minimized. But all therapists have limits, and any patient will experience some inhibition of her emotional range, sensing the demands of the therapist's privacy on her freedom of expression.

I have never heard of a therapist who did not charge a constant fee. When the therapist raises the fee, it is nearly always a major disturbance in the work; it generally requires a major disturbance initiated by the patient to compel a therapist to lower the fee. This seems appropriate to me, for the fee is the place at which the therapist's and the patient's needs most clearly clash. The same piece of money belongs now to one member of the dyad and now to the other; the point of transfer is an explosive one, arousing both individuals' natural, healthy greed, an appetite we would do well to value, for it has much to recommend it. The Tibetan Wheel of Life contains a cock, a pig, and a snake at its center: lust, greed, and envy make the world go round. When the therapist cannot acknowledge his own greed and feels compelled to behave as though he were a saint, the patient's freedom to explore *her* greed is seriously undermined. Therapists do their work for many reasons, some that go deeply into their souls and other more superficial ones; money is one aspect of the work. Both members of the therapeutic pair naturally fear its powerful shadow, but if it is not consciously confronted, it will unconsciously seep into the work and limit it.

The therapist's feelings about money will affect the cancellation policy he constructs. The most rigid policy requires the patient to pay for all scheduled sessions. Robert Langs and Arnold Goldberg, a Self Psychologist, both work with this policy. A common variant among analysts holds the patient responsible for all hours unless the therapist fills them. Many therapists require simply 24 hours notice for a cancellation, a policy that has never made any sense to me: presumably a patient would be charged for a true emergency at the same time that she is given almost unlimited freedom to act out negative feelings about the therapy. Some therapists take each cancellation as it comes along, trying to analyze its meaning with the patient and to charge for "illegitimate" cancellations and not for "legitimate" ones. My experience with that attempt left me feeling frequently manipulated: after the patient and I had discussed the cancellation at length and I had agreed to accept it, some "minor" piece of additional information had a way of surfacing. Moreover, any such "flexible" cancellation policy inevitably puts the therapist in the role of judge.

A rigid cancellation policy has the value of bluntly confronting the business aspect of the therapeutic relationship. The therapist does, in fact, make a living from his work, and regardless of the amount of notice he receives, he typically cannot fill a cancelled hour if he needs also to hold that hour for the patient's return. Although having to pay for a missed hour is upsetting, it seems to me to be a legitimate distress that can profitably be suffered. It is not the therapist's meanness that causes the upset, but the accurate facts of therapeutic work: the therapist does earn a living by accompanying the patient on her inner journey. This face is painful for the regressed patient, for it calls into question the therapist's authentic concern. It raises basic issues of splitting: how can someone want to make a profit on another's suffering if he genuinely cares about the other person? How can one make peace with an ambivalent object, neither ideal nor diabolical? This question lies at the heart of all mature relatedness. It will inevitably be worked over extensively in any therapeutic work, if not around cancellations then elsewhere. A tight cancellation policy offers one vehicle for working it over.

The ultimate rationale for such a cancellation policy, however, is the therapist's need, not the patient's. As I became increasingly capable of devoting myself emotionally to my patients, I came to want the reward of a reliable, steady income. The money seemed to be the *only* element in the work that was legitimately mine, and I strongly wanted it as I renounced more and more of the various subtle emotional demands for gratification therapists frequently make on their patients. I also wanted to find a position in which my self-interest—my greed—was in no way affected by any judgments I made about the patient's behavior, for this gave me the greatest possible chance to avoid making value judgments about her behavior. What we call "acting out" is sometimes—perhaps always—out of the patient's control and should be accepted along with other painful symptoms. I can do this only to the extent that I protect myself, at least financially, from being injured by the patient's behavior.

One analyst I know never charges for cancellations. He is busy enough to welcome a free hour in his day, and when he believes the cancellation represents some kind of acting out on the patient's part, he maintains they can talk about it. Certainly it is true that if they *cannot* talk about it, the work is in dreadful trouble. In making his statement about his relationship to his own greed, this analyst reveals an authentic image of his personal struggle to live a materially modest, richly spiritual life. It is not a denial of his greed. If a less-developed therapist wishes to avoid facing the inherent conflicts of interest that exist between oneself and one's patient, a loose cancellation policy will enable him to do so, but it will also limit the work, for it will represent a permanent, ingrained lie about himself that both he and the patient must pretend to believe in order to work together.

A tight cancellation policy arouses tremendous feelings in many people. Therapists who take a "flexible" approach to cancellations often are as deeply outraged by a rigid policy as are patients caught in its intensely constricting grasp. The fantasy is that a rigid policy frees the therapist from stress: he no longer need concern himself with ordinary fluctuations of income. In fact, the policy exposes the therapist to tremendous stresses. The amount of money one gains from a rigid policy in the course of a year may actually be quite small. The intensity of the narcissistic and borderline rage and grief that the policy mobilizes can be awesome at times. Each year my policy precipitates one or two crises in my office which demand depths of energy that tax my soul to its limits. Aaron's rage (Chapter 4) focused to some extent on my cancellation policy, although its actual roots were not in the therapy at all. I realized recently that whatever additional income I was guaranteeing with my policy did not begin to compensate me for the additional work I was taking on with it.

Why, then, I wondered, was I doing this? Once one has set the policy, one cannot abandon it in response to a patient's emotional eruption, for to do that would be to agree with the patient that the borderline rage which it mobilizes is beyond one's capacity to tolerate. To cave in to pressure here would be to establish a collusive contract promising that the analytic work will not touch certain painful places, and this would pollute all future work. But there is no reason I cannot decide that I no longer wish to work with this policy in general, that we will connect with these chaotic pockets of terror and rage through other triggers. If I cannot, in good conscience, capitulate to Aaron's demands (for example), I can certainly walk into my office on January 1 announcing to everyone that in the future I will work with some different policy; when we're both in town, for example, we'll meet. But I can feel my deep unwillingness to do this, my increasingly rooted commitment to my rigid policy which insists that the patient view his time with me with the same attitude as he views the rent on his home: whether he is in town or out, he preserves this central space to return to.

Partly I want the patient to make this religious commitment to the work that I am making and so I insist on at least its outer form. But more basically I think my policy offers me an arena for my own shadow. The therapist's most central task is to be authentically present with the patient. If I am truly to *be there* with my patient I need space in the room for all of me, just as I must create a large enough space for all of her. I am not a saint. Issues of greed and power are raised inside myself in relation to cancellations and my policy enables me to experience and share all of myself in the context of my analytic role. The money I gain from my policy does not compensate me for the stress it adds, but this emotional freedom and richness does.

The element of a fixed time for the therapeutic hour is a frequently disrespected aspect of the frame. So many things come up in both patient's and therapist's lives to make the regular time inconvenient! What can one say? First, that it is true. Many things do come up, legitimate conflicts of interest. But, second, utterly unconscious anxieties about the experiences being generated between the two participants have a way of calling up remarkably legitimate conflicts of interest. I wrote in Chapter 4 about taking a religious attitude toward the work. Truly extenuating circumstances exist; even the Pope will grant a dispensation at times. But a religious attitude will lead both participants to cherish the time that has been set aside for this very special work, regardless of the passing inconveniences that it may cause. Honoring the work, allowing it to inconvenience us, bending our lives to *it* rather than asking the work to bend to our lives, both fosters and marks the religious attitude depth work requires.

Privacy is another element of the frame much honored in the breach. Therapists confer with referring physicians, social workers, and teachers. They collaborate with other therapists (therapists of the spouse, the parent, the child, the couple). They talk with other family members in a crisis, even with friends. These are literal leaks in the container, allowing bits of the process to slip out. Instead of a hermetically sealed vessel, the therapy is a sponge, capable of holding a certain amount and no more.

Efforts to consult with other professionals are meant to provide the patient with the best possible care, by giving the therapist access to the greatest possible range of information. These consultations are predicated on a belief that information about the patient is the crucial healing aspect, rather than the interpersonal process between patient and therapist. If the patient is concealing or distorting something, either consciously or unconsciously, the central therapeutic issue involves mutually exploring and working through that resistance, not circumventing it. Resistance is a legitimate part of the psyche, too. In addition, collaborative efforts are inherently disrespectful of the patient, for they begin with an assumption that someone else knows more about the patient than the patient does. Ideally, the only collaboration the therapist needs is with the patient herself. In the real world, one also often needs some consultative support in order to be there for the patient, but that can be provided only by a fellow professional who is a stranger to the patient.

Answering the phone during an hour is another tear in the work's container, a simple, ordinary action that welcomes total strangers into the room. It disregards the needs of the regressed patient, who must have her being fill the entirety of the hour. When the patient is regressed, she will protest these intrusions most "unreasonably"; when she is not, she will be reasonable and adult about them. And she will not regress.

Meeting together in a set position, either face to face or using the couch, is an element of the fixed frame that is ordinarily adhered to naturally. Both the patient and the therapist tend to take a constant place in the room. But variations do occur, and as we discuss this element we move toward the variable frame, where variations have either creative, growing meanings, or resistant ones, or both at once. Sometimes patients who are on the couch, like Cara in Chapter 4, want to sit up; often this comes at a point when the intensity of the emotional experiences being generated is frightening, and the wish to sit up is an attempt to reassert adult controls. Certainly that is "resistant" behavior; it possibly also represents a safety valve the patient *needs* as she lowers herself into the depths of her psyche.

Sometimes regressed patients, struggling to express preverbal experiences that are close to inexpressible, look for bodily forms of communication. Winnicott's work contains many examples of this: Margaret Little (1985), describing her analysis with him, tells of an hour in which she got off the couch and wandered around the room, looking desperately for some way to communicate something that could not be articulated. The search culminated in her smashing a large vase. We must certainly call her behavior "acting in"; it was also a huge emotional experience for both participants and therefore offered at least the possibility of greatly deepening their connection.

I have known two adult patients who interrupted work on the couch to spend time sitting on the floor doing play therapy. In one case, the patient settled in on the floor and played with blocks, clay, and crayons for several months before returning to the couch. In the other case, the patient moved back and forth, now free-associating on the couch, now symbolically living out her associations by playing on the floor, again for a period of several months. Especially in the second case, some resistance was doubtless being expressed in the bobbing around, but the depth of connection these patients offered their therapists greatly outweighed any resistant elements in their behavior. In both cases, an injured child was literally settling into the room, and an attempt to interfere with that child's mode of entry because of some theoretical bias about keeping the patient immobilized or about allowing *only* verbal forms of communication would have been a death blow to the therapy's deepening movement.

The last element of the fixed frame, confidentiality, like all other elements of the fixed frame, can never be totally fixed. Leakages occur. We all try to prevent them; we all fail at times. The option of getting a professional consultation on one's work must never be relinquished, although it is technically a break in the work's confidentiality. With some patients—particularly with patients who are therapists themselves—consultations may be significant breaks in the confidential nature of the work.

But there are other breaks in confidentiality that can neither be justified nor avoided. The emotional pressures on the therapist, generated by the projective identifications he is called upon to carry, may be intolerable. When, for example, the patient is immersed in a near-psychotic transference, as in the case of Aaron in the previous chapter, the therapist finds himself under constant, dreadful attack. I do not personally know any therapist who does not respond, at times, to this kind of pressure by draining some of it off in relatively inappropriate talk to a spouse or close friend in an informal setting. In Chapter 8, I will describe some grossly inappropriate behavior I engaged in under pressure; although I felt terrible about it, and although I still believe there is no excuse for it, the unfortunate fact is that it is not uncommon for therapists to explode a few times in the course of their careers. On the one hand, it is dreadful; on the other, it is deeply human and must be forgiven.

In trying to describe the concrete elements of the therapeutic frame, I am trying to analyze the real behavior that provides the strong, safe hold that will enable the patient to unravel down to her vulnerable core. Many therapists in the 1960s and 1970s, reacting to the rigid orthodoxy of the 1950s, threw out all the rules and focused only on the intangible emotional interplay between the two participants. Therapists took mind-altering drugs with patients; encounter groups sprang up in which people faced each other, perhaps naked, and expressed emotions in raw, unmodulated, occasionally dangerous ways. One heard a great deal about therapists having sex with patients, and even more distressing, one heard too many people imagining that such behavior might be deeply healing rather than profoundly exploitative.

But even apart from such wildly untherapeutic scenarios, well-meaning and naturally responsible therapists found themselves quite lost in a therapeutic culture that had rejected the old rules. Recognizing that countertransference was not only not pathological but ubiquitous was a healthy development in the psychological world. It represented a substantial step forward in our understanding of the therapeutic process when we could acknowledge that it was the authentic nature of the therapist's response to his patient rather than his technical adroitness that would either heal or harm the patient. But the pendulum swung way out in the direction of liberality, and the 1980s are proving to be years of re-equilibrating.

When the therapist is able to integrate a solidly grounded framework for his work, he can focus his attention on the essential emotional interaction between himself and his patient in a more productive fashion than when he is working without any clear rules of behavior. How does the therapist know when he is acting out destructive countertransference pressure if he has no firm, consistent sense of how he will behave when he is centered? Subjective certainty about one's consciousness can *never* be relied upon; the one consistent thing we know about unconsciousness is that one is unaware of it. Subjective *un*certainty is a far more hopeful sign than excessive conviction. When the therapist is skilled with dreams, both his own dreams and the patient's provide a continuous supervisory check on his behavior, but if he is entrenched in unconsciousness, he will not be able to read them. Of course, if he is too unconscious, nothing will help, but a consistent framework provides a helpful beginning for self-analysis. When one deviates, one should wonder why. Perhaps the deviation represents a creative gesture emerging from one's depths; perhaps it represents the activation of one's personal neurotic complexes, or a syntonic countertransference reaction in which the therapist is expressing either a counterproductive or a constructive impulse of the patient's. A consistent framework will not answer these questions; it simply provides guidelines within which to explore them.

The frame of the work also offers something directly to the patient that was lost in the looseness of the 1960s and 1970s. Consistency and reliability, extending over time, provide a security that good intentions alone do not offer. Winnicott describes how important it is for the infant that the mother survive the baby's instinctual behaviors—greed, lust, raw need—hour after hour and day after day. The therapist's survival in the analytic situation assures the patient, like the infant, of the manageability and safety of the patient's own authentic nature. The analyst can stand the patient, and he demonstrates this by remaining predictably himself under pressure, by holding a consistent frame.

The fixed frame I have described is the first and simplest expression of the therapist's indestructibility. The variable frame, the details of which each therapist must work out individually, is a set of guidelines for the therapist's interpersonal posture. Besides helping analysts to think about their emotional responses to a patient at a particular moment, it gives both members of the therapeutic dyad a sense of the analyst's individuality by providing a container for that individuality. Let me explore the major elements of the variable frame.

The Variable Frame

A deceptively simple, and probably universally aspired-to element, is what Robert Langs calls "physicianly concern." This expresses itself in the therapist's devotion to the patient. Although certainly including "caring," it is not at all the same as "liking." One may devote oneself to a patient one does not like, and in Chapter 8, I describe several cases in which I tried to do that. Devotion is, in limited ways, under the control of the will, but different individuals' capacities for it vary greatly. Many therapists, at some time in life, must reach a point at which they are no longer able to devote themselves to the storm of a deeply regressive analytic venture. It simply requires too much; one comes to need a rest.

We see the limitations of individual therapist's capacities for devotion in the criticisms all therapists express, at least occasionally, regarding patients' "unreasonable" behavior and demands (referring here to behavior and demands that occur within the hour, not to infinitely spiralling extra-analytic demands). The patient's sense of narcissistic entitlement needs to be confronted; endless complaints should not be tolerated. The patient is stuck in her negativity—or perhaps in her development—and movement ought to be forced in some way. The patient is manipulative, seductive, abusive. . . . The patient is being criticized for her pathology. The therapist's limitations in depth of devotion either to patients in general or to one patient in particular are endlessly rationalized in psychologically sophisticated language. Behavior on the therapist's part that is emotionally abusive to a patient is unfortunately common in this field and may be easily justified as necessary for the therapist's attempt to compel the patient into health. In Chapter 7, I analyze a case of Masterson's that exemplifies this point.

Two expressions of the therapist's devotion are full attention to the patient throughout the session and commitment to work with the patient to the point of the patient's (as opposed to the therapist's) readiness to terminate. We all try to pay full attention to our patients through their hours. We all fail, almost every hour. When the patient is really dissociated or disengaged, the therapist's ability to track her may come close to total failure. What therapist has never struggled with narcolepsy? Boredom and sleepiness need to be attended to in the same way as any other associations—as data concerning the current progress of the work. When one's mind wanders, one does best by attending to where it is going and trying to imagine what that says about where the patient is. I have had two experiences in which very boring patients worked through extreme schizoid defenses and reached a point at which I became grippingly involved with them. People really *do* change even when we cannot imagine *how* they possibly can.

The boring patient in particular may tempt the therapist to terminate the treatment, but I have heard therapists tempted to terminate the treatment of every possible kind of patient: boring, aggressive, timid, depressed, borderline, rigidly organized, and so on. Unless the pain of the work becomes intolerable, the therapist is ethically required to notice impulses to end the work rather than to act on them. The therapist's wish to flee should be tolerated and analyzed (silently) in the same way that the patient's impulses to run away from the work are analyzed (often out loud).

It is never, in my opinion, the therapist's job to terminate the work, either out of despair over the patient's progress or out of the satisfaction of believing the work done. Either position comes out of a false expertise and is more apt to reflect unconscious anxieties in the therapist than anything objective in the patient. One the one hand, the work is never done; on the other hand, the patient will know when she is ready to move on, continuing her work in other containers. Among other things, the therapist's attempts to remain on top of everything at all times, to the point of knowing when the patient should leave, is an attempt to prevent himself from ever being left. We all know how much nicer it is to initiate the leaving than to have it presented to us! The time, energy, and money the patient invests provide enough pressure to leave; when she is psychologically ready to leave, she will do so. The therapist's assessment of when the patient is ready to leave is more apt to reflect the therapist's readiness, and that assessment may well grow out of a sense that what may come next will tax his own development.

Neutrality is a widely discussed element in the variable frame. The word sounds appealing to many therapists and horrid to others. As I have listened to discussions of the concept, it has become clear to me that different therapists mean very different things by the word. Anna Freud defines neutrality as taking a stance equidistant from the patient's id, ego, and superego. Having pondered that definition for many years, I have come to imagine I have some idea of what it means, but it is a definition of the word that is fairly distant from experience. Some people take neutrality to mean an absence of emotion vis-à-vis the patient, but I hope most proponents of neutrality would not define it this way.

As I understand it, neutrality is desirable in relation to the patient's inner conflicts, not in relation to the patient. Physicianly concern implies that one is *for* one's patient—for her growth, for her life working out well, for her satisfaction and enjoyment in work, in love, in play, and in analysis. Neutrality implies rather that one recognizes that only the patient can know how to work out her life and that the route she takes may seem circuitous—or even dangerous—to the outside observer. A neutral posture implies that we will not hope the patient will stay in or leave a marriage, for example—or that we will understand a subjective emotional investment in either choice as a countertransference symptom indicating something about either the patient's unconscious wishes or our own unconsciously rooted biases. A neutral stance does not mean that we will not feel grief when a patient's child is stillborn or when a much desired professional opportunity is lost. It does mean that in either of these examples we will also find room in our own psyche to contain the patient's unacceptable emotions, such as relief, at these tragic experiences.

Neutrality meets its most difficult test when the patient is in conflict about the therapy itself, but here too, we do not know what is best for another person. Even when the patient's impulses to leave the therapy correspond to her refusing her own individuation, we must recognize that some people will not take the difficult road to consciousness, and that while we can nudge a patient in that direction, we cannot push her very far at all. All too frequently, a patient's impulse to leave the therapy proves on examination to be a healthy rejection of a therapeutic situation that is too seriously flawed to be helpful. And sometimes when the therapist has been able to leave the decision to terminate to the patient, the impulse to leave may represent a healthy recognition of the concluding stages of the therapy process. Neutrality is a concept that captures an essential dimension of a feminine approach to the work. Thinking about it in masculine, Apollonian terms may be of great assistance in our attempt to remain centered in a feminine mode.

The old psychoanalytic rule of abstinence is another element in the traditional variable frame. This rule is most helpful as a starting point for exploratory thinking about abstinence and gratification in the analytic setting. Simply stated, the rule of abstinence advises the therapist to refuse to gratify the patient's impulses and to analyze them instead. The rule is one of Freud's original suggestions regarding technique but as the decades passed, the psychoanalytic community came to use it in ways that were very different indeed from its appearance in Freud's case histories. Freud reports, for example, feeding a patient and lending a patient money, gross violations of later understanding of the rule. In its original crude state, the rule of abstinence referred most clearly to the patient's erotic impulses that all reputable therapists, then and now, agree should be analyzed rather than gratified. Beyond that I think we get into very interesting, unclear territory where there is no absolute right or wrong behavior.

As I described in Chapter 3, Michael Balint, differentiating between benign and malignant regressions, suggests that in a benign regression the patient wants the therapist to witness rather than to gratify the depth of her need. I added to that the idea that if the therapist can stay centered in his willingness to witness but not to gratify, the patient (who is inevitably torn to some degree between these two conflicting impulses) may accept witnessing and come to terms with an inner deprivation that may never be wholly gratified. Balint describes at some length Ferenczi's "grand experiment," in which he tried to fill the cavernous inner void in a deserving female patient by gratifying her infinitely increasing hungers: by seeing her seven days a week, for example, as weekend breaks were not thought to be good for her. The fact that Ferenczi died in the middle of that work is synchronistically striking: one *cannot* gratify the depths of any human being's needs, and attempts to meet the existential inner emptiness with which we all struggle by gratifying it can only come to a disastrous end.

On the other hand, it is not possible only to witness and never to gratify the borderline desires that regressive work unleashes. The patient wants an extra hour, she wants the therapist to send her a postcard during the summer vacation, she paints a picture of her inner state that she wants to leave in the therapist's office for safekeeping, she wants to give the therapist a poem to read, she wants the therapist to lend her a transitional object. Most pressingly, she desperately wants some indication, no matter how subtle, verbal or nonverbal, of the therapist's personal concern for her, something to hold onto, literally or symbolically, to keep her tie to the therapist alive and real in her heart.

It is true that agreeing to even the simplest desire for some kind of "special" gratification will lead to another, apparently reasonable, desire. At the borderline layer of the psyche, the inner void is endless and cannot be filled. But it is also true there are times one would have to be monstrously cold to refuse a simple request from a needy or panicky patient. If one always guards the classic rule of abstinence, never allowing the dictates of a softened heart to overpower the rules, the patient will never be able to trust her value in the therapist's eyes sufficiently fully to let go. It is the unique human contact between therapist and patient, the mingling of their souls, that can transform the patient's pain. Purely analytic work can only strengthen her ego's capacity to bear her inner pain. The deep interpersonal merging that heals announces its existence via unorthodox, previously unthought of responses that this unique therapist makes to this unique patient. No other dyad could have imagined quite this form of solace.

One patient regularly borrowed the afghan at the foot of my couch to hold onto through each of my vacations. It cost me nothing to lend it to her, and it is hard for me to believe, given the depth of the abandonment panic that erupted before my vacations, that lending her the blanket sealed off her pain. Over many years we worked that pain through and at last there came a vacation when she left the afghan in my office, believing she would be able to keep me alive in her mind without a concrete prop. I was never able to see what constructive function would have been served had I held to a rigid rule of abstinence. A refusal to lend the blanket would have led her at best to steel herself against her abandonment panic, developing the strength to withstand its pain. Lending her the blanket was part of a very lengthy process between us in which she came to internalize my loving presence with such certainty that the extent of her abandonment panic was actually transformed.

Many analysts have commented on the fact that classical thinking about the rule of abstinence failed to notice that therapeutic work is inherently gratifying as well as frustrating. The experience of being the object of the therapist's undivided, compassionate attention is powerfully soothing and gratifying. Beyond that, affection and even love develop within the therapist as well as the patient. Hartmann's notion that the therapeutic relationship is not a "real" object relationship (see above, Chapter 2) grows out of fear of the intensity of the relationship that is constructed between therapist and patient. Two people begin as strangers and do not experience themselves as having chosen each other in any significant way. They sit together for many years, exploring every nuance of the patient's suffering. It is an unnatural situation, but real feelings are generated in both people, and the patient's ultimate healing depends on the interpersonal connection that is forged at the deepest layers, not on its surface forms. It is actually the therapist's love, not his expertise, that facilitates transformation (as opposed to adjustment). In regressed states, that love will express itself in careful attempts to gratify at least some of the patient's needs, attempts modulated by the therapist's realistic limits as well as by his beliefs about what is required for real healing to occur.

What is crucial is not that the therapist hold to an artificial rule of abstinence, but that he work to be as clear as possible about his own limits and motivations. One severely suicidal patient wanted and seemed to need the freedom to telephone me between sessions. As her suicidal impulses skyrocketed around a personal loss, I came to realize I could tolerate her intrusions into my personal life only if I charged her for telephone time. That decision acted as a reality limit regarding how often she could afford to call me, at the same time that it provided me with enough gratification to sustain me in my attempt to gratify her. It grew out of my attempt to be true to my own limitations, for if one tries to give more than one has to give, the entire situation is apt to boomerang back on one in some dreadful way.

In addition to assessing his own limitations, the therapist must struggle to know his motivation in increasingly deep ways. When is the impulse to gratify based on the patient's needs, and when is it a response to an inner pressure of the therapist's? When I allowed my patient to borrow my afghan was I really responding to *her* need for maintaining a connection with me or was I responding to my need, for her gratitude, for example, or for subjective reassurance that I was not as cruel and heartless in leaving her as she felt me to be. Perhaps I was afraid of emotions beyond the grief and rage she was already expressing, and my gesture functioned to seal off that additional pain. There may never be any way to answer the question with total clarity—to whose needs does a given act respond? It may be that no situation is ever completely one way or the other. But asking the question and attending to all the available data regarding it is an important activity.

When the patient regresses to a predominantly preoedipal level, the classic rule of abstinence is no longer relevant, for that rule is based on the idea that the analyst, via interpretations, gives the patient understanding of her inner conflicts. Understanding is expected to take the place of tangible gratification. But as Balint demonstrates, when we deal with a regressed patient, interpretations do not offer understanding; they are experienced as "an attack, a demand, a base insinuation . . . [or] as something highly pleasing and gratifying, exciting or soothing, or as a seduction" (Balint 1968, p. 18). Whatever theories we may cherish about how preverbal experiences are *supposed* to be turned into verbal symbols—about how that is *the* road to emotional healing—must give way to the data of reality: the regressed patient does not hear words the way adults do, the analyst's words have a concrete rather than symbolic impact. Every interchange between patient and therapist is a foray into virgin territory where the therapist inevitably either gratifies or cruelly deprives the patient. No neutral ground exists.

Anonymity has been a traditional companion of abstinence. In an attempt to keep the consulting room antiseptically clean, the patient was to know nothing about the therapist. If the therapist were well trained, nothing of his individuality would show through his skillful expertise, and any competent analyst would provide *exactly the same* experience for the patient. While no one any longer holds this rigid classical view, there seem to be analysts who still imagine they can conceal essential facts of their nature from their patients. Sigrid R. McPherson (1986), a Jungian analyst from southern California, has described her first therapy with a Freudian analyst. She emigrated to this country from Germany, having grown up during the Second

World War under Hitler. Suffering an intolerable guilt over Germany's genocide against the Jews, she asked her analyst, early in the treatment, whether he was Jewish. He refused to answer, maintaining that he needed to be available to be whatever she needed him to be for her. But McPherson intuitively knew he was Jewish, for he reacted in particular ways to her stories about life under Hitler, and she therefore experienced his attempt to remain anonymous as an attempt to stay disengaged and separate. It also frightened her, for it made her question the reality of life in the United States—was it really safe to be Jewish here? As the treatment progressed, the analyst began implicitly to acknowledge his Jewishness in various comments.

In the course of a lengthy analysis or therapy, all therapists occasionally share personal reminiscences with their patients (Searles 1986). In the nurturing atmosphere created by his devoted attention to his patient, both the therapist's yearnings for attention and concern and his impulses to confide something of himself to the patient are activated. The extent of this activity will vary depending on the therapist's natural inclination to openness, the patient's receptivity to his confidences and the therapist's trust in his patient.

While much attention is ordinarily paid to the patient's need to trust the therapist, little has been paid to the issue of the therapist's trust of the patient. When a patient's hostility is largely unconscious, the therapist cannot predict the outcome for himself if he lets the patient see some bit of his private vulnerability. As the treatment proceeds and the therapist comes to know the patient better, he will maintain an anonymous facade most rigorously if he feels, perhaps in an inarticulated way, that his patient's aggressive impulses will seize any opening with unconscious malice. But even a classical therapist, if he comes to trust his patient's love and good intentions, will occasionally reveal himself in some important way. Hence McPherson's therapist's unacknowledged shift from anonymity to an implicit acknowledgment of his Jewishness after he had come to know her and to trust her.

Breaks in the therapist's anonymity have intangible value for the therapy's progress when they occur in a situation where all attention is normally focused on the patient. Obviously, the therapist's wish to talk about himself comes out of his own neediness at least as much as from his desire to heal the patient. But they also reflect his willingness to be vulnerable to the patient, to accept the patient's wishes to share the role of healer and to welcome the patient's attempt to love her therapist. Winnicott has movingly described the child's need to have its love received, a need at least as powerful as the child's need to be loved. Harold Searles and Robert Langs have also written extensively of the patient's unconscious wishes to heal the analyst. When the patient sees her therapist's vulnerability and feels tenderness toward her therapist/parent, she is experiencing her own inner goodness in a direct way and can begin to believe in herself.

Often the therapist's confidences represent unique, human interchanges that enable the patient to know she is special. The wish to be special is often described pejoratively in the literature. It does come out of the patient's most primitive layers where her deepest wounding lies, and so it can easily be seen as pathological. But the wish to be special also arises from an archetypal knowledge of what is required for the healing of the deepest wounds. Therapists know there are limits on how many patients they can especially cherish, and they fear acknowledging the limits of their offerings. If, however, the therapist accepts the fact that the patient needs to be cherished in order to change, he may be able to see how each patient can in some way, over a long enough time, come to be special to him. The impulse to share some personal reminiscence with the patient marks the patient's emergence as special to the therapist.

The final element of the variable frame is the agreement between patient and therapist to seek a purely psychological solution to the patient's difficulties. On a gross level, this means that medication or hospitalization indicates an abandonment (perhaps limited) of the therapeutic contract. More subtly, it means that while it may seem greatly to improve her life, getting the patient into or out of any external situation (Alcoholics Anonymous, a good/bad marriage or job, etc.) is a diversion from the analytic task for which the therapist has been hired. If the analyst, by staying attuned to the patient's inner reality, enables her to connect with her true self, the patient will be able to work out her own external reality in her own way.

James Hillman (1964) writes grippingly about the need for a consistently psychological attitude with a suicidal patient. Certainly when suicide threatens, our commitment to a psychological solution can be most stressed. The rather cliché Jungian understanding of suicide is that it is an attempt by the psyche to be reborn: some old adaptation needs to die in order for the person's life to continue in a meaningful way. The individual, despairing of working out that inner rebirth, has concretized the wish to die. Hillman argues that the analyst's task is always to be under the patient, deeper, inviting her down, down, down into the depths. The urge to suicide must be explored and experienced in all its fullness if the psychological transformation that is sought is to be found. When the analyst turns to medication, he is cutting off that descent, implicitly stating that the patient's depths are too dangerous to explore. When the patient asks for medication, she is always asking two questions at the same time—Will you give me something to shut off this terrible torment? And, can you bear to stay with me through this terrible torment or is it too much for you? Both aspects must always be present. Although the second question is ordinarily unconscious, I have seen a number of cases in which the therapist's refusal to assist the patient in getting medication led to great relief on the patient's part—although it may have left the therapist roiling around in a storm of anxiety. It does seem that if there is anyone who will side with the patient's impulses to *know* herself and to *be* all herself, it should be her therapist.

On the other hand, any lengthy therapy probably includes some nonpsychological approaches to the patient's pain. None of the framework rules can ever be absolute. A depth analysis is closer to a marriage than to any other relationship. To attempt to define its parameters must inevitably fail. The only rule that seems to be universal, always applicable, is the ban on sexual contact between therapist and patient. All the fixed and variable frame elements I have elaborated offer the therapist a way of orienting that is usually but not always optimal. These elements provide a point from which to begin thinking about the work when it is difficult and not at all routine—a starting point that may not always be a final one. In each case, we must think about them anew and be aware of nuances in their implications, particular ways this or that element effects a patient, requiring us to adjust our attitude accordingly.

The Role of Reason

In my analysis of therapeutic work, I am relegating interpretations, traditionally the heart of analytic work, to an auxiliary role but I do not want to imply that they are unimportant. The regressed experience centered in the feminine principle provides the deepest healing of the therapeutic experience; this feminine work must be contained and supported by the dynamic masculine principle's rationality, just as it is contained and supported by the static masculine principle in the form of the frame.

Although a great deal of the analytic literature deals with interpretations, very little of it explores the underlying, irrational nature of interpretations' effects. There are attempts to analyze when an interpretation should be made, how it should be formulated and validated, how it should be presented, and so on. Because it is clearly the major *activity* the analyst engages in, the assumption that it is the most important expression of the analyst's expertise has been largely unquestioned. Because the analyst believes that what he is doing in interpreting is explaining some piece of the unconscious to the patient, the function of interpretations was assumed, for many years, to be the fostering of understanding. For decades Freud's famous dictum, "Where id was, let ego be," captured the prevailing therapeutic fantasy on the therapeutic action of analysis: consciousness heals. In more recent years, some psychoanalysts, notably the Kleinians, have begun to talk about other aspects of interpretation, such as the way an interpretation may be experienced as feeding. I have twice cited Balint's observation that to a regressed patient interpretations may be experienced in a myriad of ways, none of them involving understanding.

Winnicott suggests that interpretations may be most important in letting the patient know the limits of our understanding. This formulation is typical of Winnicott, the theorist of transitional objects and experiences. It offers us a transition, a link between the masculine activity of interpreting and the feminine activity of empathic understanding. Its corollary suggests that a major function of interpretations is not so much to offer the patient understanding per se as it is to let her know she is understood, she is not alone. To an extent, the cognitive understanding supplied by an interpretation creates an inner state in the patient in which her experiencing ego is no longer alone because her observing ego is there to hold her hand. This inner development reflects the interpersonal experience of the therapy, where the therapist's interpretation connects the patient to her own experience in the container of the therapist's compassionate hold.

Interpretations are important as the patient spirals slowly down toward her core. The patient thinks aloud about herself, saying what comes randomly to mind as well as thinking in a more directed fashion about herself. The therapist listens and, from time to time, contributes, often interpreting but also being directly empathic or mirroring. His cognitive interpretations may have some value in expanding the patient's self-knowledge; more importantly they form the concrete, continuing expression of the therapist's interest and concern. Just as a parent bathing a baby expresses his love in the interest he accords every tiny variation in the baby's physical form, so the therapist expresses his love via the interest he accords every tiny wrinkle in the patient's psyche. As the hours of analytic activity build up and the patient comes to know she can trust the therapist's good intentions and concern, she becomes increasingly able to open up parts of herself she has never before felt safe enough to expose, either to another or to herself.

There are also times when the cognitive communication contained in an interpretation is itself truly valuable for the patient. We see this, for example, when the interpretation offers the patient some perspective on the therapeutic process that enables her to take a more constructive attitude toward it. The argument of this book focuses on therapeutic work within which the patient's unconscious attempts to heal herself predominate. I take as axiomatic a philosophical view of the psychological organism that is basically optimistic. There is always a counterproductive impulse, too, and that negative, self-destructive trend will predominate, in some cases consistently through the work, in all cases at some points in the work. The patient's envy floods her psyche and her wish to triumph over the therapist leads her to destroy the therapist's work: the patient cuts off her nose to spite the therapist. Or fear of one's own inadequacy so immobilizes the patient that she aborts all inner impulses to grow, preferring to wallow in her emptiness rather than risk an inevitably frightening connection with her inner material. Every case contains some variant of this kind of unconscious refusal to grow and, in response to this situation, reason may be of some assistance.

In the early stages of the work, the patient often devotes her energy to examining her complexes *from a distance*. She wants to analyze them, not experience them. Indeed, the one place in her life that seems clean is the analytic field, and she may want very much to keep it clear of her complexes. One woman, severely conflicted regarding her dependency needs, wanted above all to avoid becoming dependent on me. She described at length how destructive her dependency could be, leading her to abdicate all responsibility for herself, driving people away, opening up her emotions to impossibly excessive demands on others. It represented an important marker in the work when she could cognitively understand my suggestion that she needed to allow herself to have her complex with me, for only if her disturbances were in the room, alive between us, could we hope to work them out. This cognitive understanding, clearly arrived at through an interpretation of mine, enabled her to take a more helpful attitude toward her work with me. One's attitude is the dimension of one's psyche most amenable to conscious control; rational thinking about what attitude would be optimal may be helpful in taking up a maximally constructive attitude.

Whenever the therapy is stuck, a rational analysis of the roots of the patient's immobilization is called for. If we can take a basically hopeful view of the psyche, remembering that there is always some inner impulse to growth pulling against the stuckness from within, it will help us to sit with an apparently futile situation with considerable patience. Often the patient's own healing capacities will produce the rational understanding that can jog her back into a constructive track. When the patient can resolve her own resistance, aided only by her therapist's patient hold, the patient's constructive impulses are strengthened.

When that does not happen—when a self-destructive pattern entrenches itself and seems destined to repeat itself endlessly—the therapist must take the lead in analyzing that pattern. This is the most obviously important role of reason in therapeutic work but even here reason is of limited value. We can try to nudge a patient into doing the work, but it is her own inner drive that really matters and there is not much we can actually do about the strength of that drive. Reason is the only tool we have, but we should not hope for miracles from it. It is often inadequate in a difficult situation.

When the therapeutic process is working, when the patient has regressed to the point where the current of her libido is carrying her and her therapist along, the cognitive dimension of interpretations is less clearly relevant. The patient makes interpretations to herself, and the therapist expands them, hopefully focusing primarily on how the patient's psyche manifests inside the treatment container rather than outside. The temperature of the interpersonal experience continually rises as the patient's libido takes now one form and now another in its attempt to bond ever more deeply with the selfobject/therapist who is carrying her projected unconscious. The therapist continually assures the patient of his interest in and approval of this profound attachment through his accepting interpretations.

Reason, whether originating with the therapist's or the patient's interpretations, offers a soothing hold for the patient's inner chaos, but each element of that inner chaos must be directly felt before it can be contained. When an element of the patient's psyche has come deeply alive, has been fully lived in the analytic situation, a cognitive understanding of what has happened is clearly valuable in fixing the experience in consciousness. This cognitive understanding seems to come naturally as a symptom of the completion of the experience. Sometimes, when the therapist can offer understanding of an ongoing painful experience, the understanding can resolve a chaos that has become stuck.

But most therapeutic work suffers from an excess of reason, from an abuse of reason. Interpretations and rationality are used as a substitute for experience rather than as a container for it. The emotional reality must be lived before it can be soothed. In the earliest days of psychoanalysis, when rational formulations were being made for the first time—as, for example, in either Freud's or Jung's self-analyses—these cognitive containers for experience inevitably followed deeply felt emotional events. Today, patients as well as therapists may begin with complex and sophisticated cognitive "knowledge" about the psyche which serves to block rather than to facilitate a personal connection with it. Interpretations may often reinforce these kinds of defensive structures; rather than opening blocked channels, reason may shore up dams.

When the transference takes a negative form, the cognitive layer of the interpretation may become important. In general, a pull for cognitive understanding draws the patient out of the experience. When the therapeutic process becomes embroiled in negativity, it is possible for the constellated hatred and rage to destroy it, and in that case a pull for cognitive understanding may be necessary to preserve the work. As with suicidal impulses, however, considerably more hatred and rage can probably be contained than one might imagine. The possibilities depend largely on the therapist's subjective feeling of readiness to take it on—which depends on his capacity to experience his own hatred and rage.

When the patient has lost all perspective regarding her experiences of the therapist—when she believes that she feels abandoned, for example, because the therapist is objectively and concretely abandoning her—she will not be able to stay in the treatment unless some perspective can be found. The therapist cannot actually provide that perspective when a delusional transference is negative, but he can urge the patient to reflect on her experience and to ask herself whether her feeling of being abandoned is a realistic assessment of the therapist's behavior and feeling toward her. When a delusional transference is positive—when the patient believes, for example, that the therapist is actively making plans to leave his family for the patient—the therapist may be under less urgent pressure to correct the delusion and can hope that the patient will regain some measure of observing ego over time. It may be possible to interpret a positive delusion directly, but it is a delicate operation, for the narcissistic wounding risks constellating in consciousness the negative delusion that lies behind its opposite. In these situations of psychotic transferences, the same regression that therapist and patient sought for its healing potential threatens to swamp the patient and therapist if it is not modulated to some extent by an adult ego. With regression, as with every element of the work explored in this chapter, the most sought-after element may also be exactly the wrong thing.

I have tried to explore in this chapter the role of the masculine principle in therapeutic work. In addition to the concrete content of this chapter, this entire book is saturated with the Apollonian thinking the masculine principle values so highly. In urging us to retrieve the feminine wisdom of the ages from the garbage heap to which it was consigned by the Enlightenment, I do not want us to throw away the marvelous developments in the Masculine that same Enlightenment has wrought. What is needed is a marriage of equals between these two great orientations in which each can be accorded the infinite respect it is due.

Chapter 6

An Archetypal Perspective

Jung's most fundamental contribution to psychoanalysis was his addition of an archetypal perspective to Freud's personal one; but, despite its apparent simplicity, none of Jung's ideas have been less adequately understood than this core concept. What does it mean to take an archetypal perspective on the psyche, on life, on analysis? I want to turn, in this chapter, from the living clinical reality to a discussion of that theoretical orientation on which is my work is grounded. In my attempt to differentiate the realm of the feminine from that of the masculine, I am, among other things, taking an archetypal perspective. I am suggesting that the division of the inner world into masculine and feminine elements is an archetypal given of the human condition. All people, everywhere and at all times, sort the world into these two categories. Although some of that sorting may be biologically determined, most of the *content* of our notions of "feminine" and "masculine" is culturally determined. What I have been describing is largely a cultural expression of an archetype that could be expressed in other ways in other cultures. Can we try to look at the archetype itself that lies beneath its expression in this particular culture?

Because of the abstruse nature of most of Jung's writings, it is left to others to demystify them. I want to make the concept of archetypes comprehensible and reasonable. I would like to demonstrate the ways in which an appreciation of the archetypal layer of the psyche and an openness to archetypal processes in the analytic work enriches and deepens psychotherapy. By way of example, I shall describe the operation of one archetype (that of the mother) in the course of normal human development. The implications of an archetypal viewpoint for one's model of the psyche will be explored, and the ways in which an archetypal perspective converges with and diverges from the other analytic models will be detailed.

I am offering here one way of looking at the psyche. I do not intend to imply that this is "the correct" viewpoint. At most, it adds something to more familiar analytic ideas; it does not replace them. Many elements of this perspective are familiar to any depth psychologist; only the terminology is unusual. By explicitly labeling a dimension of experience that is usually assumed in a more inchoate fashion, this terminology may enable us to explore a fundamental psychological layer more thoroughly.

The collective unconscious is composed of the archetypes. These two Jungian concepts are equivalents: 1) the collective unconscious is composed of the archetypes, and 2) the archetypes are the building blocks of the collective unconscious. The enigma surrounding these concepts stems partly from Jung's failure to define his terms clearly and consistently. Jung always spoke for the reality of the psyche's paradoxes and for the necessity of accepting the contradictory nature of psychic life rather than trying to resolve psychic paradoxes to logical states. Consequently, many Jungian concepts need to be apprehended repeatedly, from many angles.

Jungian thinking is often feminine in nature, progressing in spirals, circling around an image or an individual or a state; it does not move linearly from A to B to C as mainstream analytic thought attempts to do. This meandering mode of thought attempts to approach the subjective state of the human psyche, where A is not necessarily discrete from B, opposites turn out to be mirror images of each other, and logical necessities may fail to materialize. We need to live with Jungian concepts, to meditate on them rather than memorize their definitions; this is one reason for the widespread disregard in "scientific" circles of Jung's work.

Jung defines the archetype as "a typical basic form of certain ever-recurring psychic experiences . . . [that] formulates them in an appropriate way. . . . A psychic expression of the physiological and anatomical disposition" (1921, par. 748). The archetype "is an inherited organization of psychic energy, an ingrained system, which not only gives expression to the energic process but facilitates its operation" (ibid., par. 754). Archetypes are typically misunderstood to be inherited images within the psyche. They are not images but "*forms without content*, representing merely the possibility of a certain type of perception and action" (italics in original, Jung 1936a, p. 66). The infant is born, in other words, not with preformed images or ideas, but rather with the capacity and tendency to think, feel and perceive in certain ways—in human ways—in response to the typical and recurring experiences with which life confronts each individual anew.

An archetype "is determined as to its content only when it has become conscious and is therefore filled out with the material of conscious experience. Its form . . . might perhaps be compared to the axial system of a crystal, which, as it were, preforms the crystaline structure in the mother liquid, although it has no material existence of its own" (Jung 1938, p. 79). The archetypal layer of the psyche—the collective unconscious—consists of "a substrate which uses sensory experiences in predetermined ways to produce typical imagery" (Scott 1978, p. 306). The archetypes are "the unconscious images of the instincts themselves. . . . [they are] *patterns of instinctual behavior*" (italics in the original, Jung 1936a, p. 44).

There are, in these definitions, actually two differing uses of the word "archetype." The archetype is a "form," which implies a fixed or static (nonmaterial) thing; and it is an energic source where the individual's vitality originates. It is both the wellspring of our life energy and it provides the channels through which that energy can optimally flow.

Case Example

Before I attempt to develop the theoretical implications of this concept, or to explore the ways in which non-Jungian analysts have understood or failed to understand the archetypal layer of the psyche, I want to suggest the concept's clinical meaning through a case example. I shall describe the archetypal layer of one woman's development, using four dreams that occurred over a period of about seven years of analysis. These dreams have few personal referents, and those that do appear may easily be seen as subsidiary to the archetypal processes occurring in her psyche and recorded by her dreams. My hope is that this presentation will highlight the archetypal nature of the healing process outlined in Chapter 3. This innate impulsion to become whole carried her along. To emphasize the transpersonal nature of her process, I shall include no personal information about her. I will call the patient Eve, the name of woman qua woman. Her problem was a negative mother complex—something that characterizes most of the people I have ever seen, although Eve did have a particularly difficult case to grapple with.

About six months into the analysis, Eve had the following dream:

> *Two flying saucers are landing on the lawn. My nephew [a young man in his twenties] and I are watching them through my mother's huge bay windows. They are whirling saucers of light, very large, with distinct turrets. I'm yelling to my husband to come see it. I'm exasperated that he doesn't get in there, but he is trying to call the police. He's calling from the bedroom and can't see a thing. My nephew and I are exhilarated, speechless.*

In this dream, we see Eve contained in her personal mother complex. She is in her mother's house, looking at the world through her mother's viewpoint. Instead of presenting the ordinary, "real" world, the dream's landscape is suddenly dominated by the arrival of objects from outer space, luminous objects whose powerful energies cannot be captured in words (she is speechless) and which exhilarate—enliven—her. Archetypal energies—the psychic manifestation of her core instinctual processes—have burst onto the scene.

In order to understand the meaning of watching the event with her nephew, we would have to know about Eve's relationship with the sibling whose son this is and about her relationship with the boy himself. As a personal, rather than a collective image, it rests on personal rather than collective associations. Similarly, her husband is a particular person in her life—in her case, he is a man who does *not* see the archetypal layer of life, who tries, in fact, to call the authorities of the objective, outer world in an attempt to shut off these energies, to get rid of them.

We see in the dream the interrelated quality of the personal and collective layers of the psyche. Any image must contain both strands but in greatly varying proportions. Eve's nephew and husband are personal images: these two living men did embody the roles in which the dream casts them. Eve's husband is a practical, reality-based man, far removed from the inner world of dreams, visions, mercurial emotions, and intuitions. Her nephew, on the other hand, had struggled with emotional difficulties and had spent more time in the world of flying saucers than in the "real" world. Beneath the personal images of husband and nephew lies an archetypal dimension, a universal psychic organization: the two men embody two poles of a conflict within herself, a split in the "masculine" side of her nature, the part of her being she subjectively experiences as other—as not-me, the opposite of me, the opposite sex, the deep *un*conscious. The inner conflict the two figures capture was a particular personal conflict of Eve's, but the organization of her inner life, within which members of the other sex are called upon to carry a subjectively alien level of experience, is universal—archetypal—in nature.

To return to the dream, the central image, the flying saucers, is predominantly archetypal in nature. Eve has no personal experience with flying saucers and no significant personal associations to them. They are the subject of a modern mythic belief system, one Eve does not share. Because they are archetypal rather than personal images, their meaning is contained in the symbol itself rather than in Eve's personal experiences with the image. If Eve were personally involved in flying saucer mythology, her idiosyncratic associations to them might overshadow their universal import, but this was not the case. In understanding the dream we can focus on the natural reverberations of "flying saucers" in our own psyches, for the image taps into universal human layers that link Eve to us rather than differentiating her from us.

They are round, a shape that has signified wholeness in mythology the world over, a shape with no beginning and no end, complete unto itself. They are "whirling saucers of light"—sources of light/energy/life—with "distinct turrets." We might see this as a phallic image suggesting the power radiating from them; or we might think of breasts with prominent nipples, an association that also suggests great power, but feminine rather than masculine in nature. Here we need Eve to clarify the size and prominence of the turrets. In either case, the core implication of the dream is the same: caught in her destructive mother complex, Eve's unconscious is erupting with the universal human energies that will ultimately rescue her.

We shall see as we look at the dreams that follow that the conflict enacted by the two male figures was indeed a central one and that this dream images the path of Eve's ultimate healing, as well as the state of the injury that needed to be healed. The men are split in their attitude toward the inner versus the objective world and the dream presents the resolution that will eventually save Eve. Flying saucers, objects with no objective reality, dominate the real, outer world in this dream. The man whose waking connection is only to the objective, outer world is far from the awesome events unfolding in the dream's real world—he is shut away in the inner reaches of the house, cut off from the view, lacking vision. The dream implies that Eve's understanding of what is "real" needs to be reworked.

One year later, following a failure in empathy on my part, Eve had a powerful dream that presents an archetypal image of the specific nature of her personal mother's destructive qualities.

> *Someone is telling me how a little girl was walking along a road and got attacked savagely by a big person (who feels like my mother) or a wolf. The girl is killed.*
>
> *An unknown woman and a child are at the murder site, picking things up, as though they're on a nature walk. The woman turns over the gashed shoulder of the dead child. She is shocked and looks at me with horror. I'm sitting off to the other side and explain to her that that's the dead child.*
>
> *There is a party going on at my mother's house. I'm trying to get together things to go. I'm putting candies, cakes, cheeses in a box. Party people come up. I say it must be late and guess it's about 9:30. They tell me it's 1 a.m.*

> *I'm surprised it's that late. I promised I'd take the little girl's body home. This chills me as I would have to leave the house and go out into the dark where the girl's body is. I'm thinking: my husband is at home asleep, waiting for me. I'm scared to go get the body and take it home, so I decide to stay in my mother's house.*

The parallel with Little Red Riding Hood, whose cheerful (partying) (grand)mother conceals a ravaging wolf leaps to mind. This particular experience of being a child with a mother is not unique to Eve; it is a scenario that has been played out for millenia the world over. At the same time, it is her deepest and most personal experience, shaping her identity at its foundations.

Eve associated the unknown woman with the child to me, and it was, unfortunately, a fair picture of my state at the time. I did not appreciate, for the first few years of our work, the depth of Eve's wounding; I was out on a nature walk, oblivious to the dangerous forces at work in her psyche. Perhaps partly because of my inadequacy, Eve is still caught in her mother complex, trapped in frenzied, manic defenses against the horrors of the Terrible Mother who brings death as well as life to us all.

She imagines it is early in the evening but it is later than she thinks; it is 1 a.m., an hour that underscores the urgency of the task but that also increases its terror. Again we glimpse the archetypal background of the dream and consequently of Eve's inner state. While an individual might have a specific personal association to 1 a.m. (Eve did not), there is a universal human experience of that time, of going out into the middle of the night. In the Western tradition, that experience is vividly captured by St. John of the Cross in his description of his long, dark night of the soul. Eve faces an eternal human task, both imposed and assisted by her archetypal inheritance, the task of going out in the dead of the night, into the dark forest of her soul, to retrieve her wounded inner child as a first step toward healing that child and integrating her into her larger self.

Two years later, Eve dreamed:

> *I'm uncovering old archeological stones, primitive sculptures of men, women and animals. They belong to a bull or young cow with horns. I'm intruding on her territory and she's angry at that. A young helper girl helps me. I'm especially taken with a globby statue with round details. It's unclear exactly what it is. It's like Aztec stuff—ornate and carved.*
>
> *The bull changes into a beautiful young girl, lying on her stomach on a bench. I'm holding her down by the left shoulder while the helper girl makes a deep incision in it. We've convinced her to our ways—that we should preserve these*

> *old things. The girl feels betrayed and groans. I feel bad at having gotten her into this—this is some kind of initiation.*

Eve is no longer caught in her personal mother complex; she has moved into the territory of the archetypal mother. The bull appears widely in mythology as the consort of the Great Mother (in Minoan imagery, for example) and the cow, of course, is everywhere a mother symbol. The Little Red Riding Hood dream pictured her (our) immobilization in her mother-wound, but in the ensuing years she has come a great distance. Eve is no longer caught in the manic defenses against her pain that were the best solution her mother's house had to offer. She has moved far into her self, deep into her history, not as Eve Jones of 1421 State Street, but as Eve the Woman, who is herself a mother and who can find her wholeness by connecting with the Universal Woman inside herself. Out of the depths of Mother Earth, Eve is extracting archetypal images of the human condition, ancient icons to worship, from which her psyche, unconscious as well as conscious, can receive guidance in its task of healing her mother-wounds. The fact that it is an Aztec image that captivates her has to do with a violent destructiveness that existed in her family and that is spoken to in Aztec imagery and mythology.

Eve's attitude has changed. The attempt to call in the police to seal off the energies of the flying saucers has been given up. She has become convinced of the need to "preserve these old things," to look inward to her psychic roots for the life patterns that have worked for people historically. The new attitude leads to an initiation, an introduction into secret knowledge, into the society of those who have developed inner sight. This transformation is painful. The same shoulder the wolf tore open—the site of her mother-wound—is being cleanly incised to let the old poisons flow out. The shift to a new attitude cuts deep; old adaptive patterns and cherished beliefs are sacrificed. Initiation into the mysteries of the archetypal realm implies the sacrifice of her dependence on her ego and its *will* as her center of being; there is a shift to an attitude of cooperation with the deeper forces of her psyche even when their thrust is not the one she would have chosen. Sacrificing her mother's manic defenses against pain, Eve is submitting to an intense experience of the authentic pain of life.

In the months following this dream Eve did, in concrete reality, find a statue of a Mexican mother goddess with which she became powerfully emotionally involved. She "worshipped" it, imagining what kinds of thoughts, attitudes, and guidance it might have for her in various life situations. There was nothing delusional about this process; the deep regression implied by her behavior was contained in her analysis. Her functioning in the world was never in any way impaired. This experience, in which she allowed her psyche to communicate with her conscious ego in its own imagistic language extended over more than a year. Rather than trying to interpret or analyze the fantasies that the activated collective unconscious generated, she and I focused on experiencing them as deeply as possible. Rather than labeling or understanding these psychic products, the attempt was to actualize the new attitude that the dream presents, to open her ears to the voices of human wisdom contained in her own depths. Certainly we talked extensively about her experience, trying to put words to all the powerful inner emotions shaking Eve's psyche at this time, but very little energy was directed to "interpreting" the experience in any narrow sense of that word.

In the years following this dream, I became pregnant and had a baby, a significant trauma for most of my patients. It was in the context of the displaced and abandoned feelings my pregnancy and maternity leave stirred in Eve that she worked through the bulk of her personal negative mother legacy. Had I not become pregnant, the same issues would have been worked through in the less dramatic context of the normal abandonments and failures of analysis: the ends of the hours, the vacations, the failures in empathy, the glimpses of other patients, the inexorable appearance of the bill. But the pregnancy imposed my private life on her and, consequently, in this next dream that occurred three years after the previous one, Eve's integration and healing are pictured as originating in my daughter Abby's eyes.

> *I'm holding Abby on my lap. I look into her eyes and see that the pupils are half blue and half green, like my green eyes. In the dream Barbara [i.e., the analyst] has green eyes like mine and she explains that Abby's eyes are half hers and half her husband's blue eyes. In the blue part of Abby's eyes you can see a pine tree. It's so clear you can even see the pine cones. It's actually in her eyes, it's not a reflection. The image is in her eyes, the image is the real thing. There's a dark rim around the pupils, unifying them, so that the two colors are not too weird.*

The disparate sides of Eve's nature are coming together: her conflicting tendencies—blue and green, male and female—are unified and contained in a dark circle. Her healing appears in the masculine side of the circle, coming out of the not-me layer of the psyche, out of the unconscious. Her wholeness is imaged by a tree, again a collective symbol. Its roots reach deep down into Mother Earth and its tip reaches high up to Father Sky; its trunk forms a bridge between these two worlds of matter and spirit, body and mind. This particular tree is a pine tree, evergreen, promising eternal renewal.

But the absolute key to her healing lies in the fact that the tree is "actually in her eyes, it's not a reflection. The image is . . . the real thing." Eve's flying saucer dream had invited her to recognize what this dream presents as a demonstrated fact: the inner world is the fundamental reality, not the objective, outer world she had been taught was "real." In this last dream, Eve has worked her way through to an appreciation of the reality of her psyche and this provides her with a solid foundation on which to build her life, the foundation her childhood mother had been unable to offer.

At the time of this dream, Eve's presenting symptoms, severely troublesome psychogenic somatic problems, had largely dissipated, and many of the less tangible outer difficulties with which she had struggled had improved considerably. But her inner emotional life remained fixated at a particularly injurious childhood trauma. In the weeks following this dream, she returned to the scene of the trauma and repeated it in vivid imaginative activity as thoroughly as she could. This served as a final working through of her old tragedy. I continued to see her for two more years and have heard from her and of her occasionally in the several years since then. The trauma, which until then had functioned as a major source of agony, has given her little trouble since, and her symptoms have not recurred. She is leading a vital life, filled, of course, with human suffering, but also filled with joy.

A Theoretical Example

Keeping this case in mind as a reference point, let us return to a theoretical exploration of the meaning of the concept of archetypes. When we talk about archetypes and the collective unconscious, we are talking about the ways the human psyche, like the human body, is genetically programmed to develop in a somewhat typical way into a somewhat typical shape. Each individual is unique, and yet all individuals are the same. Just as the human body conforms to a basic, universal pattern, so the psyche, inextricably intertwined with the body, falls into collective—archetypal, universal—patterns. Throughout life we all face difficulties that human beings have confronted from time immemorial. We are born and socialized, we marry and reproduce, we mourn the losses in our lives and ultimately prepare to die ourselves. The broad patterns for the resolution of these recurring dilemmas—the viable approaches to the constants of human existence—are laid down within our psyches. Jung called these innate patterns "archetypes."

Let us take the mother archetype as an example. The infant has inborn psychic needs for love and affection that parallel its physical needs for warmth and milk. Just as its body requires an environment that contains a minimal level of oxygen, its psyche must be enfolded in a maternal psyche. The baby is born with the need and the capacity to fit with a mother. It is not that the baby has a picture of what a mother will look like or how she will behave. It is rather that there are, within broad limits, ways she *must* behave to meet the infant's psychic needs. How she *does* behave is organized by the developing psyche as the beginnings of a "mother complex"—a pattern of relatedness engrained in the psyche's foundation. The concept "mother complex" offers a particular way to label the psyche's innate capacity to correlate and integrate mothering experiences as psychic structure. The mother's behavior with her infant realizes pictures—affect-laden pictures, colored by all five senses, not simply sight—in three-dimensional picture frames waiting to be filled.

Experiences that do not involve the personal mother fill out part of the mother archetype: the warm, comfortable crib, for example, becomes part of the positive mother, and the gas pains that make some afternoons a torment become part of the negative mother. The environment as a whole, inner as well as outer, colors the mother archetype's emergence and actualization in an individual's unique mother complex. The infant's experience of existence in matter (from the Latin *mater*, mother) shapes the psyche's native energies that flow through the broad channels provided by the mother archetype.

It is not simply sensory experiences that the mother archetype organizes within the psyche. The psyche's natural imaginative tendencies elaborate sensory experiences at an unconscious level and these innate imaginal activities are governed and organized by their appropriate archetype, in this case, the mother archetype. Winnicott offers us an example when he hypothesizes that the nursing infant pictures his effect on his mother's body, imagining that he is creating a hole inside her chest as he empties her breast of milk. The accuracy of Winnicott's fantasy can never be assessed, of course, but what he is hypothesizing is that the psyche converts sensory/emotional experiences into imaginal pictures as naturally as the body converts nutrients into tissue. This is one major activity that Jungians postulate as "archetypal."

The psyche's waiting picture frames must be filled in somehow. The child whose mother never expresses anger or hate will not evade the experience of the negative mother. From the extraverted perspective of classical thought, beginning with the outer rather than the inner reality, we could say that since the mother does, of course, feel anger and hate, at least unconsciously, a perfectly pleasant mother is frightening because the child senses the hidden energies that become all the more feared since they are too frightful for Mother to allow.

Interacting with this extraverted level of personal experience is an inner archetypal reality. Since the child is born human, he has a psyche that will inevitably experience anger and hatred; he is therefore also born with an inchoate knowledge of this fact of human nature and therefore with an awareness of the inevitable existence of terrible, hateful mothers, wicked witches, as it were. It does not matter for our purposes here whether we accept the notion of a death instinct organizing *inborn* hateful urges, or whether we conceive of these destructive impulses as reactive to the inevitable frustrations of infancy. In either case, it is universally part of the human condition to experience murderous rage, at least as early as the first weeks of life. If the child's personal mother does not humanize this fact by embodying a wicked witch of manageable proportions, this archetypal space is left to be filled out by overwhelming impersonal forces elaborated by the psyche's natural fantasy activities. The negative aspect of the archetype must be available in age-appropriate dosages so that the inevitably present terrible capacities of human nature can be experienced and imagined in manageable proportions.

In this example of the mother archetype, I am describing how a mother complex develops around its archetypal core. "Complex" in this context is not a pathological term. The psyche is organized in complexes, each complex forming around and filling out an archetype. The archetype provides the glue that holds the different experiences, inner as well as outer, of "mothers" together. It is the inherited factor that limits what experiences *can* be integrated as "mothering," what mothering experiences *must* occur in one form or another for the psyche to survive, and how these experiences will be imaginatively elaborated by the unconscious mind. We know from Renee Spitz's work (1945, 1946) that infants whose physical needs are adequately met will die if their psychic needs are ignored. The concept of archetypes expresses that fact: the psyche is real and must be reckoned with, it is not a blank slate that can receive any kind of programming.

In addition to organizing the experiences that make up an individual's personal mother complex, the mother archetype, at the core of the adult's formed mother complex, can provide the raw energies that can supplement the experiences which an individual *did* have with those crucial ones he missed. In Eve's analysis, we could say on the one hand that she had certain experiences in the transference relationship that, because they reverberated at a deep enough level and because they differed from her childhood experiences, were able to heal old wounds. Specifically, the abandonment my pregnancy imposed upon her was temporary and repairable, whereas the ways in which her actual mother had abandoned her had not been. However, there is an inner dimension to this experience, too. Eve's ability to experience the repair of my abandonment was founded on the existence within her psyche of archetypal patterns that can contain and process such information. Her nature, in other words, was wired to imagine the possibility of a temporary rift that could be healed. Perhaps there are experiences that human beings cannot imagine and about which we know nothing. But those experiences we can receive are contained, in implicate form, within the psyche. Through the dreams and imaginative activity constellated in her relationship with me, Eve was able to connect with a quality of mothering she had personally missed, one that she needed. Her receptivity to this healing maternal energy was crucial in constellating my capacity to offer that energy; some patients, for constitutional or environmental reasons, cannot receive the restorative energy they need and when this is the case, the therapist will be unable to love them in the ways that would redeem them.

A corollary of this is the fact that, just as the mother archetype organizes the infant's experiences with the mother, it also organizes the mother's experiences with her baby. We are all familiar with the fact that the personal mother complex organizes the mother's experiences with her baby: a mother's handling of her children tends to duplicate the way she was handled by her mother. The archetypal mother complex will also be activated in the mothering situation. What Winnicott called the "maternal predisposition," or what is crudely thought of as the maternal "instinct," can be conceptualized as a function of the mother archetype. It is possible for a woman to be a better mother to her baby than her mother was to her. She will not achieve this by reading childcare books, however, but by turning inward to her own natural mothering impulses.

Implications of an Archetypal View, I: The Reality of the Psyche

When we talk about our instinctual nature in terms of an archetypal structure, we are approaching the individual through the psyche rather than through the body. We recognize that the psyche is as real as the body, even though it has no demonstrable material existence. This is not to say it has no material ramifications. Physical shocks or wounds frequently have powerful emotional—psychic—effects, and psychic states can greatly disturb or enhance somatic functioning. There is always a physical expression of any psychic state. When we feel a feeling, think a thought, perceive an object, hope, remember, fear—each and every subjective psychic experience expresses itself in some kind of electrical or chemical change in the body. Although such a change may trigger an emotional response, it is also possible to imagine that an emotional response triggers the chemical/electrical effect. The fact that one is associated with the other does not tell us which came first; it tells us only that the psyche and the body invariably affect one another and that any change in one will reverberate in the other.

There is a subjective experience of being a living individual, and describing its physical manifestation—the hormonal or neurological activity that accompanies psychic life—does not negate the subjective experience. It exists. A description of the physical expression of a psychic happening will, in fact, not tell us anything at all about the psyche itself. We must look at the psyche to learn about the psyche. Jung created the concept "archetypes" to describe the building blocks of the psyche, comparable to the organ systems that form the building blocks of the body. It is a concept, not a concrete thing, and is justified only heuristically, by the way in which it brings the psyche's real existence into clearer view.

The reality of the psyche frightens us. Its denial is deeply ingrained and pervasive in our culture; it includes, of course, the denial of the fear of the psyche's reality. Distressing emotional states are "all in your head"—meaning, not real. It is un-American to acknowledge defeat on psychic grounds. "Where there's a will, there's a way," as though there were no psychological limits to one's capacity. Mind over matter, the power of positive thinking. The conscious ego is assumed to comprise the whole of the psyche. Visions of utopian environments that will transform human nature and eliminate greed, hatred, envy, and malice are widespread among parents and educators, often in fairly sophisticated forms. Such fantasies are based on the idea that, since it has no material substance, the psyche has no inherent substance at all. We do not imagine that a utopian environment is capable of creating a human being who could run as fast as a horse, or swim like a whale, because we know the body is an objective, real fact. The psyche is just as real as the body, although it is infinitely harder to investigate and describe, partly because it *is* nonmaterial, and partly because it is in continual flux, moving, with no apparent difficulty, from one mood or idea to a logically inconsistent other state. "Psyche," in fact, is the Greek word for "soul," and we all know how unfashionable it is in intellectual circles to believe in the soul these days.

To describe the psyche by describing the physical manifestations of its existence—the somatic equivalents of psychic events—is comparable to describing Leonardo's *Mona Lisa* by analyzing the chemical composition of its pigments and canvas. Certainly this says something "real" about the painting. But just as certainly, this tells us nothing significant about the painting as a painting. Reducing a gestalt to its basic material ingredients is not the most helpful way to understand the nature of the gestalt. When a woman suffering from a menopausal depression is described as having a "hormonal" rather than a "psychological" problem, an enormous chunk of her experience is ignored. The contents of her hopes, fears, fantasies, dreams, grief, despair, rages, memories, disappointments, and yearning, to name only some of the psychic experiences that accompany and express her disorder, exist as real data that must be included in addressing her state if her experience is to be made emotionally meaningful. The fact that her psychic life can be altered by drugging her or shocking her does not mean that her subjective feelings do not exist or that they are not primary. Her life is impoverished at the same time as it is simplified by eliminating its psychological dimension.

On the one hand, everyone acknowledges the reality of the psyche. On the other hand, even sophisticated psychoanalysts sometimes raise questions that are symptomatic of the ingrained inability of the Western mind to accord a nonmaterial reality the same validity granted the body. A therapist's denial of the reality of the psyche is often glimpsed in attitudes that stem from fear of the psyche. For example, we find therapists engaging in endless and futile debate about whether a given patient's traumatic memory "really" happened or was "only" imagined. This question is at the heart of the conflict that split Freud's thinking into two major eras and that continues to be debated throughout the contemporary depth psychological world. It is the issue that fueled the Jeffery Masson *cause célèbre*: did Freud's patients' imagine their childhood sexual abuse or did these things "really" happen. In the excitement of the early clinical discovery of the power of unconscious impulses, Freud imagined that a full recognition of that power rested on a rejection of the idea that outer traumas are responsible for inner disturbances. He fell into a trap, imagining that *either* inner *or* outer events impact on the psyche. A century later we are freer to see that the tremendous power of the unconscious can be acknowledged at the same time as we recognize that outer traumas also effect people deeply.

But the basic question is, Why has this detective work been so compelling for the analytic community and for therapists in general? Its effect these days is typically to distance the therapist from the patient and to shield him from sharing the patient's emotional experience. Rather than recognizing the power of the unconscious, the idea that a "memory" is really a "fantasy" is frequently used to suggest that the patient is exaggerating his distress. If it didn't "really" happen, all the fuss is surely excessive. Therapeutically we need to assess the impact of an event by evaluating its state in the individual's psyche, not by doing detective work in the outer world. As therapists we could more profitably maintain that the patient's fuss is evidence that his trauma really did happen (without getting caught up in worrying about whether "really" implies outwardly, inwardly or symbolically). Of course this would expose us to a direct experience of the terrible suffering the patient is enduring; we would have to acknowledge the reality of the psyche.

A similar denial of the psyche's reality may be seen in the way analysts and therapists get caught up in the manifest content of a patient's material, in the concrete details of his outer life. When we accept the reality of the psyche—which means the reality of the unconscious psyche, of course—we must recognize its ever-present nature.

> We must bear in mind that free association is not really free. The patient remains under the influence of the analytic situation even though he is not directing his mental activities on a particular subject. We shall be justified in assuming that nothing will occur to him that has not some reference to that situation. (Freud 1925)

Freud wrote these words in 1925, and Robert Langs has developed their implication extensively (1978). Despite the apparent simplicity of the idea, despite the fact that "all" analysts "know" it, no one could ever hope to maintain a living connection to this psychological layer of reality at all times; many therapists and even some analysts never connect to this metaphorical layer of the work.

The essential idea behind this insight is that the psyche is always trying to transcend its immaterial nature, to be seen in the outer world. This attempt is made on a conscious level when an individual tries to tell another something about herself—when a patient, for example, tries to communicate what her mother was like for her. But the attempt is also being made, at all times, on an unconscious level, and at that level the psyche is trying to describe its immediately current state using manifest content in the same way that a dream uses the residue of the previous day. On this level memories of the mother or of yesterday's encounter with the auto mechanic may provide equally valuable vehicles for conveying the individual's current subjective experience of life. An inner drama unfolds continuously, an unconscious dream is being dreamt: one feels oppressed, cheated, pursued by the Nazis, adored by the Mother, honored by the Father.

Willy nilly, the therapist is sucked into the patient's inner drama and participates in it. Is there an opening for a bossy, castrating mother? I will (ever so sweetly) offer some advice. Do we need a cold, rejecting parent? I become powerfully aware of the need to maintain a silent, neutral stance, losing touch with the need for a human response. As the therapist/analyst's skills increase, he is less apt to be flagrant in enacting such dramas and is often even able to refrain from enacting them at all. At this point the psyche's transferential capacities come into play, and the therapist is *experienced* as cold and rejecting or bossy and castrating even when the outer data do not seem to support that view.

The patient tries to tell the therapist about his immediately current subjective state by talking about . . . whatever comes to mind. The rude checker at the supermarket and the daffodils that miraculously survived the flood are images of the state of the patient's soul, expressions of the patient's continuing yearning to be seen and known so that he can see and know himself as real, so that he can appreciate the reality of his psyche at a deeper level than the one he has thus far reached. How often do we listen at this level, and how often do we lose our way and think, or even say,

- You told me this same story last week.
- You're distorting you husband's (teacher's, supervisor's) meaning.
- This isn't important—you should be talking about your marriage (your mother, your work, your children).
- And so on.

It is so easy to miss the delicate, ephemeral image the psyche is trying to paint of itself.

The psyche's reality is confusing, upsetting, frightening. We see the fight against it in the endless analytic struggle to offer a "correct" interpretation. We can talk about interpretations that are helpful or destructive, because we can sometimes gauge these kinds of effects of our words. But when we try to assess the correctness of an interpretation, we are making the psyche into a material thing with a fixed shape, to be correctly or incorrectly perceived. This is a function of our inability to accept the *in*substantial, ever-changing psyche as fully real. In the inner world, today's correct interpretation will be superseded by tomorrow's contradictory and still correct interpretation.

Let me give an example from my own development. Very early in my analysis I had a dream in which I was driving up a steep hill and found that I could not make it to the top because "the brakes wouldn't hold." It occurred to me to interpret this as a pun, and it connected me with an intense feeling that the mess that my life was in was a reflection of the fact that "the breaks hadn't held" for me—I had been unlucky. I now see this as a relatively superficial interpretation. It seems more meaningful to think about how my *brakes* hadn't held—that I was being pulled down into depths of despair and darkness by an unconscious inner need to connect with my self. But the naive interpretation was meaningful for me at the time; it helped me to weave a sustaining fantasy about myself that had enough congruence with my outer life to be effective, for a while at least. It provided a way to experience myself as personally connected to the missal carried from my unconscious to my ego by the dream. To imagine that my more sophisticated interpretation is correct would be to imagine that I have now reached The Bottom—that I have gone as deep as there is to go. But there is no bottom to the psyche, there are only infinite depths; no view will ever be correct just as no analysis is ever complete.

How is one to feel secure in this intractable universe? How shall we make peace with our helpless, infinitesimal status?

Recall Eve's final dream, in which her ultimate healing is pictured as emanating from her discovery that the image of the tree really is inside the psyche, it is not a reflection of an outer object. The reason this recognition can be so powerful in integrating one's damaged self, is that it allows one to be wholeheartedly who one really is. Instead of agonizing guiltily over the fact, for example, that I hate my mother while my brother loves her, and searching endlessly for the external data that will pronounce one of us correct, I can instead say that if I truly feel any given way, then I must accept that reality; it must reflect something authentic about the mixture of my mother's psyche with my own, and I must come to terms with this manifestation of who *I* am and of who she is for me regardless of what it reflects about who *she* is objectively or for herself.

We can find our roots in the reality of our inner natures, by turning inward to our psyches for guidance in our development, rather than by looking outward to psychological experts or to logical imperatives. Eve found the basic materials for healing her mother's damage within herself, in her dreams and fantasies. Lacking an adequate experience with her personal mother, she had the components of an adequate mother within herself and was able to contact and integrate them to the extent that she could acknowledge the reality of the psyche.

The widespread fear of the psyche, which leads to its denial, is rooted in an unconscious appreciation of the psyche's power. Psychic injuries are often more crippling and intransigent to treatment than physical ones. And they are much more shameful, since they effect one's sense of identity at a much deeper level. It is possible to lose a limb or an organ and to recover psychologically to the point of feeling like a whole human being. One cannot feel whole if one's psyche is missing a piece—if, for example, one's aggression has been denied, or if one has been cut off from one's true nature and is living out of what

Winnicott called a false self. In these cases a subjective sense of integrity can be authentically developed only if the missing psychic pieces can be contacted and integrated. Our personhood is more fundamentally a psychological state than a physical one.

The fear of the psyche should be respected, but our heroic masculine orientation rebels against admitting that we are weak and puny before the awesome power of our nature. One manifestation of our denial appears in our refusal to confront the issue of therapeutic failure. The medical world has begun, in the last few years, to admit that death *does* come eventually, regardless of expert medical intervention. (Although the attempts to conquer heart disease and cancer often do sound as though someone continues to carry the fantasy that if we do not die of these diseases, perhaps we will never die.) While there is at least an intellectual acceptance of the fact that some illnesses are fatal, there is virtually no recognition of the comparable, and equally valid, psychological fact: some psychological illnesses are fatal and will end in suicide, *even if the case is handled ideally, even if all treatment conditions are optimal*. Perhaps even more distressing is the fact that no psychological illness—dis-ease—is completely "curable." Psychological pain will leave its scars and wounds, although treatment may profoundly alter one's relationship to one's suffering, and some of us can experience healing that we would call transformative. Still, we can no more undo the damage our emotional injuries have wrought than we can smooth out the wrinkles that time and life have etched on our faces and hands. To recognize the reality of the psyche is to face the terrible limits of our lives, our relative impotence in the face of the forces of life. In our culture's masculine orientation there has been little support for that attempt.

Implications of an Archetypal View, II: The Spiritual Instinct

We can see that archetypal—psychological—requirements shape the developing human being at every stage of life. The individual needs cultural or familial forms within which to mate and reproduce, to eat and to eliminate, to contribute to the vitality of the society through work, to grieve, to rejoice, and eventually to die. The fact that human nature is malleable must not obscure the fact that it is also limited. Grounded in the body, there are innate erotic and assertive/aggressive drives. An archetypal perspective addresses the fact that there are also innate affiliative and spiritual drives grounded in the psyche.

The channeling of psychic energy into cultural forms is a universal human pattern leading to a profound subjective sense of satisfaction. Cultural and spiritual expressions of the psyche need not be reduced to defensive sublimations of bodily drives. They can be seen instead as authentic and primary manifestations of the psyche's own nature, of our yearning to affiliate (unite) with our deeper selves. We can think of the human condition as resting on two sets of drives, physical and psychic, that intertwine with and depend upon each other at the same time as they are separate from and even opposed to each other. They develop and unfold in the growing individual in ways that are partly determined by the person's genetic heritage (in both its unique and universal aspects) and partly by environment. While different cultures have developed widely varying forms for the expression of these two sets of drives, it is the universal human condition to be torn between the demands of mind and body. This is, in fact, a crucial element in our humanity. Animals are rooted sufficiently firmly in their bodies as to experience little or no psychic conflict in the expression of their physical drives.

Grounded in the post-Enlightenment West, Freud tried to describe the human condition as though the body's drives were primary and the psyche's impulses were reactive. Philosophically, this is a materialist approach. The opposite conception of the universe, idealism, was described by Plato in his metaphor of the cave, where he suggests that the material world is a shadow or reflection of a nonmaterial ideal image that precedes its incarnation in matter. Strange as this idea may seem, we would do well to remember that the vast majority of the human race historically has accepted idealism as thoroughly as we accept materialism. The Eastern mind posits the soul as the basic building block of the human being, incarnated in a transient and insignificant body. We are equally certain that the body is the basic reality, producing an ephemeral and insignificant psyche. Either approach is simply axiomatic. Neither philosophy can be objectively demonstrated.

The work of modern nuclear physicists has put into question our deeply ingrained bias. Light, we know, cannot be understood either as matter (particles) or as nonmaterial waves; it can only be described as both, despite the obvious logical impossibility of this hypothesis. Matter, in fact, is not simply matter at all. It is almost all "empty" space filled with awesomely powerful energy fields. Matter, as investigations are proceeding to more and more primary layers of it's nature, seems "really" to be energy. Current thinking has gone beyond Einstein's famous equation describing the interchangeable nature of matter and energy and suggests that energy has more primacy than matter.

On a human level this would imply that the psyche may indeed existentially precede the body. Pragmatically, at this point in history, it would seem more useful to conceive of the body and the psyche as two equally authentic manifestations of the same thing. All human beings develop cultural/psychic patterns that interact with the body's impulses, at least from the time of birth. What effect will it have if we accept the reality of the psyche and its drives as equivalent to the reality of the body?

We know that the body's drives develop; the sexual drive, for example, moves from the oral, to the anal, to the genital area. We do not imagine the "real" human sexual impulse is oral and that further developments are simply a result of environmental pressures. Similarly, psychic impulses to symbolic creativity, increasing in complexity as the individual grows, whether they take artistic, religious, or other cultural forms, can be seen as part of the inherited nature of the human being. An archetypal psychology attempts to synthesize a recognition of our material nature (the instinctual drives) with an appreciation of our psychic nature, the spiritual drives. These spiritual drives are an introverted expression of the affiliative drive postulated as primary by all object relations psychologists. They enable the individual to express his essential nature in forms comprehensible to others; they both urge and assist one to connect with others, both external and internal others, in psychological forms. In this model the mind and the body are posited as a unity, two sides of one coin, neither one preceding the other. The concept of archetypes enriches the concept of instincts by explicitly recognizing the psyche as the body's equal partner in life.

An instinct is generally understood to be a narrowly prescribed impulse. Instinctive behavior in the animal kingdom is behavior that does not vary from individual to individual. All male cranes perform the same mating dance in their attempt to woo their mate. One must never get between a mother bear and her cub because all mother bears are intensely protective of their young: they have a strong maternal instinct.

We find ourselves in a different realm when we try to talk about human "instincts." What has been called the "sexual instinct" in man may express itself in a variety of forms, including masturbation, perversions of all kinds and an enormous range of homosexual and heterosexual activities involving every orifice, limb, and acrobatic possibility of the human body. It is also true that the individual can suppress the expression of the sexual instinct or can use sexuality in the service of any emotional aim: greedily, soothingly, hatefully, enviously, reparatively, etc. We have come a long distance from the male crane's ritual mating dance, a distance that is entirely psychological. It is not that our bodies have more flexible requirements for survival than those of other animals, but rather that our psyches are more powerful as determining factors in our behavior. When we talk about archetypal patterns rather than instinctual behavior, we are recognizing this fact.

Let us recall some of the descriptions of this concept offered above. Archetypes, the "unconscious [i.e., psychological] images of the instincts," are originally potential images. They are without content until they have been "filled out with the material of conscious experience." Thus, the individual's experiences with a human mother are elaborated into fantasy images of different mother-states, images that appear in richly developed forms in the religious art of different cultures. We see Kali, the death-mother, dancing with bowls of blood in her hands and with a girdle of human skulls; Diana (Artemis) of Ephesus, the infinitely nourishing mother, with fifty or a hundred lactating breasts covering the front of her body; Rangda, the Balinese witch, with her flaming tongue and necklace of entrails embodies the mother whose selfish needs would devour her child; the Virgin Mary actualizes the selfless spiritual devotion that the loving mother can sometimes offer her child.

Such images are collective, products of a culture rather than of an individual artist, although each artist paints them from a personal viewpoint. Their impersonal, collective nature carries the paradoxical capacity to speak movingly to the individual. One need not know Balinese mythology to be deeply shaken by the masks depicting Rangda. One knows about her—we have each experienced Rangda because these archetypal images embody the part-objects of our preverbal lives. These are not real people. They are the Kleinian Good and Bad Breasts, elaborated over centuries by the artistic and poetic talents of the entire population. These images are based partly on the infant individual's perceptions of real, external people, but they are also based on inherited channels for fantasies about the nature of people. These inherited channels are the archetypes. Larger than personal experiences, larger than life, gods rather than mortals, each image depicts one facet of the mother archetype which would be fully developed if we were to add eight or ten more images from other cultures. We would fill out the range of possible human experiences of the mother, a range founded on and limited by the inherited nature of our species.

Historically, these images that express the mother archetype most directly are religious. Eve's archetypal images also have a religious quality: flying saucers are the central symbol of a modern religious or mythic cult; the "old archeological stones" that she unearthed in her third dream were religious (e.g., Aztec) statues. I have called the archetypes "three-dimensional picture frames" waiting to be filled in by life's experiences, but they may equally be thought of as the channels through which the psyche's native energy emerges. From this perspective, they are experienced as the source of our aliveness, as the numinous and awesome centers of our existence, as, anthropomorphically, our Creator. Historically, these innate channels have been seen in projection rather than through direct introspection. Because the archetypes rule our psychological lives, because we are subject to their direction rather than in control of them, and because they provide the patterns that can make life work, they have been personified as gods. More powerful than our personal egos, they are the ground out of which our personal selves emerge.

Religious imagery as an expression of the archetypal layer of the psyche must be understood not primarily as wish-fulfilling, or as world-explaining, but rather as psychically-organizing. Religious stories describe the patterns into which our life energy naturally and profitably flows. By studying mythic stories across cultural boundaries, we can hope to discover the ever-recurring patterns of human existence that can work for us.

Take for example the Greek myth that describes the progress of the sun across the sky. Apollo is said to harness his horses to the chariot of the sun and to drive it from the eastern horizon, through its noontime zenith, to the western horizon. A secondary story tells of the tragedy that occurred when his mortal son, Phaethon, attempted to drive the chariot and fell instead to his death after nearly destroying the world with his inability to control the powerful horses that pull the sun. Now this story explains nothing about the natural world; it is not a primitive attempt to address the sorts of questions asked by modern science. It tells us only what we already knew, that the sun travels across the sky every day. The myth of Apollo elaborates a familiar sensory experience in poetic imagery. The second myth invents, again in poetry, an imaginary event. To hypothesize that the second invention was triggered by a very hot day is to miss the point that it tells the story of a day far hotter than any day that occurred in the outer world.

While these religious stories tell the believing listener nothing about the natural world's material essence, they connect people to the natural world in psychologically meaningful ways. The first story takes a concrete outer event and makes it a human event. The story can then function within the psyche in a variety of ways: as a metaphor, for example, for the progress of a person's psychic energy through the course of life, or as a bridge, connecting one personally to the outer world. The second story elaborates the first and describes the danger that befalls the individual who tries to drive his life energy with his conscious, mortal will, rather than recognizing that he is subject to his psyche's forces which can be driven only by "a god"—the historical word for an archetype. In other words, religions, the historical repositories of the images of the archetypes, fill two main functions: they convert the sensory world into a psychological experience and offer a viable pattern for the individual's relationship to both inner and outer worlds.

Convergences and Divergences with Other Analytic Schools

Reading the Freud–Jung letters is like witnessing a Greek tragedy: the final break is inevitably prefigured in their early relationship, in the fact that Jung, no more than Freud, could remain anyone's disciple through his mature years. But in addition to the emotional determinants of the break, intellectual issues were involved, and it is instructive to examine them. In 1912 Jung published the book *Wandlungen und Symbole der Libido* ("Transformations and Symbols of the Libido") which was ultimately translated as *Symbols of Transformation*. Attempting the impossible task of surveying the mythology of the world, Jung laid down, in a relatively chaotic form, the basic ideas that were to develop into his archetypal perspective. Intellectually, the break between Freud and Jung was founded on Jung's explicit denial of the sexual nature of libido. Jung sees libido simply as psychic energy that moves through any number of forms, no one being any more real than any other. This is the basic notion on which a recognition of the psyche's spiritual drive, and of the psyche's reality, must rest. This is the notion that the Freud of 1912 could not accept.

Today, Jung's formulation is commonplace, even among orthodox Freudians. The rupture between these two psychological giants is no longer intellectually significant. Many conventional psychoanalysts have independently come to the essential views behind Jung's break with the psychoanalytic world of 1912. Freud himself moved some distance from his 1912 position by the time of his death in 1939.

The system-ego that Freud struggled with his whole life is a very different concept from the person-ego-self that such disparate theorists as Erikson, Winnicott, Guntrip, Fairbairn, and Kohut explore. Freud's early insistence on the primacy of the body has been rejected by many, perhaps most, contemporary analysts who implicitly, if not explicitly, begin with the psyche as the basic unit of investigation and as a real object in its own right. It is always a matter of emphasis: there is a body and a psyche, and all thinkers recognize both to one degree or another. Do we, however, start with a biological drive that grabs a handy object for its expression, or with an object whose emotional significance draws the biological drives toward it?

Because the reality of the psyche seems to me the essential Jungian concept, I am impressed with the similarity between Jung's thinking and that of other object relations thinkers. Both perspectives see the psyche as a microscopic universe in which the individual's life experiences, molded by fantasied elaborations of them, live on, shaping current experiences. Jung's "complexes" are what non-Jungians describe as "self-images" bound to "inner objects" (or "object-images") by an "affective valence."

Many non-Jungians have described aspects of the archetypal layer of the psyche without recognizing it as Jung's collective unconscious. Spitz, for example, talks about psychic "organizers"; Klein's hypothesis of unconscious phantasies operating from birth is equivalent to the hypothesis of archetypally determined psychic concomitants to physical experiences; Piaget's idea of "innate schemata" depicts the operation of the archetypes in human cognitive development. All these notions describe the existence of certain limits and patterns of human nature. Any developmental psychology, in fact, that purports to describe universal patterns of human psychological growth must rest on an implicit use of the concept of an archetypal foundation to the psyche. There are broad limits to our nature, innate patterns that underlie our unfolding as human beings. If a human mother were to attempt to raise a baby chimpanzee as a human, she would not wind up with a nonverbal baby, she would be stuck with a chimp. The concept of archetypes simply describes this fact.

One major value of an archetypal perspective lies in the greater clarity of thought that an explicit conceptualization offers over an implicit recognition of this layer of the psyche. Spiritual imagery and experiences can be studied as phenomena in their own right. When patients try to communicate that layer of their experience, they need not be dismissed as defensive. We can avoid reducing numinous energies to bodily instincts in ways that degrade transcendent experience.

The archetypal layer of the psyche is the psyche's foundation, its most primitive strata. Studying the world's mythology gives us story lines and imagery to support our attempts to contain a patient's frightening descent into these infantile layers. We are confronted with quantities of suffering in our work that seem insupportable. When we can call up a mythic parallel to an individual's ordeal, we can find a container for our own terror that may enable us to hold someone through an experience we would otherwise need to seal off. When one woman lost custody of her daughter, her therapist found the strength to sit with her in her anguish rather than medicating it away only by remembering the tale of Demeter: Persephone's loss shattered Demeter, making a desert of the entire earth. By holding onto the myth's graphic picture of totally devastating despair, remembering that Demeter's emotional death was navigated, the therapist was able to hold her patient through to the patient's spiritual rebirth (Beth Barmack, personal communication). We can see the future—or at least one possible future—when we are connected to the patterns of human development painted by mythology.

An archetypal perspective leads us also to a unique conceptualization of the self. Jung defines the self as both the center and the totality of the psyche. It is an archetype, the psyche's ruling archetype, that organizes the individual into an integrated whole. It is supraordinate to the individual person, it carries forces to which the individual must accede rather than attempt to dominate. Unlike object relations perspectives, which do not typically differentiate between the ego and the self, an archetypal viewpoint enables us to differentiate the two concepts. In Jungian terminology, the term "self" is used to refer to an archetype that rules and organizes the formation of the individual. The "self" the non-Jungian object relations thinkers talk about is conceptually closer to the Jungian "ego." This is the person's "I," roughly equivalent to the conscious self. The ego must be related to the larger self, but psychological health requires that the ego defer to the self, to the tremendous forces of the psyche that we can never dominate and that absolutely determine our lives. The fascinating and awesome power of the self that leads to its projection in such images as Yahweh, Christ, Buddha, the atman, and so on, is not discussed psychologically, as far as I know, outside of Jungian circles. This differentiation comes out of and highlights the supremacy of the unconscious in the psychological life of man and invites us to relate to our depths rather than try to dominate them.

If Jungians, however, have described the numinous, transpersonal quality of the self in a manner that other object relations thinkers have neglected, these other thinkers have detailed the personal incarnation of the self much more thoroughly than the Jungians. Taking the mother archetype and complex as our example again, the Jungian focus often tends toward the archetypal and spiritual qualities of one's experience of the Mother; object relations thinkers emphasize the specific qualities of the personal mother that have shaped one in an exact way, or the primitive, infantile layer of a person's experience, that elemental personal level where one's individual life emerges from the universal—archetypal—energies of the species. The viewpoints are complementary and mutually enriching.

Implications for Work with Dreams and Images

In explicitly recognizing the archetypal layer of the psyche, Jung was hypothesizing that mythic imagery works directly on the psyche's unconscious foundation. While interpreting a symbolic image may be a valuable and interesting activity for psychologists to engage in, the image itself contains the psychological power to shape the viewer's psychic energy at its source.

There are conflicting senses through the analytic world regarding the depth of healing one can hope for in this work. Psychoanalytic circles discuss this in terms of the possibility of making "new identifications" as an adult. The question is whether changes can be hoped for in the deeper layers of the psyche or whether one must content oneself with learning about the deeper wounds, accepting them, and compensating for their effects with one's rational capacities. A feminine approach to the work is based on the belief that even in an older adult, the psyche's core is accessible and mutable (although not, of course, infinitely so). I have been discussing in this chapter a Jungian view of that core, an archetypal perspective, which offers us some sense of how transformation occurs by suggesting a continuous process within which symbolic imagery, the language of the dream, changes the psyche's core at the same time as it proceeds out of it. One the one hand, a dream is like an x-ray of the soul, depicting the current state of some inner segment. On the other hand, when the dream's imagery is consciously engaged—when the ego allows a dream experience to resonate powerfully in waking life—the dream's potency can be brought to life in a way that enables it to feed back into the dreamer's depths and modify these fundamental layers in some way.

A cognitive attempt to interpret dream material is one way to engage with a dream, but it is not ordinarily the most powerful way. If we seek transformative change in the psyche's structure, an appreciation of the inherent power of the image itself will typically lead us away from interpretive work on primary process material. Classical work attempts to translate primary process thinking—the image in its original form, in the native language of the archetypes—into secondary process thinking. A feminine approach seeks psychological change that grows from core layers of the unconscious upward, and it asks our secondary process minds to learn (or relearn) the primary process language of the soul. It is not that we will not talk about the dream imagery, but rather that we will talk descriptively, emotionally, resisting cognitive understanding that would settle its meaning once and for all.

In *The Interpretation of Dreams*, one of Freud's basic hypotheses is that the psyche translates secondary process thoughts—disguising them—

into primary process images. At the same time, the very names he gave to the two modes of psychic expression would indicate the opposite: primary process is the psyche's native language, while secondary process—directed, logical, and verbal—is a later development. Primary process thinking is primitive, uncivilized, blunt, and shocking. The secondary process thought, "I'm angry with Paul," is leagues away from the primary process image a dream presents, in which Paul turns into a doll whose head is snapped off by a stray mongrel. The secondary process thought is bland, a cognitive formulation without life unless the emotion behind it emerges in the speaker's tone of voice or gesture. The dream image takes one's breath away, it triggers a living reaction because the emotional reality of the anger is inherently contained within it. Certainly there are disguises, even in the dream image, of its unconscious—nonverbal and preimagistic—roots. "I" did not snap the doll's head off, the vicious mongrel grabbed the doll, it was an "accident." But as soon as we agree that each dream image captures a part of the dreamer's psyche, it becomes an undisguised, straightforward picture of the psyche as it is naturally experienced. "I" (i.e., my conscious ego) does not want to snap Paul's head off, it is a despised, impure (mongrel) side of my animal nature that surprises me as well as Paul with its viciousness.

What is the purpose of translating the image into secondary process language? One major impact of the interpretation is to distance the emotions contained in the image. The translation creates the illusion that the ego controls the situation (*I* am angry) and denies the reality which the image presents, that the anger has a life of its own to which I, like Paul, must respond. In reality my best hope is to work out a cooperative truce with this vicious mongrel side of myself, such that I contain it rather than being overwhelmed by it and acting it out. Our masculine values rebel against the need to recognize our smallness, our lack of control, and we therefore try to dominate the image by interpreting it, as though that will fix it in our power.

This formulation provides an example of working with the image in its own language. Cognitive understanding is a by-product, not the primary thrust. A translation of the image to secondary process language is typically an attempt to seal off the vicious mongrel, to be rid of it once and for all. Eve's husband, calling the police in an attempt to suppress the energies carried by the flying saucers, is the quintessential secondary process man. An imagistic method attempts to open up and expand the ego's connections with the raw energy expressed in the fearful image, hoping thereby to tame its wildness and also to have continuing access to the wild, archetypal energy within it. Interpreting the images of the psyche in intellectual formulations is useful for some purposes, but it runs the risk of draining the psyche of its life. It is like the difference between a hot bowl of chili and the recipe for chili. For some purposes the recipe is more valuable than the chili, but to imagine that the recipe can substitute for the food is to declare that a description of life is the same as living.

When the focus is on translating psychic imagery into adult thought, the attempt is to actualize Freud's famous maxim, Where id was, let ego be. The classical Freudian Leo Stone is explicit on this point: he works for "a gradual replacement of the primitive mechanisms by the special functions of speech and cognitive understanding" (1980, p. 191). But the primitive mechanisms of primary process thought, the teeming chaos of the id, are expressions of the source of life itself, of the archetypal ground of the psyche. To replace with "cognitive understanding" the zest and energy that flows in endless profusion out of one's archetypal core into one's dreams is to cut oneself off from the joy as well as from the agony of life.

Secondary process thinking is, by nature, not alive. It is not that it is dead, it is simply nonliving. Like a piece of petrified wood, it may capture the essence of a moment in life and preserve it permanently. It is fixed and clear. But it does not suddenly shift in meaning, it does not vibrate with indefinable nuance, it does not surprise one by suddenly turning into its opposite. These mercurial qualities are the essence of any living entity, and they form the core quality of primary process products. Rather than subjugating the territory of the id to the will of the ego (in any case, a hopeless task), we can work toward a harmonious coexistence based on open lines of communication and cooperation. Instead of translating the psyche's images into secondary process thoughts, we can bring our secondary process capacities to bear in an attempt to develop fluency in the psyche's own language. This offers the possibility of an integration of these two forms of mental expression, not sacrificing one or the other. Instead of attempting to get the "meaning" of an image nailed down (thereby killing the vitality of the image), we can work to open channels through which the image's multiple implications resonate in our hearts in ways that can be partly captured in words but that will always remain partly nonverbal. Rather than *replacing* the psyche's primitive mechanisms, an archetypal, imagistic approach enables us to use our cognitive capacity to establish a dialogue with the primitive psyche, to bring fresh life to our jaded adult egos at the same time that it leads to modifications in the structure of the primitive psyche.

Chapter 7

Two Clinical Examples[1]

The feminine principle has been disrespected in the practice of therapeutic work in proportion to its abasement in our culture at large. Societal rejection of the Feminine is itself symptomatic of the wounded Feminine inside each of us. For many of us, in one way or another, healing that injured inner woman becomes a lifelong task of central importance. I began this book with two examples of individuals, Sydney, a woman, and Stanley, a man, for whom this struggle to heal the wounded Feminine formed the core of their individuation process. We could describe one central element in this book as an exploration of the way therapeutic work has been distorted by the injuries each of our inner feminine capacities have sustained. On a personal level, this book is one part of my attempt to repair the wounded feminine therapist inside myself.

In Chapters 4 and 5, I tried to describe the broad outlines of a therapeutic attitude grounded in the feminine principle. In Chapter 5 especially, where I delineated some masculine ground rules for the therapist's approach, we found repeatedly that nothing absolute could ever be said. In some situation, imperfectly imagined in advance, anything might be appropriate. In the field as a whole, every reasonable and valuable guideline is sometimes misused by some therapists at all experience levels to justify behavior that is harmful to their patients. Because we are exploring a field that is more an art than a science, individual case examples are crucially important. Because we are exploring a field that deals with the most private, vulnerable reaches of the human soul, case examples are extraordinarily difficult to share. In this chapter, I will present the development of the transference/countertransference relationship in one case of my own, that of Christina. Some of the theoretical ideas presented in Chapters 4 and 5

---

[1]A portion of this chapter appeared in Stevens (1986).

should come more fully to life in this extended example. I shall also analyze a piece of James Masterson's work, the case of Lynn. His work misses the value of the feminine principle in sweeping ways and I present it to amplify the destructive potential of a one-sided, masculine approach.

Christina

When I first saw Christina, I was struck with the many ways she seemed to be a Kohutian case example come to life. The immediate issues leading her into therapy were an inability to begin a major creative project in her work and a sense of futility and chaos about the meaning or direction of her life. About nine months before calling me, she had left her husband and two preadolescent children and rented temporary living space. Her despair, which had grown steadily throughout her marriage, had not significantly lifted after leaving it, which led to further despair. Realizing that no new birth would come from simply leaving her family, she called me for therapy.

I saw Christina as an intelligent, talented, professionally well-functioning woman with severe narcissistic difficulties. She presented herself in disorderly bits and pieces, jumping from topic to topic, apparently unable to remember what we had talked about in our last hour or to connect emotionally with what she did remember about yesterday or last week; subjectively, she felt fragmented and lost. Two months into the work she presented a dream that revealed the depth of the wounding to her wholeness:

> *I did a long narrow painting that reminds me of the drawings in the children's book,* Four Fur Feet. *At the top was a washy kind of sky and at the bottom was grass, with deer and a woodsy place. An idyllic scene. On the right hand side of the painting I put in a figure in plastic. It was a little like a figure eight—like those three-dimensional candles you put on a child's birthday cake—with arms and eyes [see illustration].*

> *This is the one part of the picture that can't be changed, for it's plastic. As I made it, I thought, "I'll put the hand here so it's clear it's not masturbation." I showed the painting to a woman and she showed it to people and they praised it a lot. I gave the woman credit for inspiring me.*

The fixed plastic figure reminded Christina of a diagram she had seen in Jung's work:

She thought her image was like Jung's, divided into two halves.

Jung uses this diagram as a map of the archetype of the self. This interpretation of the plastic figure eight as an image of Christina's self is supported by her association to an eight-year-old's birthday cake. Four is typically a number of wholeness (the four points of the compass, the four seasons of the year, for example). Eight is double four. In associating her one unchangeable element to a *divided* Self, Christina is expressing (without affect or understanding) her unconscious despair of ever unifying herself.

Her essential disunity is further expressed in the elements of the doubly spiralling figure eight. The eye is in the top half and the hand in the bottom. The eye cannot see what the hand does; the hand is cut off from the eye's direction. The hand's position, which we must assume is fixed like all else in this image, makes clear that what is happening is not masturbation. Thus the hand's position also precludes masturbation. Christina is permanently unable to give herself pleasure, to love her body, to make love to herself.

These deeply sobering pessimistic implications are softened by two positive elements in the dream. First there is the idyllic rural scene forming the backdrop to the painting. *Four Fur Feet*, the book Christina remembered, is the story of an unidentified furry animal who "walked around the world/on his four fur feet/ and never made a sound—O" (Brown 1961). Just so, Christina as a small child must have experienced herself as "never making a sound" in the sense that no one ever seemed to hear her. But the pictures of the round, round world around which the four fur feet walk are delightfully rich in variety and color. This world includes wild animals and fish, cities and railroad trains, meadows, rivers, and a brilliant warming sun. The four fur feet travel all around a wonderfully intact, vital self.

The second hopeful dream element is Christina's relationship with the other woman, a relationship we can hope to bring to life in the course of our work. This other woman, apparently simply through her interest in Christina and her work, inspires her to paint the state of her self. Although at this early stage of the work Christina could not emotionally appreciate the meaning of her dream, the image was permanent and would be there when Christina could truly see it, with the eyes of her heart as well as the eyes of her intuitive perception. Seen by others, the painting leads to praise and this allows Christina to feel good about herself and generous toward the woman who helped her. She is filled with love as a result of receiving praise, love for herself and love for her companion. Paradoxically, the immutable, plastic self will have been changed if Christina can love herself. Seeing the brutally divided state of her soul, facing the deepest hopelessness about her condition, may lead, the dream informs us, to her healing.

The dream's instructions seemed clear: I was to infuse Christina with the inspiration to paint herself in the deepest possible way; I was to see the painting she made and to communicate to her my appreciation for her effort. In the simplest of terms, Christina needed to be cherished and esteemed—loved—by me. In order for her to develop a sense of her identity as a whole human being with a reliable, on-going center of initiative located inside herself, she needed to be seen and mirrored as a unit, paradoxically intact in her deep, inner disunion. If I could empathically share her experience of life, if I could take that experience into my body and vicariously live it for the fifty minutes we spent together, I would be able to reflect her wholeness back to her by embodying it.

It is not a simple thing to empathize with another person's experience, however, and for the first two years of our work I had great difficulty aligning myself with Christina as a woman who had left her children. In terms of Jung's alchemical pictures, we both had trouble getting our clothes off and getting into the bath together because we were each afraid to see ourselves reflected in the other. Initially, I did not appreciate the intensity of my response to this woman who had "abandoned" her children. But looking back, I remembered that a friendship of mine had collapsed not long before when my friend left her child. I had not been able to absorb the horror the image of a mother leaving her child contained for me. It is an awful image, and Christina shared with me a strong condemnation of any woman, herself most certainly included, who would do such a dreadful thing. To look such a woman in the face, any mother must confront her own impulses to leave her children; we must each face the ways in which our mothers abandoned us. Resonating to Christina's plight meant sympathizing with the woman who was playing the role of the Bad Mother in this human drama.

The most immediate information we ever have about what is going on in a case is countertransference data, and the most interesting countertransference experience I had with Christina in the first two years of our work was becoming physically cold in my hours with her. I realized it was invariably when she was talking about her children that I started to shiver, and from there it was a short step to realizing that the incidents she was describing were those in which she was shockingly cold toward her children.

This insight, however, had no warming effect. For this beginning phase of the work, the theoretical attitude I was taking toward her, around the issue of her children, could be summed up as follows. Because she had been unable to contain her rejecting, hateful feelings toward her children, her feelings had possessed her and led her to leave the children with no warning. I saw my task as helping her to face and accept those rejecting feelings as legitimate parts of her self. In retrospect, it is clear to me that my attitude was cold; beneath the psychological language, I was distancing myself from her. "Face up to the fact you are a witch of a mother," I was implicitly saying. I was afraid to open myself up to an alchemical merger with her, afraid of the ways her shocking behavior might transform me.

Had I not been so horrified by the external sight of a woman who leaves her children, I would have been freer to pay attention to its psychological implications. Early in our work, Christina had dreamed of being on a long journey, a metaphor for the journey she was starting with me. As the bus she was riding turned the corner toward her home, its progress stopped. Chris saw an ambulance and a police car beside an overturned child's doll carriage: a little girl had been hit by a car and severely injured or killed. The wounded little girl had been playing at motherhood, enjoying and delighting in her maternal instincts. This tragic accident, the smashing of the mother-child bond, blocked Chris's way to her home, to her sense of belonging, of having a place, a center from which to meet the world.

This violent running-over of her inner child was repeatedly enacted in our work. For example, in the first months, when she started to think about coming three times a week, she worried about whether or not that would be "good" for her. She felt childish talking about it and remembered the girl who had been run over by a car. She was sure coming more often would be good for that child, but was not at all sure it would be good for *her*. This formulation reflected one of the splits within herself, a way in which she stomped out her inner child, dissociating from her infantile roots, from her vulnerable, young center, from her feelings, from her self. Caught up in the negative aspects of her interaction with her outer children, I became distracted from the fact that her cold, abandoning attitude toward them was a pale reflection of her cold, abandoning attitude toward her own child self.

My physical coldness reflected the fact I had caught her emotionally cold and unempathic attitude toward herself. Thoroughly saturated with self-loathing, she was more than willing to collaborate in a image of herself as a hateful mother. But as I became less eager to join her, I began to realize how utterly helpless she had felt in her marriage. She had reached a point where she would drive to the supermarket to do the week's shopping only to find she could not get out of the car because she could not stop crying. She had repeatedly asked her husband for a separation, wanting him to leave the house and children, and he had repeatedly refused. At last, feeling she was drowning in that suburban home, believing the only possible way out was to jump out quickly and feeling subjectively unable to take her children with her, she brought herself to make the ultimate sacrifice and wrenched herself away from her children in a desperate attempt to save her essential self.

This is quite a different perspective toward her behavior from the righteous stance I had started with, demanding that Christina take responsibility for her behavior and own up to her hateful, rejecting impulses. It was not that she did not have hateful, rejecting impulses toward her children. All parents suffer those feelings. But she could integrate them only by centering herself in the fact—which was a fact—that leaving her children had been a terrible loss. Christina had reached a point at which she felt she had to choose between her life and her children, and she and I both needed to appreciate how that impossible choice had led to a dreadful wounding of herself. In order to find this empathic point of view inside myself, I needed to recognize that I, too, could be vulnerable to a terrible self-wounding, that circumstances could arise that would require a sacrifice in order to save another part of myself without which I could not live. Empathizing with Christina's leaving her children meant, in other words, that I had to accept a quality and level of suffering beyond my previous limits, and my physical coldness reflected my resistance to experiencing that. As I came to understand these dynamics, I found I was no longer subject to chills in my work with her.

In terms of the alchemical imagery that I am using as a thread to guide us through the development of the therapeutic bond, working through this countertransference difficulty allowed Christina and me to immerse ourselves, naked, in the bath. For the next three years, we flowed in and out of an emotional merger, suffering despair-unto-death and being occasionally soothed with the healing moisture of hope. These themes repeated themselves in an infinite variety of forms, some of which I will describe.

The issue of coldness reflected Chris's basic injury: there was a cold, dead part of herself. Her feeling function had suffered a terrible wounding in her childhood when she received every privilege that money could buy and no empathy for any of her emotional experiences. She emerged unable to empathize with herself and unable to evaluate the importance of events from a feeling perspective. A little girl had been run over, and Chris could not say with any certainty whether this was an important or a trivial event.

A major root of Chris's frigidity was fear of her destructive potential. Although her hatred and rage were ordinarily turned solidly inward against herself, she needed to maintain an impenetrable coldness toward others in order to protect us from that hatred and rage. This coldly distant stance also protected her from my hurting her, as well as shielding her from feeling the pain of her loneliness.

As the months and years of our work passed, the frozen territory inside Chris began to thaw. I needed to restrain all of my impulses to *do* things: I needed to *not* interpret her dynamics, to stop myself from trying to help her or to make her feel better. I worked to suffer the pain of empathizing with her *just as she was*, and she responded by introjecting that self-directed empathic capacity. Her self-loathing for a long time led her to try to analyze herself, tearing herself to pieces and harshly critiquing each piece. As she began to develop a different attitude toward herself, she dreamed she came into my office and found Jung sitting on the couch. There were raw gems scattered around on the floor and he was polishing one of them. "That's what we Jungians do," he told her. "We polish."

Holding and accepting herself as a unified person enabled Chris to share herself increasingly intimately with me. One strand of that sharing involved criticizing me, hesitantly turning a faint echo of her frozen hatred and rage in my direction as I encouraged this increasingly authentic expression of her true nature. She expressed a gamut of feelings about my various therapeutic inadequacies: I was inept in my capacity to work with dreams, I was too young to be wise, I was the wrong sex to be powerful, my master's degree was woefully inadequate. Because she came three times a week, and because her income was limited, I did not raise her fee in the five years I saw her. As time passed, her fee became low by contemporary standards. The fee, then, became clear evidence of my second- or third-rate status. She knew when she started with me that I was a candidate at the Jung Institute, and this was also used to discredit me: perhaps she had not fully appreciated the implications of the fact that I had not yet completed my training, that I did not yet know how to do this work. For me, one of her most compelling depreciations was her attitude toward my Jewishness, an attitude faintly colored by her father's direct anti-Semitism. I was accorded here an intimate view of upper-crust WASP culture I had never had before.

In the last year of our work, Chris realized that these depreciations reflected primarily the ways she depreciated herself. But while this insight was useful, the main value of her criticism lay in the experience itself. She turned her human nastiness in my direction and I survived. Although she hurt my feelings at times, my positive sense of self was strong enough to withstand her destructive impulses. I was able to maintain my affection for her, pretty much unbroken, through her assaults, and that was crucial in helping her develop and maintain some affection for all of herself, including her darker side.

The other side of her sharing herself intimately with me was more directly positive. As we held and polished her selfhood, she became able to express a variety of dependency needs toward me. She talked about the despair that flooded her when I abandoned her by going away on vacations or by ending each hour. She shared with me her wishes to come home with me and to be my child. With considerable distress and anxiety, she told me about sexual feelings toward me. At about the time I worked through my coldness toward her, Chris had an erotic dream in which she did not have an orgasm. The dream continued, and in it she began telling me her dream. The process of telling me about it led her to have an orgasm. My feeling for her constellated her capacity to feel for herself. The warmth of our relationship brought to life her frozen ability to enjoy her body and her self. The parallel with Chris's early dream of the divided self seemed vivid: I have become able, both within her psyche and within my own, authentically to play the part of the early dream's appreciative audience that enabled her to love.

Some of our most moving hours revolved around her sharing herself with me on a bodily level. In an hour that occurred in the last six months of our work, she noticed I had a corn pad on my little toe. Mastering her embarrassment, she managed to tell me the insulting thought about my physical grossness that popped into her mind. Then she went on, in an easy, intimate way, talking about the various gross disabilities of her own body, such as what her hemorrhoids looked like recently when she examined them in a mirror. (One can see, in this sequence, the way the expression of negative, critical thoughts can open the door to a positive, interpersonal connection.) This verbal sharing of her body has been important *not* for the psychodynamic "meaning" of the content, but rather because of the interpersonal experience it generated. This kind of utterly intimate view of another person's body is normally available only to the mother of an infant. Telling me about her private physical self was one way a deep merger was created and maintained between us. The fruit of that intimate connection was pictured in a dream in which she was giving birth to a baby girl. I was standing at her feet with my hands deep inside her, helping the baby out.

In terms of our alchemical pictures, Chris's communications, both the critical ones and the loving ones, express the fact that we had merged in a union that was both pleasurable and painful. As the dream of giving birth would indicate, Chris had experiences in our work of being reborn. These experiences alternated with long stretches of immersion in her pain, periods in which we lay locked in grim agony in the tomb. Together we cycled between the deathly experiences in the tomb and the soothing experiences of renewal which follow them many times.

I saw Christina for five years. In terms of outer signs, one would consider our work highly successful, though on an intrapsychic level it remained incomplete. Externally, her relationship with her children was transformed. When I first met her, she saw her children rarely—once every three or four weeks—and the visits were a nightmare for all concerned. Every member of the family was in an on-going rage at every other member of the family. By the third year of our work, she was seeing her children several times a week and was almost as involved with them and with their day-to-day concerns as a custodial mother could be. Their contacts became primarily positive and loving and were clearly enjoyed by all participants. Her relationship with her ex-husband shifted from a rageful symbiosis to a disengaged but reasonably cooperative connection that worked well in relation to their two children. By the end of our work, she had completed the creative project she had been unable to begin and was offered a job that represented a substantial promotion professionally. Unfortunately, it also involved a geographical move that interrupted the analysis somewhat prematurely. But Chris clearly felt better and more intact and was presenting herself much more coherently than had been true when I met her.

It is my belief that the dramatic improvements in her life were a direct result of the transference experience she and I navigated together. In our last hours, Chris struggled to express what our work had meant for her. I tried to point out the improvements of her life, but she decisively rejected that measure of our work. In fact, she felt sorely misunderstood by my intervention. She finally formulated it for herself: "These years have been filled with pain for me. There's been pain with the children, pain at work, pain with my ex-husband, and pain with my lover. Our work has offered me a container for all of that pain. Here I have felt soothed and held." In her relationship with me, Chris developed the capacity to know and hold her whole self by introjecting my capacity to see and hold her, to unite with her without being injured by her fearful impulses. In the container of our relationship, she explored more and more of her inner world, expanding her familiarity with herself and her ability to be the whole person she naturally should be.

Lynn

James Masterson exemplifies an approach to therapeutic work rooted almost solely in the masculine principle. As a therapist, he tries to sort patients into clear-cut categories (neurotic, borderline, narcissistic, etc.). He attempts to devise a treatment plan based on his diagnosis and to devise interventions that will impact on people in predictable ways. He does not seem to consider holding, receiving, yielding to, or containing patients to have significant curative value. Merger is a negative (i.e., primitive) state in his system, and an Eros-centered "entering in" to the patient's experience is not accorded any significance in his theories.

Masterson's work on the borderline syndrome and its developmental roots is invaluable in describing the dynamics of the preoedipal psyche's twin terrors, abandonment and engulfment. His belief that there are people who have matured beyond these fears is inaccurate. When one is unconscious of these fears within one's psyche, their power controls one and dominates one's behavior; when one can consciously experience the pain of these infantile terrors, one can hope to contain them rather than being run by them. But abandonment and engulfment are primary risks in all intimate relationships and can never be outgrown. Masterson's therapeutic approach relies heavily on confronting people with the ways in which these primitive fears are dominating their lives. I consider his basic attempt futile, for he hopes to enable people to *transcend* this elemental layer of the psyche rather than to integrate it. In so far as the patient attempts to meet this requirement, a splitting of his or her psyche may result, a narrowing of self rather than an expansion of capacities to hold woundedness within his or her soul. I will look here at the case of Lynn, presented in Masterson's *Psychotherapy of the Borderline Adult* (1976, pp. 286–336). It is to his credit that he has the courage to present his cases in process-level detail—although I must say I am troubled by the issue of privacy raised by that detail, an issue he seems to ignore.

The patient, Lynn, is a 33-year-old college teacher at the beginning of her five-year therapy. Masterson diagnoses her as borderline because she is emotionally dominated by her fear of abandonment and her consequent clinging defenses. There is no evidence of the violent rages often associated in the literature with borderline personalities, or of the unstable splitting some people demonstrate, within which the same person is perceived as fluctuating between all-good and all-bad valuations. She is successful in her career, although not completely satisfied with it, as the therapy starts. She is unhappy with her husband and finds most of her satisfactions in her relationship with her five-year-old daughter, Margaret, and in an extramarital affair. Whatever diagnostic label one might choose for this woman, she is functioning quite adequately and there is no reason to imagine she is not capable of running her life and making her own assessments of it.

The focus of Masterson's presentation is on her relationship with her daughter. The first year of therapy dealt primarily with her marriage and affair. The patient then decided to get divorced and "her clinging to Margaret increased. . . . I [i.e., Masterson] began confronting its destructiveness to the daughter" (p. 291). It was the therapist, in other words, who decided to make the mother–daughter relationship the focus of the therapy, presumably because he believed the patient's pathology was most clearly expressed in that relationship. For the remainder of the therapy, the major topic addressed is Lynn's mothering of Margaret. Masterson is very problem-oriented, deeply involved in a medical model that focuses on addressing and curing the patient's pathology. He sounds at times like a detective, focusing his attention on seeking out information regarding how Lynn is or is not clinging to Margaret, using Margaret as an inner mother to replace the loving mother Lynn never had, saddling the child with pathology that belongs to the mother.

For whatever reasons of his own, Masterson chose to see himself as therapist to *both* Lynn and Margaret, even referring to his work as "the treatment of Lynn and Margaret" (p. 300), although he was hired to treat only Lynn. It is disturbing to recognize that the needs of a mother and a daughter, like those of a husband and wife, may diverge. Any mother will need, at times, to express her neurotic complexes in her relationship with her children. Ordinarily, the therapist's job in that situation is to use the material the patient presents as a vehicle within which the patient can grow toward inner change, toward an authentic resolution of her neurotic complexes. When a mother abuses her child, the therapist may need to abandon the therapeutic role and take some action on the child's behalf.

There is no evidence that anything remotely like abuse was occurring in this case. A single mother with significant separation anxieties was contributing to difficult but reasonably age-appropriate separation problems in her daughter. When Margaret (age seven) has trouble separating from Lynn to go to day camp, Masterson tells Lynn she is holding onto her daughter as a defense against her own separation problems. He bluntly informs her "that she was sacrificing her daughter's welfare to the demands of her neurosis" (p. 294). Lynn, who had been a high-achieving, compliant child, follows Masterson's advice and insists that Margaret remain in camp. In the next interview, Lynn talks about how abandoned she felt as a child when her mother insisted she go to camp, how she "cried [her] way through the whole summer" (p. 294). She continues with a flood of abandonment memories, in which her rage is masochistically turned inward, leading to suicidal fantasies and self-destructive behavior. She reports what is apparently a life-long fantasy of starving herself to death, feeling this would be the only behavior that would move her coldly rejecting mother to sympathy.

Of course Masterson is aware of the existence of the unconscious, but he can imagine it only as something *out there*; he does not seem open to the idea that the patient has brought her unconscious with her into the treatment room, that the material rising to the surface of Lynn's mind is an expression of her unconscious reactions to the way in which he is currently, *in here*, dealing with her. In this example, the therapist abandons the patient by allying with her daughter's needs instead of with hers. The patient responds by detailing the abandonments of her history. Lynn goes on to talk about the way her mother was always unavailable to hear any of her angry feelings and about how her mother never listened to her, always making her stick it out, continuing on with things regardless of her lack of internal strengths. We can see here an easily understandable reaction to Masterson's approach.

He describes his technique as relying heavily on confrontation, but one feels a serious limitation in his ability to empathically imagine the patient's emotional experience of his confrontations. Lynn pleads that she doesn't want to "force [Margaret] to do things" (p. 295). In addition to the constructive aspect of this conscious wish for her daughter (a constructive aspect Masterson seems to miss), there is a plea here that he present a more sympathetic approach toward her. Let her grow in her own way, at her own pace, she is saying. The therapist responds by telling her this is simply a rationalization "for holding on to Margaret"—something the mother of a seven-year-old who has just recently lost her father in a divorce might naturally wish to do. Lynn responds to this critical assessment of her behavior by remembering the way both her husband and her mother withdrew from her at the time of her daughter's birth. This current situation, like that old one, realistically leaves her with Margaret as the only person available for a close, loving relationship.

There is no need to go through Masterson's notes in detail on this point. He repeatedly interprets her material (accurately) as expressing her "fear of being engulfed or abandoned if she should allow a real close relationship with a man to develop" (p. 301). He consistently focuses on the manifest layer of the hours' content, attending to Lynn's behavior (whether neurotic or healthy) with *Margaret*, unable to hear her commentary on his engulfing and abandoning behavior that is constellating her fears. He enters her life with no apparent ambivalence, confident of his ability to assess the health versus the pathology of her behavior, and Lynn feels engulfed. She responds similarly to his undoubtedly well-intentioned efforts to be helpful to her by instructing her on how to behave maturely. When her therapist focuses on the needs of her concrete, outer child, ignoring the emotional needs of her lonely inner child, Lynn feels abandoned. Lynn complains that she wants " 'a man to support [her]' " and he tells her she is being childish and unrealistic, she must grow up and be independent (pp. 304–305).

On the one hand, Lynn's pathology has clearly constellated a syntonic (complementary, meshing) countertransference in her therapist. But this is also Masterson's preferred style. His attunement to borderline issues is acute and probably has the advantage of rapidly constellating any patient's borderline fears and defenses. Once these primitive levels are opened up, however, Masterson's focus is on curing them rather than containing them and we can see, in his relatively unconscious style, the way his own borderline issues catch him unaware, from behind, and infuse his work. The infantile layer of the psyche can no more be "cured" than a tree can be detached from its roots.

The central experience in this therapy was Margaret's death. Two-and-a-half years into the treatment, "Lynn was making excellent progress when Margaret suddenly fell acutely ill" (p. 308) with leukemia. One year later, following some fluctuation in her condition, she died. In a strange way, Margaret's death can be seen as a logical conclusion, in symbolic form, to many of the difficulties in this therapeutic work. Let me enumerate here the data which can be imagined in this way.

Let us start with Lynn's suggestive childhood fantasy, mentioned above, of starving herself to death in order to win her mother's sympathy. Since this was a continuing conscious fantasy, one may infer that, like a repeating dream, it captures something of the basic organization of her psyche. As Masterson points out, Lynn experiences him in the transference as her mother. Lynn continually and consciously tries to win his sympathy and she consistently receives criticism from him for it. It seems likely that she unconsciously believes that only if she can starve her child-self to death will she ever be loved by her therapist-mother. Margaret's death, then, represents the fulfillment of this self-destructive impulse. This does not, of course, imply that her death was caused by that impulse.

It is chilling, however, to see that Masterson repeatedly lays the credit for Lynn's "cure" on Margaret's death. Summarizing and introducing the case, he says, "In this strange, poignant way the daughter, through her love and her death . . . enabled the mother . . . to separate, individuate and find her true self" (p. 288). Some part of Masterson agrees with Lynn that Margaret's death was necessary if Lynn was to find her own developmental path. But there is considerable reason to question Masterson's belief that Lynn has found her true path in his work. While Lynn certainly renounces hope of gaining Masterson's "regressive" sympathy, it is not clear that she has given up, at her treatment's termination, the belief that a parent's love can only be hoped for if one pleases the parent by committing suicide.

The symbolic rightness of Margaret's cancer, however, is most centrally related to Masterson's inability to accord the psyche substantive reality. He is unwilling to allow psychic space for Lynn's pathology to express itself, and the pathology consequently can find no resting place outside the concrete body of the admittedly symbiotic mother–child pair. If we recognize the reality of the psyche, we recognize that the psyche's illnesses can no more be wished away than the body's. The psyche's pathology is, of course, all in one's head, but one lives in one's head, one's head contains a real world that will not change simply because one recognizes that the inner world is not congruent with outer reality. A refusal to experience the psyche emotionally will not make the psyche go away. It will force it into another channel: a compulsive piece of behavior, for example, a symptom—or a psychogenic physical illness that really exists in the body. The essence of Masterson's therapeutic technique lies in his confronting the patient with the unrealistic nature of her symptoms and emotions. The idea that cognitive awareness of the neurotic nature of one's state can resolve the neurotic problem reflects an inability to recognize the powerful reality of the inner world, an inability which is probably based on fear.

When Lynn complains, for example, that she does not *want* to grow up, that she wakes each morning at dawn in a state of terror, Masterson tells her "that her failure to set reality limits to her anxiety . . . was dramatizing and perpetuating it." Stop being anxious, he is saying. Lynn responds by reporting a dream.

> *I went to the office this morning and found it filled with my old clothes that I had gotten rid of and I was upset and shocked. I asked my new secretary how they got there and she said the Salvation Army returned them.*

Masterson interprets the dream: "The old clothes were her projections of the mother image on me which she had to put behind her in order to perceive me as I am: a psychiatrist" (p. 305).

Masterson's interpretation is accurate, but it misses the point of the dream. The clothes are returned by the Salvation Army because Lynn's ultimate salvation would require her to change her attitude toward her pathology (her projections) and make room for it in her soul. It is understandable that Lynn consciously shares the common American prejudice that pictures health as a result of the amputation of one's illness: send it away to the old clothes man. That Masterson would share this attitude is tragic. In her dream, Lynn's unconscious psyche is attempting to transform their attitude, but Masterson cannot hear the music of the soul.

Her pathology, now expressed in her transference neurosis, is to be junked. She must see him for what he is, a psychiatrist. I am not being in any way original when I say that the great majority of depth therapists, from any orientation, agree that the power of the treatment to resolve neurotic complexes resides in the transference neurosis's existence. When the patient sees the therapist as he or she really is—sensibly and simply "a psychiatrist"—the treatment and the therapist have no leverage in the patient's soul. True, the job of the treatment is ultimately to resolve the transference. But, again, the transference will not be resolved by denying its existence. The psyche and its products really exist, they carry real power to effect the material outer world just as surely as do tangible things. Somehow patients must grow into a resolution of the transference from deep inside themselves, not from the head down.

Masterson repeatedly acknowledges (e.g., p. 310) that while Lynn's behavior with her daughter changed from symbiotic clinging to a "realistic" recognition of Margaret's existence as a separate person, Margaret's position in Lynn's psyche was unchanged. The Margaret-within retained her position as Lynn's selfobject good mother, an integral part of Lynn's self. Lynn's situation, then, was such that her supposedly pathological tie to her daughter could not be acted out behaviorally, and she was subjected to intense criticism by her highly cathected selfobject therapist if she even attempted to explore with him the nature of this pathological tie. Don't feel those feelings, don't think those thoughts, he repeatedly insists. Where, exactly, were those thoughts and feelings to go? The only avenue available to them, if they were to insist upon their reality, was the body. Masterson himself unconsciously makes this connection when he says, "Lynn was making excellent progress when Margaret suddenly fell acutely ill" (p. 308). Lynn's "excellent progress" was actually a sham, a heroic attempt to meet her therapist's expectations. Lynn's inner psychic structure had not changed, she had simply been learning new roles to enact, ways of being that were not based on anything authentic in her inner self.

I do not wish to deny Masterson's contention that Lynn's relationship with her daughter was excessively enmeshed. But I do want to modulate it and depathologize it. Separation-individuation is not something that "happens" in the first few years of life. The mother–daughter tie is the closest possible parent–child bond. The daughter emerges from her mother's body and is *the same as* her mother. A son experiences each of these merging experiences with a different parent. The mother–daughter bond constellates the most intense merger normally found in a parental relationship. Separating from one's mother is something that any child, but most especially any daughter, does over and over again throughout life, each time gaining a new sense of self as an autonomous individual. That separation is never completely effected. And there are lovely things about the merger, as well as some terrible ones.

Having lost her daughter, Lynn becomes involved with "a more appropriate man with whom there seemed . . . some realistic chance of a close gratifying relationship" (p. 287). Lynn and Robert get married, and she terminates treatment, leaving with her new husband for a summer trip. Masterson tells us that Robert offers Lynn an opportunity for a mature, healthy relationship, and Lynn reports the kind of intensely positive feelings one has when one has fallen in love ("It's like being wrapped in whipped cream" (p. 333)). But people are certainly capable of falling in love with destructive figures. Lynn's final dreams are not positive in nature, and her associations to them should give us pause in accepting Masterson's statement that this therapeutic experience has led to reconstruction of her psyche's structure.

A month before her treatment's end, Lynn reports the following dream:

> *I was on a bus alone with the driver. The driver took the wrong direction and left me out in a deserted place on the edge of the water and, as I stood there all alone, a snake appeared and I screamed. I woke up screaming.*

In what seems to be her last hour, she reports this dream:

> *I was in a terrible awful dark rain forest looking for Margaret. Nobody was there except you. You didn't realize I was looking for her. You said there were*

snakes all over in cages. I thought I was OK because you wouldn't let them out but you did and I woke up terrified.

Masterson interprets these dreams as imaging the fears that Lynn clearly felt about ending her treatment and separating from him. Still caught in his inability to recognize the reality of the psyche, he evaluates her fears as "all in her head." But Lynn's associations are more ominous.

All that she can say of the first dream is, "I don't know what it means" (p. 334). Perhaps her inability to think anything at all about the dream reflects her fear of the thoughts that might arise regarding it. The snake is not personally meaningful to Lynn, but it appears the world over as an image of the cold-blooded instinctual psyche out of which wisdom (e.g., the snake in the Garden of Eden) and healing (e.g., the caduseus) can emerge if the psyche is respectfully treated. The driver of the bus can be thought of as the energic force that has been propelling Lynn's therapeutic work along, and the therapist, whether as directive as Masterson or not, is apt to receive this projection. Here, this energy has gone in the wrong direction and the patient finds herself alone, confronting her unconscious (the water) and her authentic inner nature (the snake).

Lynn's association to the second dream is startling. "I thought I trusted you and I was wrong in the dream. Now I have the same thoughts about you and about Robert. I realize they're crazy and atrocious. I begin to get feelings he married me to be mean to me" (p. 335). There is no way to shape this dream into a psychic confirmation of Lynn's readiness to terminate treatment, though this treatment may seem too flawed to salvage. In "a terrible awful dark rain forest," where the whole world is weeping, Lynn is searching for her lost child. Her therapist is so ignorant of her inner state he does not know she still seeks the warm and loving maternal bond he had prohibited as regressive. And then, in a final betrayal, he releases the natural psyche from its cage. He has repeatedly assured her through his behavior and attitude that it is possible to keep one's deepest nature locked permanently away. As the therapy ends, Lynn must face the fact that this is not possible: her psyche really exists and must be confronted, even if her magician-psychiatrist insists he has abracadabra'd it away.

Chapter 8

The Disliked Patient[1]

There is a profound problem with the argument of this book. The central orientation rests on the assumption that the patient's healing energies predominate in his or her own inner developmental thrust, and in the real world that is not always true. We all get caught at times in self-destructive or at least counterproductive eddies. Some people seem entrenched in patterns that lead nowhere. The therapeutic attitude I have been espousing invites the therapist to identify with the midwife and to position himself in such a way as to facilitate the birth of the patient's self. But sometimes the patient is not pregnant (Stein 1984) and the therapist who waits patiently will never catch a birthing baby, for there has been no conception to bear fruit.

It is not clear to me that there is anything constructive to be done about the patient who is really caught in what we could call the death instinct, in an unconscious determination not to grow. The therapist can interpret the situation, can confront the patient with it, can construct double binds with which to pressure the patient—but ultimately the therapist's power seems limited to giving the patient a rather mild nudge in a constructive direction. If the life force is working inside the analysand, perhaps it can be brought to the fore, but it is the analysand's inner energies that heal, not the analyst's, and if those will not work, nothing can be done about it.

As I emphasized earlier, however, the extent to which the patient's own constructive energies will emerge cannot be predicted in advance. If we do not turn people away for their apparent untreatability, we will find ourselves with some number of patients who are not doing simply wonderful, exciting work every moment of the hour. All of our patients will get stuck sometimes, in patterns that reflect their complexes mixed up with ours. Many hours will involve some demand on the therapist

[1]This chapter is a revised version of Sullivan (1987b).

to do something beyond simply being with the patient, to help the patient in some way to get unhooked from some thorn catching him on his path. In this book, I have emphasized the demands on us to be with our patients because that side of our work has been so severely undervalued by our profession and our culture, but my arguments may be a pendulum swinging as far from center in a feminine direction as our field had gone toward the Masculine.

It would take another book entirely to examine adequately the issue of therapeutic blockages. When is one to decide the work is stuck, how does one determine whether or not the patient herself will disentangle a knot, what is one to do about a patient who is sterile or infertile? What failures in this work are inevitable, which ones could we prevent if we were more skillful, less unconscious, a "better fit" with this particular patient? In this chapter I will examine one small segment of this topic, the problem of a patient one dislikes. I hope to take a perspective here that is compatible with the feminine stance of this book, but I also hope to attend to the ways in which my feminine stance complements rather than contradicts some more traditional approaches.

What happens when a therapist or analyst finds himself unable to like a patient? We have looked at one element after another in the therapeutic situation, always assuming the therapist's *ability* to center himself in a positive connection to his patient. But Eros was a tricky god, emerging where he chose, not where practical men might have wanted him. The "linking factor" in the analytic situation is not amenable to control. One can position oneself in such a way as to invite liking to emerge from one's psyche but, like the sun and the rain, it either comes or it doesn't. It is distressing for most therapists to find themselves disliking a patient, and we consequently defend ourselves against recognizing dislike and its more powerful variants—hatred, loathing, revulsion, etc.—when it is present. This is based on the instinctive knowledge that is it not possible to provide a healing environment for someone one does not like. It is the therapist's contained love—his liking—that activates the patient's inner emotional healing, and therapists consequently work very hard to like their patients and/or to remain unconscious of the ways in which they do not.

I am not referring to some tepid emotional state when I use the term "liking." This word covers many possible emotional qualities that can form a feeling foundation within the therapist for her end of the therapeutic alliance. "Liking" includes all the tender, nurturing emotions that lead us to cherish our patients and that ground us in a compassionate attitude. Liking implies the therapist enjoys being with the patient, but in this context, it must also imply that she does not depend on the patient to bring enjoyment into her life. She does not love the patient in the way one loves a spouse or a child or one's own—she does not expect the patient to meet her needs.

The liking factor can be disturbed in either a positive or a negative direction. If the therapist likes the patient too much, she loses her ability to be there for the patient. To some extent all patients function as selfobjects for their therapists. When the therapist falls into a state of being in love with a patient—whether this is sexualized or not—she has fallen into a place where her need for the patient has eclipsed her availability to the patient, where the patient's role as selfobject for the therapist is more dominant than is the therapist's ability to offer herself as a selfobject for the patient. The therapist is merging in with the patient rather than allowing the patient to merge in with her. Although this is a real danger for the work, the threat is minimized to the extent that the therapist is connected with her own neediness and has other arenas in which to work on it. The danger is not really excessive liking, it is excessive unconsciousness that leads a therapist to use her patient for her own gratification. The anxiety frequently expressed about being overinvolved with a patient almost invariably reflects a fear of merger, intimacy, regression, and closeness rather than a danger regarding the direction of the therapist's concern within the treatment relationship.

The situation is much more difficult when the therapist likes the patient too little—frequently a euphemistic rationalization for "not at all." In Christina's first dream (Chapter 7), people's praise for her painting—their appreciation of her ability to see and communicate the state of her self—repaired the hopeless injuries of her self. Liking, even when so intense as to be adoration, is healing. The therapist's objectivity may be seriously disrupted; she may be permanently unaware of significant areas of difficulty in the patient and neurotic collusions between the two participants may never be broken. But something good comes of being loved anyway. When the therapist dislikes her patient, a past experience, intensely wounding in nature, is being replayed and unless something happens to change the drama's course, it is hard to see what good can come of it for either participant.

Beginning with Winnicott's seminal paper, "Hate in the Countertransference" (1949), a number of authors have examined this topic. Of particular relevance is the work of Searles who is unusually open to his own negative emotions vis-à-vis his patients. But the topic has received surprisingly little attention in the literature—surprising in view of the fact that so many therapists so often find themselves saddled with one or two disliked patients in an otherwise comfortably likeable practice. When these disliked patients are presented in consultation, the conclusions typically center on the ways in which the patient is objectively distasteful. This follows Winnicott's lead. This is almost invariably the approach demonstrated in the literature, especially when the author is presenting a case of his own: the therapist's hatred is understood as rooted in some hateful aspect of the patient.

Racker (1968) discusses countertransference hate from a more subjective perspective, using *other therapist's* cases as examples. He suggests that whenever the therapist hopes that a positive transference will develop—a hope I would imagine is universal—and when that desire is thwarted in any serious way, countertransference hatred will arise. When a case goes badly, when the patient's resistances repeatedly frustrate the analyst's therapeutic intent, a variety of anxieties, often quite primitive in nature, are stirred in the therapist. The therapist typically defends himself against his own anxieties by accusing the patient of badness. His capacity to perceive his patient objectively—which, in this context, must mean compassionately, with liking—is disturbed by the activation of his own negative introjects: "the bad mother (breast) that will not give, that eats and robs, or the self-image of the 'vampire,' etc." (ibid., p. 120). Using another analyst's work, Racker demonstrates the way the analyst's hatred of the patient is rooted in his hatred of some element of his own inner world which the patient personifies for him. Racker's assessment supports my own: in this situation the analyst frequently behaves in ways that are comparable to the ways in which the patient's original bad objects behaved, thus reinforcing the patient's neurotic complexes.

In an attempt to discuss what one might *do* when confronted with one's own hatred for one's patient, Epstein (1979) urges the therapist to be maximally open to his feeling response to his patient, and then to "reduce the intensity of his feelings without attempting to eliminate them lest they become virulent" (p. 228). He does not, however, tell us *how* to reduce the intensity of our hatred.

In this chapter I want to follow and extend Racker's lead, examining countertransference dislike from a predominantly subjective perspective. As I will discuss below in more detail, I believe that a subjective approach is necessary if we are to accomplish Epstein's injunction to reduce the intensity of our feelings to manageable proportions. Unlike the typical example presented in the literature, the disliked patient is often not clearly more hateful than many of the people therapists do find ways to like. Rather than looking to the "objective" facts of the patient's personality when dislike dominates the treatment, I want to identify the dynamics that function to generate and maintain dislike in the therapist, assuming that these dynamics involve interactional pressures from the patient *on an available predisposition in the therapist's psyche*. I would think of this approach as feminine rather than masculine because it begins in a humble place of not-knowing and looks inward to one's own difficulties rather than toward outer obstacles (in the patient) to be heroically conquered. However, let us remember that both masculine and feminine modes are always needed to balance each other. When this humble, inward search is not tempered by a focused outer attention to the patient's actual being, it will rapidly swing into a masochistic self-blaming for difficulties that Hercules himself could not have surmounted.

Michael Fordham (1974) differentiates syntonic and illusory countertransference. Syntonic countertransference is an emotional response on the therapist's part conditioned by the patient's inner reality: the therapist plays a role orchestrated by the patient's unconscious. In illusory countertransference, the therapist's psyche dominates the situation, forcing the patient into a role of the therapist's unconscious choosing. Heinrich Racker (1968) makes a similar distinction between countertransference proper and neurotic countertransference. Various other analysts have expressed this same idea using various other terms. The distinction is valuable but it is also misleading, for in practice the two forms inevitably coexist. A syntonic or proper countertransference experience can only be constellated by the patient in the analyst because some bit of a neurotic complex is available in the analyst to receive it. The central thesis of this chapter is that only by attending to the illusory or neurotic component of the countertransference difficulty can we hope to resolve it. By modeling openness to our own madness, we enable our patients to turn a receptive eye toward their own.

The phobic approach to negative emotions that most therapists feel is based partly on the helplessness we all experience in relation to any emotion: regardless of our wishes, we do feel whatever we feel. When one feels a deeply unacceptable emotion, therefore, the impulse to deny it is powerful. But resisting an emotion can only function to entrench it. The psyche's basic thrust, underlying the entire individuation process, is its need to become real and actual, to exist in the material world. When the ego resists that need by refusing to experience an emotion fully—which does not imply allowing it to direct one's behavior, but rather a complete subjective exploration of the emotion in question—a stand-off is created. That strand of the psyche's development is blocked. It cannot go forward, but it will never go away. The feared emotion, be it positive or negative, can only grow in size as it attempts to force its way into existence.

Jung (1921) postulates two modes, thinking and feeling, through which the ego evaluates experiences. I take his sharp separation of feeling and emotion to indicate a misunderstanding of their relationship. Emotions are to the feeling function what ideas are to the thinking function: the raw material with which to work. The feeling function takes emotions which arise in response to perceptions or thoughts and works them over; it evaluates them, develops them, amplifies them, molds them. Where raw emotions possess the individual, driving him behaviorally in unconscious, autonomous ways, the feeling function takes possession of emotions and uses them evaluatively. When the therapeutic alliance is working, the therapist's feeling function has found a way to shape the primary emotions available to it into some kind of liking toward the patient.

What happens when the emotions the therapist has to work with can not be shaped into liking—when we *dis*like or hate a patient? My interest in this question began with two deeply distressing personal experiences.

Early in my career as a patient I worked for about a year with an analyst (Dr. X) toward whom I developed an intensely paranoid transference. I believed she hated me and wished me ill. She maintained that was not the case, but as my intense distrust of her showed no signs of abating, she urged me to terminate at the end of a year. I naturally experienced this urging as demonstrating her rejecting, hateful feelings. She assured me that wherever the problem between us resided, it did not lie in "the liking." So I left and went on, doing what I could in another consulting room to understand what had gone so very wrong between us.

Several years later I learned that one year after my termination with her, she had secretly and energetically attempted to prevent me from receiving a major advance in my career. My paranoid experience of her had either been an accurate assessment of her authentic inner state or I had constellated my worst fear. Or both. To soothe myself, I could at least maintain a righteously condemning attitude toward her and her completely unethical behavior.

Then Andy walked into my consulting room. As our work unfolded, he rapidly became for me what I had apparently been for Dr. X. I came to dislike him more and more intensely, until there was no doubt I hated him. I was unable to find the ultimate roots of my negative feelings, however, and as the pressure inside me built up, I suddenly found myself, in an impulsive moment, repeating Dr. X.'s behavior: I used my intimate knowledge of Andy in an attempt to undermine his career.

Luckily, my behavior was not objectively harmful to Andy but it caused a great upheaval in myself. I had behaved like Dr. X, who had long been established in my heart as The Bad Object. Perhaps my judgments of Andy were as distorted as Dr. X's judgments of me had been. I no longer felt certain that the parts of "Andy" I hated were objectively present in *Andy*. The pejorative assessments that had seemed so demonstrable were no longer clear to me. *He* had supposedly been "borderline"; but I had behaved in a borderline fashion.

These two experiences completely disrupted my attitude toward my own negative feelings. I no longer trusted them to reflect an objective reality about my patient. Diagnosis in general and feeling assessments specifically seemed more subjective than I had ever imagined them to be. The next time dislike arose in a case, I approached its meaning with a naively open mind.

Betty

My experience with Betty demonstrates the way in which the psyches of the patient and the therapist interpenetrate one another. In this interpenetration the patient's complexes are constellated in (projectively identified into) the therapist, and—hopefully to a far lesser extent—the therapist's complexes are constellated in the patient. This situation provides the ground from which dislike can spring, for dislike and its variants are ultimately rooted in one's dislike of some unacceptable piece of oneself.

Betty was shopping for a therapist, and I was the fourth person she was seeing. As she told me about herself, I was aware of neither liking nor disliking this 35-year-old single woman. I had only one free hour and while I felt willing to give it to her, I was equally willing to be rejected—unchoosen—by her. As she described the various therapists she had seen, I felt mildly touched. What a chaotic mass of data to sort through, with no clear guidelines for how to approach it! I made some mildly sympathetic comment, and she suddenly leaped into my lap, asserting that she wanted to work with me. As the case material will demonstrate, it is likely that Betty's sudden choice of me as a therapist was a response, at least partly, to an unconscious awareness on her part of an unconscious aversion to her on my part.

In a relatively short time I knew I did not like Betty, but it was nearly nine months before I could acknowledge I was building up hatred toward her in my heart. The aversion I felt centered consciously on her clinging defenses which covered over her tremendous fear of intimacy. I thought if she would just *leave* my office when I told her the time was up, rather than taking an extra minute or two to blow her nose and get herself together, I would be more welcoming of her presence for the fifty minutes that were rightfully hers. I was wrong in this fantasy, of course—the difficulties were much deeper than that.

But the fantasy did reflect the nature of the problem. If the boundary between us, I was saying, could be clearly drawn, I could make space for her in my life. The lack of boundaries within herself, between her various conflicting impulses and aspects, was matched in the outer world by a lack of boundaries in her relationships, and I was unconsciously frightened by the fluid merger she rapidly established between us. If the boundary between her wish for closeness and her wish for distance could have been acknowledged rather than denied, I could have lived with it, wherever it fell. I have tolerated patients who want to set up housekeeping under my skin and I can tolerate patients who want to keep me remotely distant. What I could not tolerate was the fact that her conscious attempts to merge with me were primarily a reaction formation against her even stronger wish to keep me away from her true self.

Realizing I had been evading the experience of my negative feelings, I decided to approach my hours with Betty differently. I determined to focus my energy (silently, in the privacy of my mind) on the feelings and fantasies that were being stirred in me as I sat with her, hoping thereby to get a handle on where she was grabbing me.

It is surely not an accident that I reached this point just as she first began to live with a man. Up to that time, her frequently stated experience of me and of our work was ecstatically positive. She felt loved and nourished by me, validated in her feelings as she never had been before. Now, as Roger moved into her life, the center of her dependency rapidly shifted out of my office and into their bedroom. This must have been important in allowing me to relax with her—I no longer felt constantly in danger of being gobbled up alive. She had separated from me to some extent and a boundary between us had been established.

My notes for the first hour in which I attempted to focus on my inner reactions are amazingly fragmentary. She talked of her fear of abandonment, triggered consciously by Roger's moving into her house. The losses of her life that came to her mind were emotional abandonments by people who remained with her physically, rather than the extensive losses she had suffered through death and physical abandonment. About myself, I noted I had felt some sympathy for her, some irritation and some envy but by the end of the hour, when I was writing out my notes, I was not sure to what I had been responding with each of those feelings. In fact, I could remember very little of what she had talked about and almost nothing I had experienced. Despite my best intentions, I had scarcely been there. It was not that my mind had wandered; I had simply gone unconscious and had been nowhere for much of the hour. Her fear of emotional abandonment in the context of physical contiguity had apparently been lived out in our hour. Whose complexes had shaped this experience? Was I sucked into abandoning her in ways she had experienced in the past, or was she unconsciously perceiving my attempt to focus on my inner state more primarily than hers? Was my unconsciousness a reflection of an unconsciousness that Betty lived with, a permanent abandonment of her self, a noninvolvement in her own emotional existence? Was there something about Betty that touched something in me I could not bear to look at, some part of my self that, Medusa-like, turned me to stone? Were all of these possibilities activated, and perhaps others as well?

Our next hour preceded a one week vacation of mine. Betty talked frantically of her fear of Roger's leaving her if he were to know how terrified she was of his leaving her. She felt she would lose him unless she could stop feeling her anxiety about being abandoned—and she also knew that only by feeling the pain of her anxiety would she ever get past it. She was in a terrible, hopeless dilemma. I wondered if she was having any feelings about *my* leaving. She touched briefly on that and then returned to her panic around Roger. I described the ensuing sequence in my notes:

> Me: I don't know this happened, but you left me and went back to him [i.e., by changing the topic].
> Betty: Began to talk with great authenticity, in a very moving way, of her terrible fear of burdening me with her need for me, that I won't like her, I'll get burned out on her and quit practicing altogether, that she'll destroy me.

What I actually said to Betty was probably something like, "I don't quite understand the sequence, here—first you were talking about my vacation, and now you're talking about Roger again." But it seems significant to me that I described it in my notes as Betty's "leaving me" for him.

We can summarize the case to this point: Betty had behaved in a powerfully clinging fashion that had constellated intensely rejecting feelings in me. At the same time as she had moved to a point where she was relaxing her leechlike clutch on me, I had moved to a point where I was able to face my negative feelings more fully. At this turning point, I began to reach for her and she began to draw away from our connection. We were changing places in our work.

In the next few weeks, Betty dreamed twice of having an abortion, once of adopting and nurturing a very sweet baby, and then of accidentally dropping a baby she was caring for in a tub of water. As the baby's head slipped under the water, Betty felt a great lethargy in herself, an inability to mobilize herself to rescue the baby. The prognosis for Betty's treatment was severely in question. I had begun to feel quite fond of her, I was liking her more and more, and she was having clearer and clearer negative feelings about the therapy and about me. I had never succeeded in capturing any particular emotional fantasies regarding her; my feelings had shifted partly in response to the shift in her dependency and partly in response to my inner emotional acknowledgment of their extent. In Betty's dream her lethargy prevented her rescuing the baby. In our work, my lethargy—my uncontrollable slip toward unconsciousness—prevented my grasping a clear, tangible sense of where she was or had been getting me. Again the impossible question presents itself: whose complex was dominating our interaction?

Then, one year into the work, Betty had a dream which seemed to clearly state that however I was collaborating in her difficulty with being in therapy, it was her difficulty that we were confronting. She was walking through apartment complexes, going back over ground she had previously covered and descending. Suddenly she realizes, "I've gone way past where I meant to go. I'd gone too far and too deep. . . . Blocking my way back was an animal: a rodent, like a weasel, with huge teeth, snarling." She talked in that hour extensively about her negative feelings about therapy. Emotions were being stirred in her that she did not feel able to contain. Where she had felt accepted and nourished by my welcoming her emotions in the past (i.e., in the months during which I had been feeling rejecting toward her and her emotions), she now felt frightened of her inner state.

In the past, I had carried this vicious rodent for her: I had had vicious, hateful feelings toward her which, though they had never been openly acknowledged, had been unconsciously reassuring to her. Betty had felt safe with me when I was a vicious rodent because that allowed her to completely disidentify with that capacity in her own psyche. Now that I was liking her, her equilibrium was upset. Where was our work leading, she worried; her anxieties seemed bottomless.

I suggested that the emotions with which she was struggling might be more successfully contained in the therapy if she came more often than once a week. I summarized her response in my notes:

> She is afraid of coming twice a week, partly because of the money but also because she is afraid of what she needs to face—i.e., this vicious rodent. She thought coming more often would be like going into a cave with spiders, snakes, and chocolate. I was pretty silent, but I felt that if she doesn't come more often than once a week, she might as well stop. It's wrong for me to feel this way. I need to be neutral, let her come at her own pace. I'm carrying some inner figure of hers, ordering her to leap all the way in or get completely out.

I had developed considerable cognitive insight into the way in which I was an absorbed participant in her inner drama, but I was not able to disentangle myself fully. This inability on my part can only have been rooted in the ways in which her inner drama meshed with unresolved—unconscious—aspects of my own. In the months when I had been caught in my negative feelings about her, I had been utterly trapped in the unconscious complexes she and I shared. This had been the source of my dislike—I had hated myself when I was with her for I had been living out a hateful figure in her psyche, a figure that also belonged to me.

As her unconscious withdrawal provided me with enough space to find myself, I became more able to see her compassionately, as an ordinary, suffering human being, and I became more able to understand some of the negative dynamics between us. Intense fears of abandonment and engulfment had see-sawed back and forth between us. I thought I knew about and had experienced my fears of abandonment and of engulfment. What I had not been able to face was the fact that these fears can never be fully known. Their extent is always somewhat unconscious and when their ambivalent intensity cannot be consciously contained I, like Betty, will use one half of my impulse (the clinging or the rejecting half) to defend against the other side. Like Betty, I can be inauthentic, I can be allergic to the truth. This unconscious splitting, that possessed Betty so deeply and that is described so pejoratively in the psychiatric literature, is a universal human phenomenon that varies only in degree. It was shocking to (unconsciously) confront it in myself, and I had deeply disliked the woman who generated it in me.

Having seen it, however, and made some additional peace with it, I no longer needed to reject the woman who had mirrored that capacity of mine to me. I found myself during one hour fantasizing cutting my hair in her style, and I realized I had come to love her. My negative, rejecting anti-identification had turned into a simple appreciative wish to be like her.

Betty terminated her work with me 15 months after we had begun. There had been several objective improvements in her life of some substance: a significant promotion at work, the first live-in love relationship of her life. But the kind of basic character reorganization that analysis at its best can offer had certainly not occurred. In terminating, Betty directly expressed her sense that her anxieties were infinite and needed to be left alone. There is no way to assess this judgment from outside; perhaps she was right.

In this work, Betty's difficulties with intimacy were constellated in the transference. The countertransference problems I have described were syntonic in nature; they reflected a way my psyche molded to hers rather than a way my personal problems distorted her process. But what I have wanted to emphasize here is the fact that she could constellate my emotional response only because the kernel of it already existed within me.

Dr. X's betrayal of my confidences left me permanently unable to trust any therapist's negative judgments about his or her patients, including my own. The shift in my feeling for Betty was an amazing experience for me. The dislike or hatred I felt for her in the first months of our work was clearly the kind of emotion that had led me to act out against Andy and, I feel sure, the emotion that led Dr. X to act out against me. I believed, and could easily have demonstrated through her own material, that Betty was severely disturbed, a borderline personality. After my feelings had shifted, the *content* of my diagnostic assessment of Betty remained unchanged, but its tone was transformed. Certainly, she is borderline, but all human beings struggle with a borderline layer. It is no longer clear to me that her problems with abandonment and engulfment or her tendencies toward splitting are significantly more severe than those of some of my fellow analysts. What did become clear to me, as soon as I came to like Betty, is the fact that evaluating the extent of her disturbance, in the sense of putting a label on it—measuring it—is irrelevant. My need to do that had come out of my need to distance her from me, which, in turn, came out of my fear of the similarities between us lying below the surface.

We are all simply human at base and we all contain bits of all diagnostic categories. My use of diagnosis in this case supports my contention that diagnosis is typically used in the service of distancing the more distressing elements of the human condition from ourselves. In theory labeling Betty "borderline" was an attempt to guide my treatment approach to her. In fact, when *any* person is struggling with issues of abandonment and engulfment, one must take a certain approach to him, and diagnosing him—defining him by the issues with which he is struggling—serves only to differentiate him from oneself. *You* have problems with intimacy, the label asserts; I don't.

Although Betty made significant gains in her outer life, this work cannot really be considered successful. In her own way, she rejected the painful road to deep inner change. The premature termination was distressing for me, for I had become so fond of her by the end of our work, but it was not as though she had stopped growing. She was ending her involvement in an analytic process designed to intensify the pace and depth of her growth. What path her life has taken since then, I cannot know. In any case, Jung suggests that we can learn more from our failures than from our successes and my disappointment at Betty's termination was tempered with a strong sense of having gained something substantial from her regarding my understanding of counter-transference dislike. Not only had the problem of dislike been writ large for me to study, I had actually worked it through.

In struggling with dislike, I have found it consistently detrimental to focus on its objective justifications. Only in so far as one can approach the *subjective* factors in dislike, can one hope to change the field that is nourishing it, and only by changing this field can one hope to change the patient's inner world. The inner world develops initially as a mirror of the outer world of infancy. As the psyche acquires shape, it in turn shapes its outer world into a mirror of itself. This endless process, within which inner and outer realities reflect each other, forms one basis of our work. By bringing consciousness to bear on the bipersonal field of the analytic situation, we hope to change the outer configuration enough to impact on the patient's inner state. But we can only change the outer reality through the medium of our own psyche. When the analyst situation is stuck in a negative place, we must look to inner change of our own if we hope to effect it.

We tend to think of projection as a pathological mechanism—and so it is, when operating indiscriminately or to excess. But projection is also the basic relationship-creating mechanism. We can only empathize with another's pain by allowing that pain to resonate with its mirror image in our own psyche; by projecting our parallel experience. Projections are a bridge to understanding when they function constructively, just as they destroy understanding when they function inaccurately. We can know a quality in another only because it exists in ourselves and it is because of this that we find ourselves liking—or disliking—another. These emotional reactions arise only in relation to ourselves. Insofar as a quality belongs to an other, rather than to our self, it is interesting—its valuation emerges from its resonance in our selves. What we dislike in our patients are parts of our selves.

*Dis*liking a patient or, more commonly, some aspect of a patient, offers a rich opportunity for both the therapist's and the patient's growth. Liking is not a static quality; it is a fluid one and it will inevitably change. It is the changes in the quantity and quality of liking that must be attended to. While it is true that the therapist's liking forms a rich basis for the patient's healing, healing can also flow from situations of dislike if they are faced and worked through.

When a therapist dislikes a patient, his instinctive response may be an attempt to stiffle his feeling judgment. My experience with Betty suggests that attempting to sink deeply into our negative emotions is a more fruitful approach. In a worst-case scenario, the attempt to stiffle unacceptable emotions leads to the kind of destructive acting out both Dr. X and I engaged in vis-à-vis our patients. By working to create as much space for our negative feelings within ourselves as we possibly can, by seeking to explore them thoroughly and deeply, to totally *have* them, we make room for them to develop and change, to grow. We must create the same kind of inner space for our disliking selves that we create in the consulting room for our patients. I cannot emphasize too strongly that I am not advocating discharging negative feelings by telling the patient about them. It is a silent, inner exploration, as contained as possible, that I believe to be fruitful.

The patient will constellate in the therapist whatever negative emotions his complexes need to mesh with. If the patient and the therapist can stay consciously in their difficult situation, liking may eventually emerge. But liking will come only on its own terms, when all the emotional factors that were blocking it have been paid their full due.

Again I am explicitly calling into question the attempt to assess patients in initial hours, in this case the attempt to assess the patient's likeability. Rejecting a patient, no matter how skillfully the rejection is managed, is hurtful to the patient. While there are situations that can justify rejecting a patient anyway, an initial not liking is not adequate. When therapists feel, either initially or in the course of the work, that they cannot *stand* the patient, a rejection is in order. Our work is legitimately difficult and demanding, but it is not supposed to be torturous.

When one has reason to believe that specific complexes of one's own are touched—complexes that other therapists do not share—one might consider rejecting the patient. But the situation is tricky; in theory one can separate illusory and syntonic countertransference, but in practice they only exist together. When one dislikes a patient, the patient knows it, at least unconsciously. If he chooses to stay in the treatment nonetheless, one's dislike is probably ego syntonic for him in some way, and it is not unlikely that other therapists will dislike him, too. Whatever neurotic element may be constellated in the analyst is apt to rest on an objective difficulty in the patient. My patient Betty is not so unusual in her need to evoke dislike. I do not think she could have stayed with a therapist who liked her. Indeed, her flight from therapy was at least partly in response to my working through my dislike of her too rapidly for her to tolerate. When one's complexes mesh with a patient's, the patient may be better off elsewhere. Or this may be exactly where he needs to be.

Therapists are too easily sucked into attempts at omniscience. To reiterate: we do not know who is analyzable and who is not. We can know who we like initially, but we do not know how we are going to feel about someone six months or several years down the road. We must all have had the experience of coming to dislike a patient we initially liked; those of us who do not reject patients we initially dislike may have had the surprising experience of coming to like initially distasteful people.

Finally, I question whether anything is gained by attempting to screen patients for likeability. One's practice reflects one's psyche. Each hour of the work week brings to life some piece of one's inner world, some part of a complex that needs to be known. The tragic Greek vision seems as true today as it was in its own time: attempts to evade one's destiny can only serve to bring that destiny home with a terrible vengeance. If one can go naked into the world, prepared to meet and accept the burdens Fate has prepared for one, those burdens may magically turn into treasures. It is perhaps shocking to think we might simply accept as patients those people who call us when we have time to see them. But I am convinced that a simple, passive approach will produce a practice as rich and as likeable as will any attempt to screen people.

A primary tenet of analytic theory is the notion the therapist must function as a participant-observer, allowing himself to become emotionally involved with the patient to some extent while retaining an objective, separate viewpoint. Throughout this book I have suggested that objectivity and separation are less possible than we would like to believe. At some very profound level, the two individuals in the therapeutic situation are always merged. The patient knows his therapist's psyche from inside, through the deep unconscious merger that is rapidly and inevitably effected in the clinical container. It is not possible for a therapist to assess a patient objectively, either from a thinking perspective or from a feeling one. When two psychic systems meet and engage, there is no ultimate way to differentiate which system is the original source of any given quality.

Now, some separation is needed if one is to have any chance of seeing another person at all. Usually, enough objectivity is available to the therapist to enable him to function effectively with his patient. What we think of as negative countertransference difficulties can be seen as problems in separation. Sometimes these problems are idiosyncratic: this particular patient stirs this particular therapist's complexes in a way that overwhelms the therapist, obliterating his sense of his own boundaries and his consequent capacity to perceive the patient compassionately. Something of his own shadow has been constellated and he is unable to live with those parts of himself this patient evokes.

Often, however, countertransference problems are more general. Borderline, narcissistic, and psychotic patients confront most therapists with severe problems because these patients constellate the borderline, narcissistic, and psychotic layers of the therapist's psyche, layers of his self he has been unable to face and integrate. Healthier patients, working in these difficult, primitive areas, similarly trigger our own elemental anxieties. We all carry within our selves islands of madness we have never had the strength or the courage to explore.

From this perspective, when the therapist's dislike is aroused, it is counterproductive to focus on the patient's pathology in an attempt to locate the source of the dislike. It is the therapist's pathology, evoked to complement the patient's, that must be attended to if this deadlock is to be transcended. Only by facing and accepting our own madness can we hope to help our patients face theirs.

In understanding countertransference dislike, it has been most commonly theorized that the patient is using projective identification to put an intolerable piece of himself into the therapist. The formulation I am suggesting differs from, without contradicting, that idea. Rather than attending to the dreadful piece of the patient that has been injected into the therapist, it seems more clinically helpful to attend to the piece of the therapist available to receive the patient's projection. Something ugly is constellated in the therapist, and it is too easy and too destructive to project that back onto the patient, saddling the patient with all the illness while we retain all the health.

The cases that constellate the greatest countertransference difficulties may offer us the greatest rewards. By studying those cases, we can learn the most about the difficulties of the ordinary case. Jung suggests that until the two people in the analytic container have become a mutual problem for each other, the analysis is not working. By studying those cases in which the patient becomes a *tremendous* problem to the therapist, by immersing ourselves deeply in the problems that those patients bring, we can hope to gain insight into the fundamental troublesome dynamics of the analytic situation, dynamics that exist in all therapeutic work but that are writ large only occasionally.

Despite the trenchant, earthy tone of this book, I would hope the reader could reflect on its content in a symbolic, intuitive state, viewing my ideas through somewhat blurry eyes. Just as no fixed rules can be devised for the therapeutic situation, none of my ideas can hold up for patients-in-general or even for any given patient at all times. The excitement of analytic work rests on the fact that no two people can ever be handled in the same way, each new case is an unpredictable foray into new territory filled with unexpected twists and unpredicted views. I hope to have contributed here a somewhat different perspective from which to view the infinitely complex and ever-shifting world of depth psychological work. But already, as I write the final sentence in the book, I am pulled away from its orientation, questioning the intensity with which I assert the centrality of Being, fascinated by the issue of when and how we must focus on Doing. . . .

References

Balint, Michael. 1968. *The Basic Fault: Therapeutic Aspects of Regression.* New York: Brunner/Mazel.

Balmary, Marie. 1982. *Psychoanalyzing Psychoanalysis.* Ned Lukacher, trans. Baltimore, Md.: Johns Hopkins University Press.

Barmack, Beth. 1986. Countertransference and the pregnant therapist. In *The Psychotherapy Institute Journal* 3:10–20.

Basch, Michael Franz. 1987. The interpersonal and the intrapsychic: Conflict or harmony. In *Contemporary Psychoanalysis* 23:367–381.

Breger, Louis. 1981. *Freud's Unfinished Journey.* London: Routledge and Kegan Paul Ltd.

Brown, Margaret Wise. 1961. *Four Fur Feet.* Illustrated by Remy Charlip. New York: William R. Scott, Inc.

Campbell, Joseph. 1949. *The Hero with a Thousand Faces.* New York: Bollingen Series, Pantheon Books.

Cooper, Arnold. 1987. Discussion. In *Contemporary Psychoanalysis* 23:382–391.

Dieckmann, Hans. 1975. Transference and countertransference. In *Journal of Analytical Psychology* 19:25–36.

Edinger, Edward F. 1972. *Ego and Archetype.* New York: G. P. Putnam's Sons.

Eisler, Riane. 1987. *The Chalice and the Blade: Our History, Our Future.* San Francisco: Harper and Row.

Epstein, Lawrence. 1979. The therapeutic function of hate in the countertransference. In *Countertransference.* Lawrence Epstein and Arthur H. Feiner, eds. New York: Jason Aronson, 213–234.

Fordham, Michael. 1974. Counter-transference. In *Technique in Jungian Analysis.* Michael Fordham, et al., eds. Library of Analytical Psychology, vol. 2. London: William Heinemann Medical Books, Ltd., 240–250.

Freud, Sigmund. 1925. An autobiographical study. In *Standard Edition of the Complete Psychological Works of Sigmund Freud*, vol. 20. James Strachey, trans. London: Hogarth Press, 7-70.

______ . 1963. *Dora: An Analysis of a Case of Hysteria.* New York: Collier Books.

Green, Hannah. 1964. *I Never Promised You a Rose Garden*. New York: Signet Books.

Greenberg, Jay R. and Stephen A. Mitchell. 1983. *Object Relations in Psychoanalytic Theory*. Cambridge, Mass.: Harvard University Press.

Guntrip, Harry. 1971. *Psychoanalytic Theory, Therapy, and the Self*. New York: Basic Books, Inc.

______ . 1975. My experience of analysis with Fairbairn and Winnicott (How complete a result does psychoanalytic therapy achieve?). In *International Review of Psychoanalysis* 2:145-156.

Hill, Gareth. 1978. *Patterns of Immaturity and the Archetypal Patterns of Masculine and Feminine*. Unpublished dissertation.

Hillman, James. 1964. *Suicide and the Soul*. New York: Harper and Row.

______ . 1975. *Re-Visioning Psychology*. New York: Harper and Row.

Hunt, Morton. 1987. Navigating the therapy maze. In *The New York Times Magazine*, August 30, 1987, 28ff.

Jung, C. G. 1921. *Psychological Types*. In *Collected Works*, vol. 6. Princeton, N.J.: Princeton University Press.

______ . 1931. Problems of modern psychotherapy. In *The Practice of Psychotherapy, CW* 16. Princeton, N.J.: Princeton University Press.

______ . 1936a. The concept of the collective unconscious. In *The Archetypes and the Collective Unconscious, CW* 9i. Princeton, N.J.: Princeton University Press.

______ . 1936b. Concerning the archetypes, with special reference to the anima concept. In *The Archetypes and the Collective Unconscious, CW* 9i. Princeton, N.J.: Princeton University Press.

______ . 1938. Psychological aspects of the mother archetype. In *The Archetypes and the Collective Unconscious. CW* 9i. Princeton, N.J.: Princeton University Press.

______ . 1943. On the psychology of the unconscious. In *Two Essays on Analytical Psychology, CW* 7. Princeton, N.J.: Princeton University Press.

______ . 1946. *The Psychology of the Transference.* In *CW*, vol. 16. Princeton, N.J.: Princeton University Press.

______ . 1954a. On the nature of the psyche. In *The Structure and Dynamics of the Psyche, CW* 8. Princeton, N.J.: Princeton University Press.

______ . 1954b. *The Practice of Psychotherapy*. In *CW* 16. Princeton, N.J.: Princeton University Press.

______ . 1984. *Selected Letters of C. G. Jung, 1909–1961*. Selected and edited by Gerhard Adler in collaboration with Aniela Jaffe. Princeton, N.J.: Bollingen Series, Princeton University Press.

Kafka, Franz. 1948. The metamorphosis. In *The Penal Colony: Stories and Short Pieces*. Willa and Edwin Muir, trans. New York: Schocken Books.

Kohut, Heinz. 1984. *How Does Analysis Cure?* Arnold Goldberg with Paul Stepansky, ed. Chicago: University of Chicago Press.

Langs, Robert. 1980. *Interactions: The Realm of Transference and Countertransference*. New York: Jason Aronson.

______ . 1978. *The Listening Process*. New York: Jason Aronson

______ . 1979. *The Therapeutic Environment*. New York: Jason Aronson.

Levene, Howard. 1982. The borderline syndrome: A critique and response to recent literature on its etiology, dynamics and treatment. In *The San Francisco Jung Institute Library Journal* 3:22–33.

Little, Margaret. 1985. Winnicott working in areas where psychotic anxieties predominate: A personal record. In *Free Associations* 2:9–42.

Masterson, James. 1976. *Psychotherapy of the Borderline Adult*. New York: Brunner/Mazel.

McGuire, William, ed. 1974. *The Freud/Jung Letters*. Princeton, N.J.: Princeton University Press.

McPherson, Sigrid. 1986. Reflections on a dream about Jung. In *Proceedings of the 1986 California Spring Conference of Jungian Analysts and Control Candidates*. Los Angeles: C. G. Jung Institute of Los Angeles.

Neumann, Erich. 1955. *The Great Mother: An Analysis of an Archetype*. Princeton, N.J.: Princeton University Press.

______ . 1956. *Amor and Psyche: The Psychic Development of the Feminine. A Commentary on the Tale by Apuleius*. Princeton, N.J.: Princeton University Press.

Perera, Sylvia Brinton. 1981. *Descent to the Goddess: A Way of Initiation for Women*. Toronto: Inner City Books.

Racker, Heinrich. 1968. *Transference and Countertransference*. New York: International Universities Press.

Sandner, Donald. 1979. *Navaho Symbols of Healing*. New York: Harcourt Brace Jovanovich.

Scott, W. C. M. 1978. Common problems concerning the views of Freud and Jung. In *Journal of Analytical Psychology* 23:301–314.

Searles, H. F. 1958. The schizophrenic's vulnerability to the therapist's unconscious processes. In *Collected Papers on Schizophrenia and Related Subjects*. New York: International Universities Press, 192–215.

______ . 1979. *Countertransference and Related Subjects*. New York: International Universities Press.

______ . 1986. *My Work with Borderline Patients*. Northvale, N.J.: Jason Aronson.

Spitz, R. 1945. Hospitalism. In *The Psychoanalytic Study of the Child* 1:53–74.

______ . 1946. Hospitalism. In *The Psychoanalytic Study of the Child* 2:113–117.

Stein, Murray. 1984. Power, shamanism and maieutics in the countertransference. In *Chiron: A Review of Jungian Analysis*, Nathan Schwartz-Salant and Murray Stein, eds. Wilmette, Ill.: Chiron Publications, 67–87.

Stevens, Barbara. 1982. A critical assessment of the work of Robert Langs. In *The San Francisco Jung Institute Library Journal* 3:2, 1–38.

______ . 1984. Jung and other object relations theorists. In *The San Francisco Jung Institute Library Journal* 5:3, 8–29.

______ . 1986. A Jungian perspective on transference and countertransference. In *Contemporary Psychoanalysis* 22:2, 185–201.

Stone, Leo and Robert Langs. 1980. *The Therapeutic Experience and Its Setting*. New York: Jason Aronson.

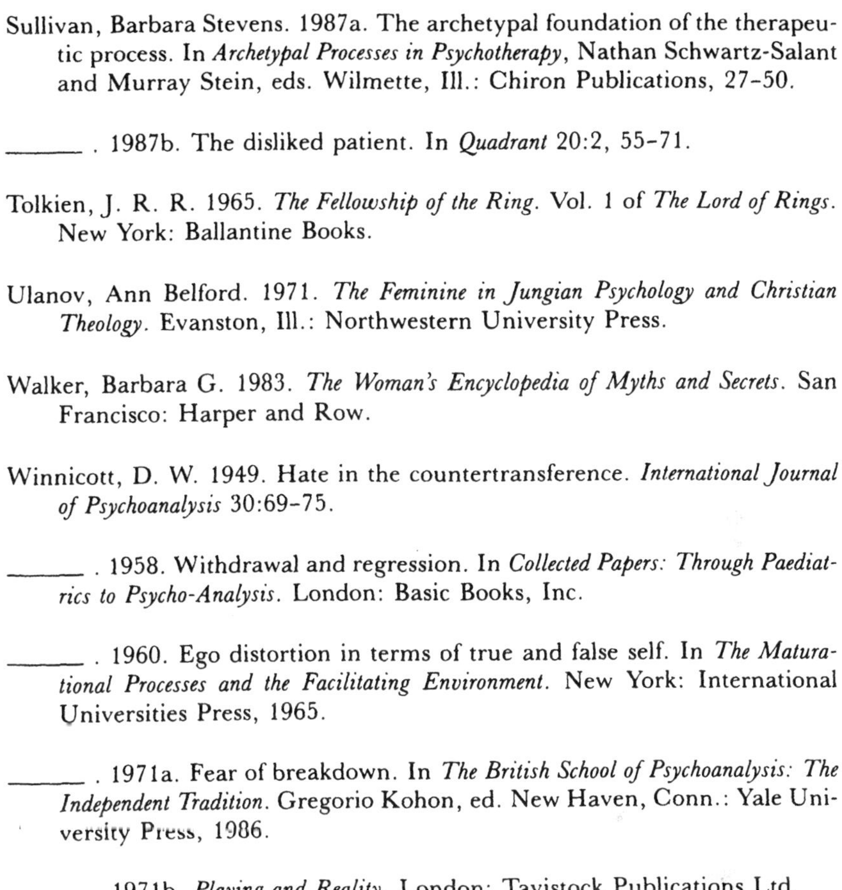

Sullivan, Barbara Stevens. 1987a. The archetypal foundation of the therapeutic process. In *Archetypal Processes in Psychotherapy*, Nathan Schwartz-Salant and Murray Stein, eds. Wilmette, Ill.: Chiron Publications, 27–50.

______ . 1987b. The disliked patient. In *Quadrant* 20:2, 55–71.

Tolkien, J. R. R. 1965. *The Fellowship of the Ring*. Vol. 1 of *The Lord of Rings*. New York: Ballantine Books.

Ulanov, Ann Belford. 1971. *The Feminine in Jungian Psychology and Christian Theology*. Evanston, Ill.: Northwestern University Press.

Walker, Barbara G. 1983. *The Woman's Encyclopedia of Myths and Secrets*. San Francisco: Harper and Row.

Winnicott, D. W. 1949. Hate in the countertransference. *International Journal of Psychoanalysis* 30:69–75.

______ . 1958. Withdrawal and regression. In *Collected Papers: Through Paediatrics to Psycho-Analysis*. London: Basic Books, Inc.

______ . 1960. Ego distortion in terms of true and false self. In *The Maturational Processes and the Facilitating Environment*. New York: International Universities Press, 1965.

______ . 1971a. Fear of breakdown. In *The British School of Psychoanalysis: The Independent Tradition*. Gregorio Kohon, ed. New Haven, Conn.: Yale University Press, 1986.

______ . 1971b. *Playing and Reality*. London: Tavistock Publications Ltd.

Index

Made in the USA
Columbia, SC
22 January 2021